BOSTON

THE MINI ROUGH GUIDE

D1649289

There are more than one hundred Rough
Guide travel, phrasebook, and music titles,
covering destinations from Amsterdam to
Zimbabwe, languages from Czech to Thai,
and styles of music from Opera to Jazz

Forthcoming titles include

Bangkok • Barbados • Japan
Jordan • Syria • Music USA
Country Music

Rough Guides on the Internet

http://www.roughguides.com

Rough Guide Credits

Text editor: Andrew Rosenberg
Series editor: Mark Ellingham
Typesetting: Helen Ostick
Cartography: Melissa Flack

Publishing Information

This first edition published June 1998 by
Rough Guides Ltd, 1 Mercer St, London WC2H 9QJ.

Distributed by the Penguin Group:
Penguin Books Ltd, 27 Wrights Lane, London W8 5TZ
Penguin Books USA Inc., 375 Hudson Street, New York 10014, USA
Penguin Books Australia Ltd, 487 Maroondah Highway,
PO Box 257, Ringwood, Victoria 3134, Australia
Penguin Books Canada Ltd, 10 Alcorn Avenue,
Toronto, Ontario, Canada M4V 1E4
Penguin Books (NZ) Ltd, 182–190 Wairau Road,
Auckland 10, New Zealand

Typeset in Bembo and Helvetica to an original design by Henry Iles.
Printed in Spain by Graphy Cems.

BOSTON

THE MINI ROUGH GUIDE

by David Fagundes
and Anthony Grant

We set out to do something different when the first Rough Guide was published in 1982. Mark Ellingham, just out of university, was traveling in Greece. He brought along the popular guides of the day, but found they were all lacking in some way. They were either strong on ruins and museums but went on for pages without mentioning a beach or taverna. Or they were so conscious of the need to save money that they lost sight of Greece's cultural and historical significance. Also, none of the books told him anything about Greece's contemporary life – its politics, its culture, its people, and how they lived.

So with no job in prospect, Mark decided to write his own guidebook, one which aimed to provide practical information that was second to none, detailing the best beaches and the hottest clubs and restaurants, while also giving hard-hitting accounts of every sight, both famous and obscure, and providing up-to-the-minute information on contemporary culture. It was a guide that encouraged independent travelers to find the best of Greece, and was a great success, getting shortlisted for the Thomas Cook travel guide award, and encouraging Mark, along with three friends, to expand the series.

The Rough Guide list grew rapidly and the letters flooded in, indicating a much broader readership than had been anticipated, but one which uniformly appreciated the Rough Guide mix of practical detail and humor, irreverence and enthusiasm. Things haven't changed. The same four friends who began the series are still the caretakers of the Rough Guide mission today: to provide the most reliable, up-to-date and entertaining information to independent-minded travelers of all ages, on all budgets.

We now publish more than 100 titles and have offices in London and New York. The travel guides are written and researched by a dedicated team of more than 100 authors, based in Britain, Europe, the USA and Australia. We have also created a unique series of phrasebooks to accompany the travel series, along with an acclaimed series of music guides, and a best-selling pocket guide to the Internet and World Wide Web. We also publish comprehensive travel information on our web site: **http://www.roughguides.com**

Help Us Update

We've gone to a lot of effort to ensure that this first edition of *The Rough Guide to Boston* is as up to date and accurate as possible. However, if you feel there are places we've under-rated or over-praised, or find we've missed something good or covered something which has now gone, then please write: suggestions, comments or corrections are much appreciated.

We'll credit all contributions, and send a copy of the next edition (or any other Rough Guide if you prefer) for the best letters. Please mark letters: "Rough Guide Boston Update" and send to:

Rough Guides, 1 Mercer St, London WC2H 9QJ, or
Rough Guides, 375 Hudson St, 9th floor, New York NY 10014.
Or send email to: mail@roughguides.co.uk

Online updates about this book can be found on
Rough Guides' Web site (see opposite)

The Authors

Born and raised in the Los Angeles area, **David Fagundes** went to college in Cambridge, MA, where he still lives. He worked as an associate and managing editor for Let's Go before defecting to Rough Guides, for whom he is also co-authoring (with Anthony Grant) a forthcoming guide to New England.

A native Californian, **Anthony Grant** attended Boston University and lived in the city for several years after graduating. He has written for *France-Soir*, *The Moscow Times*, and *The Malibu Times*, and produces the travel Web site Split (*www.splitnews.com*).

Acknowledgments

David would like to thank Tony, Andrew, Martin Dunford, the Greater Boston CVB, Caron LeBron, countless local restaurateurs, and the crew at Let's Go for professional assistance; Alex, Sonja, 1902 alums, Sean, the Cap'n, family and friends in California, the Allston Beats, and Ron for good times; and most of all to Anna, for all of the above and much more.

Anthony would like to thank his mother and mentor, Pamela, and his brother, Arthur, for their dedication and support; Andrew in New York, Martin in London and David in Boston (Cambridge, to be precise). Special thanks to Larry Meehan at the Greater Boston CVB, Ryan Nally at The Atlantic Monthly for his culinary expertise, and Virginia Adams Otis.

CONTENTS

INTRODUCTION

Boston is as close to the Old World as the New World gets, an American city that proudly trades in on its colonial past, having served a crucial role in the country's development from a few wayward pilgrims right through the Revolutionary War. It occasionally takes this a bit too far – a faded relic anywhere else becomes a plaque-covered tourist sight here – but none of it detracts from the city's overriding historic charm, nor its present-day energy. Indeed, there are plenty of tall skyscrapers, thriving business concerns and cultural outposts that are part-and-parcel of modern urban America, not to mention excellent mergers of past and present, such as the redeveloped – and bustling – Quincy Market, a paradigm for successful urban renewal. True, nowhere else will you get a better feel for the events and personas behind the birth of a nation, all played out in Boston's wealth of emblematic and evocative colonial-era sights. But the city's cafés and shops, its attractive public spaces, and the diversity of its neighborhoods – student hives, ethnic enclaves, and stately districts of preserved townhouses – are similarly alluring, and go some way to answering the twin accusations of elitism and provincialism to which Boston is perennially subjected.

As the undisputed commercial and cultural center of New England, Boston is the highlight of any trip to the region, truly unmissable because almost every road in the area leads to it (indeed Boston was, until the late-1700s America's most populous and culturally important city). It's also the center of the American university system – more than sixty colleges call the area their home, including Harvard, in the neighboring city of Cambridge – and it enjoys a youthful buzz that again belies any reputation it might have for stuffiness. This academic connection has also played a key part in the city's long left-leaning political tradition, which has spawned a line of ethnic mayors, and, most famously, the Kennedy family.

Today Boston's relatively small size – both physically and in terms of population (it ranks eighteenth among US cities) – and its provincial feel actually serve the city to advantage. Though it has expanded since it was first settled in 1630 through landfills and annexation, it has never lost its center, which remains a tangle of streets clustered around Boston Common which can really only be explored on foot. Steeped in Puritan roots, the residents of these areas often display a slightly anachronistic Yankee pride, but it's one which has served to protect the city's identity, while groups of Irish and Italian descent have carved out authentic and often equally unchanged communities in areas like the North End, Charlestown and South Boston. Indeed, the districts around the Common exude almost a small-town atmosphere, and, until recently at least, were relatively unmarred by chain stores and fast-food joints. Even as Boston has evolved from busy port to blighted city to the rejuvenated and prosperous place it is today, it has remained, fundamentally, a city on a human scale. And despite such mass-market intrusions as NikeTown and Planet Hollywood in Back Bay, and the replacement of the decrepit but beloved Boston Garden sports arena with the more impersonal FleetCenter, it looks set to stay that way.

When to visit

Boston is at its most enjoyable from September through early November, when the weather is cooler and the long lines have somewhat abated (though they are never totally absent), and in late spring – May is when the magnolia trees on Commonwealth Avenue blossom and the parks spring back to life. Summer is the most popular time to come, both for the warmer weather and frequent festivals, but you should be aware that July and August can be uncomfortably humid, and watch out for the large student influx around Labor Day and graduation time, usually early June. The New England fall foliage season – roughly mid-September to mid-October – sees a sizeable crowd hit town – Boston is a convenient point of departure to the countryside; in Boston itself the leaves change colors a bit later, sometimes well into November. Boston winters can be harsh affairs: they tend to run from late November through March, but, thanks to the moderating influence of the Atlantic, mild spells often break the monotony of chilly days and snowfall is lighter than in the interior regions of New England. No matter when you go, be prepared for sudden changes in the weather in the space of a single day: a December morning snow squall could easily be followed by afternoon sunshine and temperatures in the 50s.

Boston's climate

	°F Average daily		°C Average daily		Rainfall Average monthly	
	max	min	max	min	in	mm
Jan	36	23	2	-5	3.6	91
Feb	37	25	3	-4	3.6	92
March	45	32	7	0	3.7	94
April	57	41	14	5	3.6	91
May	66	50	19	10	3.2	83
June	77	59	25	15	3.1	78
July	82	65	28	18	2.8	72
Aug	81	64	27	18	3.2	82
Sept	71	57	22	14	3.1	78
Oct	63	46	17	8	3.3	84
Nov	52	39	11	4	4.2	107
Dec	39	27	4	-3	4.0	102

THE GUIDE

INTRODUCING THE CITY

Boston is small for an American city, and its tangle of old streets makes it far easier to get around on foot than by car, especially in the city center. Driving is particularly trying these days due to the ongoing "Big Dig" highway reconstruction project, wherein Interstate 93, which cuts through the heart of the city, is being put underground. Boston's **downtown** area is situated on a peninsula that juts into Boston Harbor; most of the other neighborhoods branch out south and west from here mainly along the thoroughfares of **Washington**, **Tremont** and **Beacon streets**.

Downtown really begins with **Boston Common**, a large public green that holds either on or near its grounds many of the city's most historical sights, including the **State House**, **Old Granary Burying Ground** and **Old South Meeting House**; nothing, however, captures the spirit of the city better than downtown's **Faneuil Hall**, the so-called "Cradle of Liberty," and the always-animated

Quincy Market, adjacent to the hall. On the other side of I-93 from the marketplace is the **North End**, which occupies the northeast corner of the peninsula; aside from being the city's Little Italy, it's home to **Old North Church** and the **Paul Revere House**. Just across Boston Inner Harbor is **Charlestown**, the quiet home of the world's oldest commissioned warship, the **USS Constitution**.

North of the common are the vintage gaslights and red-brick Federalist townhouses that line the streets of **Beacon Hill**, the city's most exclusive residential neighborhood. **Charles Street** runs south from the Hill and separates Boston Common from the **Public Garden**, which marks the beginning of **Back Bay**. This similarly well-heeled neighborhood holds opulent rowhouses alongside modern landmarks like the **John Hancock Tower**, New England's tallest skyscraper. The gay enclave of the **South End**, known for its hip restaurants, lies below Back Bay; the student domains of **Kenmore Square** and **Fenway** are to its west. The latter is home to the **Museum of Fine Arts**, **the Isabella Stewart Gardner Museum** and **Fenway Park**, and spreads out west of Massachusetts Avenue and southwest along Huntington Avenue. South of all these neighborhoods are Boston's vast **southern districts**, which don't hold too much of interest other than the southerly links in Frederick Law Olmsted's series of parks known as the "Emerald Necklace," such as the dazzling **Arnold Arboretum** and **Franklin Park**, home to the city zoo. Across the Charles River from Boston is **Cambridge**, site of the area's best nightlife, café scene and, above all, the ivy-covered walls of **Harvard University**.

The telephone area code for all of
metropolitan Boston is ©617.

Arrival

Boston is the unchallenged travel hub of New England, and if it's not the only place in the region you'll visit, it almost certainly will be the first. Conveniently, all points of entry are located inside the city boundaries, none more than a few miles from downtown.

By air

Logan International Airport is usually quite busy with services both domestic and international. It sits on Boston's easternmost peninsula, which is manmade and juts far out into Boston Harbor. The airport has five lettered terminals: you'll find **currency exchange** in terminals E and C (daily 2–6pm), plus information centers, car rental, and Automatic Teller Machines (ATMs) in all five. Each is connected by a series of courtesy buses, which also run to the Airport **subway station**. From there, you can take the Blue Line to State or Government Center stations, in the heart of downtown; the ride is about fifteen minutes (85¢). Just as quick, and a lot more fun, is the **water shuttle**, which connects the terminal buses with Rowes Wharf across the harbor (Mon–Thurs every 15min, 6am–8pm; Fri every 30min, 6am–11pm; Sat every 30min, 10am–11pm; Sun every 30min, 10am–8pm; $8). A **taxi** to downtown costs $15–20, plus an extra $4 or so in tolls.

By bus or train

Boston is well served by both **bus** and **rail** travel, with the city being the focal point of travel to New England. It's an especially common stop coming from **New York** or **Washington DC**. Both **Greyhound** buses (✆1-800/231-

2222) and **Amtrak** trains (ⓒ1-800/USA-RAIL) arrive in Boston's **South Station**, at Summer Street and Atlantic Avenue, near the Waterfront and just a short walk from downtown. The newly renovated station houses information booths, newsstands, restaurants, and a fantastic old clock, though no currency exchange. The adjacent Red Line subway can quickly whisk you to the center of town or out to Cambridge.

By car

If you're coming **by car**, be aware of the three main highways that lead into town: **I-95** (locally referred to as Rte 128), which is part of the interstate that runs all the way down the east coast, circumscribes the Boston area; **I-93**, locally called the Central Artery, is an expressway that runs through downtown and proceeds up into Vermont; and **I-90** (the Massachusetts Turnpike, or "Masspike") is a toll highway that approaches Boston from due west, a popular entryway from New York State.

Information

Boston's main public tourist office is the **Boston Visitor Information Pavilion** on Boston Common, near the Park Street subway (Mon–Sat 8.30am–5pm, Sun 9am–5pm). You'll find loads of maps and brochures, plus information on historical sights, cultural events, accommodation, restaurants and bus trips. There are also public restrooms, a rarity in Boston. Across the street from the Old State House, at 15 State St, is a **visitors center** maintained by the Boston National Historical Park (daily 9am–5pm); it too has plenty of free brochures, plus a bookstore with lots of material on

Boston, New England and Revolutionary history. In Back Bay, there is a visitor **kiosk** in the Prudential Center (Mon–Fri 8.30am–6pm, Sat 10am–6pm, Sun 11.30am–6pm). For advance information, the Greater Boston Convention & Visitors Bureau maintains the free **Boston By Phone** service, which is especially helpful for accommodation bookings (Mon–Fri 9am–5pm; ✆1-800/888-5515).

Accommodation listings begin on p.163.

The best sources of up-to-date events' listings are the "Calendar" section in Thursday's *Boston Globe* (35¢) – the premier city newspaper – and the somewhat alternative weekly *Boston Phoenix* ($1.50), published on Fridays. Both are available at newsstands throughout the city. Free publications include *The Improper Bostonian* and *Stuff@Night*, though both concentrate more on features than listings.

Getting Around

Much of the pleasure of visiting Boston comes from being in a city built long before cars were invented. **Walking** around the narrow, winding streets can be a joy; conversely, driving around them is a nightmare. If you have a car, park it for the duration of your trip and get around eitherby foot or **public transport** – a system of subway lines and buses run by the *Massachusetts Bay Transportation Authority* (MBTA, known as the "Ⓣ"; ✆1-800/392-6100, Web site *http://www.mbta.com*).

Subway

Four **subway** lines transect Boston and continue out into some of its more proximate neighbors. While not the most

Tours

Perhaps the best way to orient yourself in Boston, aside from walking, is by taking a **trolley tour**, on small open-air bus-like vehicles painted over to look like street cars. Most of the trolleys let you hop on and off at various locations and they make pick-ups at major hotels; full tours usually last about two hours, and there is little difference from tour to tour in what historical sights you'll actually see. For day trips to Lexington, Concord, Plymouth or Salem, Brush Hill Tours (see below) offers bus services and is by far the best option, unless you have a car.

Narrated trolley tours:
Beantown Trolley (✆986-6100). One of the oldest and most popular. $18.
Cityview Luxury Trolley Tours (✆363-0181). More comfortable than most. Advance reservations are available too. $18.
Discover Boston Multilingual Trolley Tours (✆742-1440). Tours in English, but they provide special audio devices that make it possible to hear descriptions in French, German, Italian, Japanese or Russian. $20.
Old Town Trolley Tours (✆269-7010). Ubiquitous, and distinguishable by their orange and green colors. $20.

Other tours:
Boston by Boat (✆422-0392). Not tours as such, but fun hourly aqua-shuttles from the Computer Museum and Children's Museum to the New England Aquarium, North End and USS Constitution in Charlestown. $5.
Boston by Foot (✆367-2345). Informative, guided

90-minute tours of Beacon Hill, Copley Square, the waterfront, North End and the Underground (which takes in disused Ⓣ stations). $7.

Boston Duck Tours (Ⓒ723-DUCK). A fleet of restored and brightly painted World War II truck-boats that make the usual rounds and then dip into the Charles River. Be forewarned: you may be asked to quack. Tours depart from the Prudential Center, at 101 Huntington Ave, every half hour starting at 9am. $19.

Boston National Historical Park Visitors Center Freedom Trail Tours (Ⓒ242-5642). Tours led by park rangers, and taking in a few Freedom Trail sights. They run on the hour between 10am and 3pm.

Brush Hill Tours (Ⓒ720-6342). A variety of day-long coach tours to surrounding towns, including Lexington, Concord, Plymouth and Salem, and run generally from late March through November.

Revolutionary Pub Crawl (Ⓒ624-6707). A two-hour spin around the historic pub locations, where the Sons of Liberty met and planted the seeds of rebellion; you can drink in their rebellious footsteps as you go. Tours on Fridays and Saturdays at 7pm at the entrance to the Aquarium Ⓣ stop (on the blue line); you must be 21 or over to participate. $10.

modern system (the Green Line was America's first underground train, built in the late nineteenth century), it's at least reasonably cheap and efficient.

See color map 8 for a plan of the subway.

Each line is keyed to a particular color and passes through downtown before continuing on to other districts: the **Red**

Line is the safest and most frequent, passing through South Boston and Dorchester to the south and Cambridge to the north; the **Green Line** hits Back Bay in addition to Kenmore Square, the Fenway and Brookline; the infrequent **Orange Line** traverses the South End and continues down to Roxbury and Jamaica Plain; and the **Blue Line** heads out into East Boston, useful primarily for its stop at Logan Airport. Free transit maps are available at any station. The fare is 85¢, payable with exact change or by tokens purchased at the station; trains run Mon–Sat 5.15am–12.30am, Sun 6am–12.30am.

If you're planning to take public transport a lot, it's a good idea to buy a visitor's "passport," for one ($5), three ($9), or seven days ($18) of unlimited subway and bus use.

Buses

Buses run less frequently than the subway and are harder to navigate, but they bear two main advantages: they're cheaper (60¢, exact change only) and they provide service to many more points. It's a service used primarily by natives who have grown familiar with the byzantine system of routes; be brave and arm yourself with the *Official Public Transport Map* and schedules available at all subway stations. Buses run from 5.30am to 1am.

Taxis

Given Boston's small scale and the efficiency of its public transit, **taxis** aren't as necessary or prevalent as in cities like New York or London. You can generally hail one along the

BUSES, TAXIS

streets of downtown or Back Bay, though competition gets pretty stiff after 1am, when the subway has stopped running, and bars and clubs begin to close; in that case, go to a hotel, where cabs cluster, or where a bellhop can arrange one for you. In Cambridge, taxis mostly congregate around Harvard Square.

Boston Cab (©262-2227) and Bay State Taxi Service (©566-5000) have 24-hour service and accept major credit cards. Other cab companies include All Area Taxi (©536-2000), Checker Taxi (©536-7000), and Town Taxi (©536-5000). In Cambridge, call ©495-8294.

DOWNTOWN BOSTON

Boston's compact **downtown** encompasses both the colonial heart and contemporary core of the city, an assemblage of red brick buildings and modern office towers that, if not rivalling the glamour of other American big-city centers, still holds a number of the city's best attractions. It's a lively area by day, when commuters and tourists create a constant buzz – although the streets thin out come nightfall, with only a few exceptions: the touristy **Quincy Market** area, which has a decent, if somewhat downmarket, bar scene; **Chinatown**, with its ever-popular restaurants; and the **Theater District**, particularly animated on weekends.

Skyscrapers aside, downtown is very flat territory, though it was once quite hilly – the name of a particularly pronounced peak, Trimountain, lives on in **Tremont Street**, long one of Boston's busiest byways. Today **King's Chapel**, on Tremont, and the nearby **Old State House** mark the periphery of Boston's earliest town center. The first church, market, newspaper and prison were all clustered here, though much closer to the shoreline than they are now. **Spring Lane**, a tiny pedestrian passage off Washington Street, recalls the location of one of the bigger springs that lured the earliest settlers over to the Shawmut Peninsula from Charlestown. The most evocative streets, however, are those whose essential character has been less diluted over the years – **School Street**, **State Street** and the eighteenth-century enclave known as **Blackstone Block**, near Faneuil Hall.

You can get the flavor of Boston Harbor, once the world's third busiest, along the **Waterfront**, now somewhat isolated on account of the unsightly elevated John F. Fitzgerald Expressway, a chunk of I-93 that's eventually to be put underground. The **Freedom Trail**, a self-guided walking tour that connects an assortment of historic sights by a line of red bricks embedded in the pavement, begins in **Boston Common**, a king-sized version of the tidy green space at the core of innumerable New England villages; close by is the ever-popular meeting place **Faneuil Hall**. South is the **Financial District**, its short streets still following the tangled patterns of colonial village lanes; west of it is the small but vibrant **Chinatown** and adjacent **Theater District**; below those is the **Leather District**, where empty warehouses and low rents have given rise to a series of art galleries.

....

**The area covered in this chapter
is shown in detail on color map 3.**

....

BOSTON COMMON

Boston's premier piazza is **Boston Common** (Map 3, D7–F5), a fifty-acre chunk of green, neither meticulously man- icured or especially attractive, which effectively separates down- town from the posher Beacon Hill and Back Bay districts. It's the first thing you'll see emerging from the **Park Street Ⓣ station**, the central transfer point of America's first subway and, unfortunately, a magnet for panhandlers. Established in 1634 as "a trayning field" and "for the feeding of Cattell" – so a slate tablet opposite the station recalls – the Common is still primarily utilitarian, used by both pedestrian commuters on their way to downtown's office towers and tourists seeking the **Boston Visitor Information Pavilion** (see p.6), down Tremont Street from the Ⓣ and the official starting-point of the Freedom Trail. The shabbiness of the southern side of the Common is offset by the lovely **Beacon Street Promenade**, which runs the length of the northern side, from the gold-domed State House to Charles Street, opposite the Public Garden.

For more detail on the Beacon Street Promenade, see "Beacon Hill," p.61

Even before John Winthrop and his fellow Puritan colonists earmarked Boston Common for public use, it served as pasture land for the Reverend William Blackstone, Boston's first white settler. It then became little more than a gallows for pirates, alleged witches and various religious heretics; a commoner by the name of Rachell Whall was once hanged here for stealing a bonnet worth seventy-five cents. Newly elected president George Washington made a much-celebrated appearance on the Common in 1789, as did his aide-de-camp, the Marquis de Lafayette, several years later. Ornate eighteenth-century iron fencing encircled the entire park until World War II, when it was taken down for use as scrap metal: it is now said to grace the bottom of Boston Harbor.

One of the few actual sights here is the **Central Burying Ground**, which has occupied the southeast corner of the Common, near the intersection of Boylston and Tremont streets, since 1756. Artist Gilbert Stuart, best known for his portraits of George Washington – the most famous of which is replicated on the American one-dollar bill – died penniless and was interred in Tomb 61. Among the other notables are members of the largest family to take part in the Boston Tea Party, various soldiers of the Revolutionary Army, and Redcoats killed in the Battle of Bunker Hill. From the Burying Ground it's a short walk to **Flagstaff Hill**, the highest point on the Common, crowned with the pillar of the Civil War **Soldiers and Sailors Monument**. A former repository of colonial gunpowder, the hill overlooks the **Frog Pond**, once home to legions of unusally large amphibians and site of the first water pumped into the city. It's really just a kidney-shaped pool, used for wading in summer and ice skating in winter. From here, a path leads to the elegant **Brewer Fountain**, an 1868 bronze replica of one from the Paris Exposition of 1855.

PARK STREET CHURCH

Map 3, F5. July–Aug daily 9am–3pm, rest of year by appointment ⓒ523-3383; free. Park Street Ⓣ.

The **Park Street Church**, which has occupied the northeast corner of Park and Tremont streets just across from Boston Common since 1809, is an oversized version of a typical New England village church. Though a rather uninteresting mass of bricks and mortar, its ornate 217-foot-tall white telescoping **steeple** is undeniably impressive. To get an idea of the immensity of the building, including the spire, walk to tiny Hamilton Place, across Tremont Street. Ultimately its reputation rests not on size but the scope of events that took place inside: William Lloyd Garrison delivered his first public address calling for the nationwide abolition of slavery (Massachusetts had scrapped it in 1783); the first Sunday school in the country started in 1818, and a year later the parish sent the first missionaries to

Hawaii; lastly, the classic ditty *America* ("My country 'tis of thee . . .") was first sung on July 4, 1831.

Park Street itself slopes upward along the edge of Boston Common toward the State House. It was once known as **Bulfinch Row** for its many brick townhouses designed by the architect Charles Bulfinch, but today only one remains, the imposing **Amory-Ticknor House** at no. 9, unfortunately not open to the public.

OLD GRANARY BURYING GROUND

Map 3, F4. Daily 8am–dusk; free. Park Street Ⓣ.

One of the more peaceful stops on the always-busy Freedom Trail is the **Old Granary Burying Ground**, the last resting place for numerous leaders of the American Revolution. Its odd name comes from a grain warehouse, which formerly stood on the site of the adjacent Park Street Church. The two-acre tract, set a few feet above the busy Tremont Street sidewalk, was originally part of Boston Common; today it's hemmed in by tallish buildings on three sides. The fourth, with its Egyptian Revival arch entrance, fronts Tremont Street.

From any angle, you can see the stocky **obelisk** at dead center that marks the grave of Benjamin Franklin's parents, but some of the most famous gravesites can only be properly appreciated from the Tremont sidewalk, at the southern rim of the plot. On the side closest to Park Street Church, a boulder with an attached plaque marks the tomb of revolutionary **James Otis**, known for his articulate tirades against British tyranny. A few tombs down is that of **Samuel Adams**, the charismatic patriot whose sideline in beer brewing has kept him a household name. Next to it is the group grave of the five people killed in the **Boston Massacre** of 1770, an event which fueled anti-Tory feeling in Boston (see p.26).

OLD GRANARY BURYING GROUND

Burial vaults and table tombs, somewhat more secure, were preferred by wealthier families. **Peter Faneuil**, who gave his money and his name to Boston's most famous hall, is interred this way in the left rear corner of the grounds. Midway along the back path is the grave of famed messenger and silversmith **Paul Revere**, opposite that of Judge **Samuel Sewall**, the only Salem Witch Trial magistrate to admit later on that he was wrong. Back across from it on the Park Street Church side, a white pillar marks the likely resting spot of Declaration of Independence signer John Hancock. Robert Treat Paine, another signatory, lies along the eastern periphery.

BOSTON ATHENÆUM

Map 3, F4. Mon 9am–8pm, Tues–Fri 9am–5.30pm, also Sept–May Sat 9am–4pm, tours Tues and Thurs 3pm; free. Park Street Ⓣ.

The best view of Old Granary Burying Ground – and an unparalleled photo opportunity most people miss – is from the fifth-floor balcony of the **Boston Athenæum**, at 10 $1/2$ Beacon St, established in 1807 and one of the oldest independent research libraries in the country. In naming their library, the founders demonstrated not only their high-minded Classicism but marketing sensibility too, as its growing stature was a potent enough force to endow Boston with a lofty sobriquet – the "Athens of America" – that has stuck. The library moved to its present quarters, a replica of the Palazzo da Porta Festa in Vicenza, Italy, in 1849. Best known are its **special collections**, including the original holdings of the library of King's Chapel (see below) and books from the private library of George Washington. **Art**, too, has a prominent place: an impressive array of sculptures, coupled with paintings by the likes of

BOSTON ATHENÆUM

17

The Freedom Trail

Boston's history is so visible that it often stands accused of living in the past, and the presence of numerous tourist-friendly contrivances, none more conspicuous – or successful – than the **Freedom Trail**, only adds to the notion. Like many American cities, Boston experienced an economic slump in the postwar years as people migrated to the suburbs. This urban flight engendered the kind of mentality that enabled civic officials to green-light a major highway that ripped through the most historic part of the city, the North End. So when in 1951, Boston residents William Schofield and Bob Winn came up with the idea of the Freedom Trail, it seemed like a sure way to lure visitors and their money back into town – and it has become Boston's chief attraction in the process.

The trail is delineated by a 2.5-mile red-brick stripe in the sidewalk, which links sixteen historical sights that reach from the downtown area up into Charlestown, and while it simplifies their identification, it belies the complexity of early Bostonian (and American) history. Though it's easy to assume each spot played an important part in the struggle to overthrow British rule, this is not entirely the case. While there's no denying the Revolutionary era role of the **Old North Church** and **Faneuil Hall**, two of the most popular stops on the trail, historians would be hard pressed to pinpoint the contributions of, say, **King's Chapel**, built nearly 100 years *before* the Boston Tea Party, or **Park Street Church**, built 35 years after it. And despite its eventual critical role in the War of 1812, the frigate **USS Constitution** ("Old Ironsides") in Charlestown was assembled fully two decades after the Declaration of Independence.

In addition, some of the touches intended to accentuate the historic appeal of the attractions do them a disservice. The people in period costume stationed outside some of the sights can't help but grate a little, and the artificially enhanced atmosphere is exaggerated by the $1 million recently spent by the city to replace most of the painted line with bright red brick and add pseudo-old signage. The Freedom Trail remains the easiest way to orient yourself downtown, and is especially useful if you'll only be in Boston for a short time. But it's still possible, perhaps desirable, to appreciate the city's most historic sights for their individual merit.

John Singer Sargent and Gilbert Stuart, contribute to the atmosphere of studious refinement. A copy of Stuart's famous "Athenæum Head" portrait of Washington, the likeness of which appears on the US one-dollar bill, is housed here.

The crowning glory of the Athenæum is the sedate fifth-floor **Reading Room**; though added in 1914 it's a throwback to a century before. Large Palladian windows afford those stunning views of Old Granary Burying Ground and the skyscrapers beyond. Paying members of the Athenæum like to roost up here, which is probably why only visitors on guided tours can visit it.

KING'S CHAPEL BURYING GROUND

Map 3, G4. June–Oct daily 9.30am–4pm; Nov–May daily 10am–4pm; free. Park Street Ⓣ.

Boston's oldest cemetery, the atmospheric **King's Chapel Burying Ground**, at 58 Tremont St, often goes unnoticed by busy passersby. Coupled with its accompanying church, however, it's well worth a tour despite the din of nearby traffic. The graves of several prominent Bostonians are here, and one of the chief pleasures of walking amongst them is to examine the many beautifully etched ancie gravestones, with their winged skulls and contemplative seraphim, such as that of one **Joseph Tapping**, near the Tremont Street side. Others include **John Winthrop**, the first governor of Massachusetts, and **Mary Chilton**, the first Pilgrim to set foot on Plymouth Rock. Near the center of the plot is the tomb of **William Dawes**, the unsung patriot who accompanied Paul Revere on his famous "midnight ride" to Lexington. King's Chapel Burying Ground was one of the favorite Boston haunts of author **Nathaniel Hawthorne**, who drew inspiration from the grave of a certain Elizabeth Pain to create the famously adulterous character of Hester Prynne for his novel *The Scarlet Letter*.

The most conspicuous thing about the gray, foreboding **chapel** that stands on the grounds is its absence of a steeple (there were plans for one, just not enough money). But the belfry does boast the biggest bell ever cast by Paul Revere, which you'll notice if you happen to pass by at chime time. A wooden chapel was built on this site first, amid some controversy. In 1686, King James II revoked the Massachusetts Bay Colony's charter and installed Sir Edmund Andros as governor, giving him orders to found an Anglican parish, a move that for obvious reasons didn't sit too well with Boston's Puritan population. The present chapel was completed in 1749, with the pillar-fronted portico added in 1789.

At the chapel's entrance is a monument to a certain Chevalier de Saint Saveur, whose burial is said to have occasioned Boston's first Roman Catholic mass. A French inscription reads that locals were not allowed to purchase the bread which members of the first French contingent to the rebel colonial town were baking for themselves, using Boston's own wheat no less. So the locals rioted, and young Chevalier was killed in the fracas. Most visitors never go past the entrance, but it is well worth a look inside, ideally during one of the weekly chamber music concerts (Tues 12.15–12.45pm). While hardly ostentatious, the elegant Georgian interior is a marked contrast to the minimalist adornments of Boston's other old churches. It also features America's oldest pulpit and many of its original pews.

WASHINGTON STREET SHOPPING DISTRICT

Map 3, G4–H6.

To a Bostonian, downtown proper comes in two packages: the **Washington Street shopping district**, namely the School Street area and Downtown Crossing, and the adjacent Financial District (see p.27). The former has some of the city's most historic sights – the Old Corner Bookstore, Old South Meeting House and Old State House – but it tends to shut down after business hours, becoming eerily quiet at night. All the stops can be seen in half a day, though you'll obviously need to allow more time if shopping is on your agenda.

Narrow and heavily trafficked today, in colonial times **Washington Street** connected the Old State House to the city gates at Boston Neck, an isthmus that joined the Shawmut Peninsula to the mainland. That ensured its position as the commercial nerve center of Boston. The best way to begin exploring the area is via **School Street**, anchored on its northern edge by the **Omni Parker House**, the city's most historic hotel. It was here that Boston Creme Pie – really a layered cake with custard filling and chocolate frosting all around – was concocted in 1855, and the hotel reportedly still bakes 25 of them a day. More mystifyingly, Ho Chi Minh and Malcolm X each used to wait tables at the hotel's restaurant.

Only one block long, School Street offers up some of the best in Old Boston charm, beginning with the antique gaslights that flank the the severe western wall of King's Chapel. Just beyond is a grand French Second Empire building that served as **Boston City Hall** from 1865 to 1969. It's near the site of the original location of the **Boston Latin School**, founded in 1635 (a mosaic embedded in the sidewalk just outside the iron gates marks the exact spot). Benjamin Franklin, a statue of whom graces the courtyard, and John Hancock were among the more illustrious graduates of this, America's first public school. Venture forth from the sidewalk to see a lighthearted **mural** that depicts them as kids on recess – Hancock is shown honing his famous signature, while Franklin experiments with a kite.

A few doors down on the left, the gambrel-roofed, redbrick former **Old Corner Bookstore** anchors the southern end of School Street as it joins Washington. The stretch of Washington from here to Old South Meeting House was nineteenth-century Boston's version of London's Fleet Street, with a convergence of booksellers, publishers and newspaper headquarters; and the bookstore itself – as home to the publishing house of Ticknor & Fields – was the hottest literary salon Boston ever had, with the likes of Emerson, Longfellow, Hawthorne and even Dickens and Thackeray, all of whom Ticknor & Fields published. One of America's oldest literary magazines, the staid *Atlantic Monthly*, was published upstairs here for many years; later *The Boston Globe* moved in. The newspaper maintained the site as *The Globe Corner Bookstore*, an atmospheric travel book shop until its demise in 1997, now vaingloriously reincarnated as the *Boston Globe Store*, where you can buy merchandise stamped with the newspaper's logo.

Old South Meeting House

Map 3, H4. Daily: April–Oct 9.30am–5pm; Nov–March 10am–4pm; $3. Downtown Crossing Ⓣ.

Washington Street's big architectural landmark is the **Old South Meeting House**, at 310 Washington St, a charming brick church building recognizable by its tower, a separate but attached structure, that tapers into an octagonal spire. Its exterior clock is the same one installed in 1770 – and you can still set your watch by it. An earlier cedarwood structure on the spot burned down in 1711, clearing the way for what is now the second oldest church building in Boston, after Old North Church in the North End. Its Congregationalist origins prescribed simplicity inside and out, with no artifice to obstruct closeness to God. This also endowed Old South with a spaciousness that made it a leading venue for anti-imperial rhetoric. The day after the Boston Massacre, outraged Bostonians assembled here to demand the removal of the troops that were ostensibly guarding the town. Five years later, patriot and doctor Joseph Warren delivered an oration to commemorate the incident; the biggest building in town was so packed that he had to crawl through the window behind the pulpit just to get inside.

On the morning of December 16, 1773, nearly 7000 locals met here, awaiting word from Governor Thomas Hutchinson on whether the Crown would actually impose duty on sixty tons of tea aboard ships in Boston Harbor. When a message was received that it would, Samuel Adams rose and announced, "This meeting can do nothing more to save the country" – the signal that triggered the **Boston Tea Party**, perhaps the seminal event leading to the War for Independence (see p.36). Today, the Old South houses a museum with exhibits that focus on freedom of speech; it

OLD SOUTH MEETING HOUSE

previously went through incarnations as a stable, a riding-school and even a bar in the meanwhile. One of the things to go in that time was the famous high pulpit; the more ornate one standing today is a replica from 1808.

Downtown Crossing

Downtown Crossing (Map 3, G6) is a busy pedestrian area, centered on the intersection of Washington and Winter streets, whose strip of department stores and smaller shops recalls the time before malls, and it possesses some fine nineteenth-century commercial architecture besides. Brimming with stores that mostly cater to lower-income shoppers and the pushcart vendors and panhandlers that pester them at nearly every street corner, its nucleus is *Filene's Basement*, a magnet for bargain hunters of all socio-economic stripes and the only "attraction" here really worth your time (see p.269). Otherwise, unless you have the money and inclination to eat at the historic *Locke-Ober* restaurant on Winter Place, you may as well move on.

Old State House

Map 3, H3. Daily 9.30am–5pm; $3, students $2. State ⓣ.

That the graceful three-tiered window tower of the red-brick **Old State House**, at the corner of Washington and State streets, is dwarfed by skyscrapers amplifies, rather than diminishes, its colonial-era dignity. This is especially notice-able if you're stuck in traffic on I-93 where the elevated expressway passes by State Street, a view that affords a spec-tacular juxtaposition of the old and new.

For years this three-story structure, reminiscent of an old Dutch town hall, was the seat of the Massachusetts Bay Colony, and consequently the center of British authority in

New England. Later it served as Boston's city hall, and in 1880 it was nearly demolished so that State Street traffic might flow more freely. It was spared that fate by the Bostonian Society, and today houses the small but comprehensive **Boston History Museum** (see below).

You can get loads of information on the city at 15 State St, home to the excellent Boston National Historic Park Visitor's Center (see p.6).

An impassioned speech in the second-floor Council Chamber by **James Otis**, a Crown appointee who resigned to take up the colonial cause, sparked the quest for independence from Britain fifteen years before it was declared. He argued against the Writs of Assistance, which permitted the British to inspect private property at will. Legend has it that on certain nights you can still hear Otis hurling his anti-British barbs and the cheers of the crowd he so energized, but museum staff have no comment. The **balcony** overlooking State Street is as famous as Otis' speech, for it was from here that royal governors made official announcements and where on July 18, 1776 the Declaration of Independence was first read publicly in Boston – a copy having arrived from Philadelphia. That same night the lion and unicorn figures mounted above the balcony were set ablaze (the ones there now are replicas). Oddly enough, just to show there were no hard feelings, Queen Elizabeth II – the first British monarch to set foot in Boston – read the Declaration of Independence from the balcony as part of the American bicentennial activities in 1976.

As for the museum, the permanent ground-level exhibit, "Colony to Commonwealth," chronicles the role of Boston in the Revolutionary War. Dozens of images and artifacts track – with varying interest – the events that led up to the

OLD STATE HOUSE

establishment of the Commonwealth of Massachusetts (though not, curiously, the US). You can see a bit of tea from Boston's most infamous party, the plaque of royal arms that once hung over Province House, official residence of the colonial governors, the flag that the Sons of Liberty draped from the Liberty Tree (see p.40) to announce their meetings, and Paul Revere's propagandistic engraving of the Boston Massacre – the most galvanizing image of the Revolutionary period. Upstairs are rotating exhibits on the history of the city and, incongruously, a display on old Boston hotels and restaurants.

Boston Massacre Site

Directly in front of the State Street side of the Old State House, a circle of cobblestones embedded in a small traffic island marks the site of the **Boston Massacre**, the tragic outcome of escalating tensions between Bostonians and the British Redcoats who occupied the city. Riots were an increasingly common occurrence in Boston by the time this deadly one broke out on March 5, 1770. It began when a young wigmaker's apprentice began heckling an army officer over a barber's bill. The officer sought refuge in the Custom House, which stood opposite the Old State House at the time, but by this time, a throng of people had gathering, including more soldiers, at whom the mob flung rocks and snowballs. When someone threw a club that knocked a Redcoat onto the ice, he rose and fired. Five Bostonians were killed in the ensuing fracas, as a result of which Governor Hutchinson relocated the occupying troops to Castle Island, in Boston Harbor. Two other patriots, John Adams and Josiah Quincy, actually defended the offending eight soldiers in court; six were acquitted, and the two guilty were branded on their thumbs.

FINANCIAL DISTRICT

Map 3, I3–I6.

Boston's **Financial District** hardly conjures the same interest as those of New York or London, but it continues to wield influence in key areas (like mutual funds, invented here in 1925) and is not entirely devoid of historic interest – though this is generally more manifest in plaques rather than actual buildings. Like most of America's business districts, it beats to an office-hours-only schedule, and many of its little eateries and Irish pubs are closed on weekends – though some brash new restaurants are beginning to make inroads. The generally immaculate streets follow the same short, winding paths as they did three hundred years ago, only now, thirty- and forty-story skyscrapers have replaced the wooden houses and churches that used to clutter the area. Still, their names are historically evocative. High Street, for example – originally Cow Lane – once led to the summit of now vanished eighty-foot-tall Fort Hill. Arch Street recalls the decorative arch that graced the Tontine Crescent, a block of stately townhouses designed in 1793 by Charles Bulfinch and unfortunately demolished by the Great Fire of 1872, which began in the heart of the district. Tucked among the relatively generic sky-scrapers are several well-preserved nineteenth-century mer-cantile masterpieces, many of them also Bulfinch designs.

Milk Street and Post Office Square

You can start your tour of the Financial District by heading south from Faneuil Hall or the Waterfront, but the most dramatic approach is east from Washington Street via **Milk Street**. A bust of **Benjamin Franklin** surveys the scene from a recessed Gothic niche above the doorway at 1 Milk St, across from the Old South Meeting House. The site marks Franklin's birthplace, though the building itself only dates from 1874. A bit farther down Milk Street, at the intersection with Devonshire Street, the somber 22-story **John W. McCormack federal courthouse** building houses one of Boston's better post offices, with a special section for stamp collectors, though an earlier building on this site gave the adjacent, triangular **Post Office Square** its name. Sneak up to the glass atrium atop the building at **One Post Office Square**; though not really open to the public, it's worth sneaking in for its jaw-dropping views of Boston Harbor and downtown – a skyline that encompasses the architectural excesses of the 1980s and a few Art Deco treats too. The best example of the former is the **Bank of Boston** tower at 100 Federal St, with its bulging midsection, nicknamed "Pregnant Alice."

The prime Art Deco specimen is nearby at 185 Franklin St, the head office of **Bell Atlantic**. The step-top building was a 1947 design; more recently the phone booths outside were given a deco makeover. If you're here during business hours, check out the fusty nook off the right-hand side of the lobby, home to a replica of the Boston attic room where, in 1875, Alexander Graham Bell first transmitted speech sounds over a wire. The wooden chamber is a meticulously reassembled version of the original that was installed in 1959; with the exception of an evocative diorama of an old Boston cityscape, it looks like it hasn't been dusted since. Likewise for the 360-degree mural in the lobby that glorifies the exciting world of *Telephone Men and Women at Work*.

Exchange Place, at 53 State St, is a mirrored-glass tower rising from the façade of the old Boston Stock Exchange; the *Bunch of Grapes* tavern, watering hole of choice for many of Boston's revolutionary rabble-rousers, once stood here. Behind it is tiny **Liberty Square**, once the heart of

Tory Boston and now mostly of note for its improbable sculpture that commemorates the Hungarian anti-Communist uprising of 1956.

THE CUSTOM HOUSE DISTRICT

Map 3, I3–J3.

The not-quite-triangular wedge of downtown between State and Broad streets and the Fitzgerald Expressway is the unfairly overlooked **Custom House District**, dotted with some excellent architectural draws, chief among which is the **Custom House Tower**, surrounded by 32 huge Doric columns, built in 1847; the thirty-story Greek Revival tower itself was added in 1915. Not surprisingly, it is no longer the tallest skyscraper in New England, but it still has plenty of character, though its observation deck has been closed since the Marriott Corporation purchased the building.

Another landmark is the **Grain and Flour Exchange Building**, a block away at 177 Milk St, a fortress-like construction that recalls the Romanesque Revival style of prominent local architect H.H. Richardson. Its turreted, conical roof, encircled by a series of pointed dormers, is a bold reminder of the financial stature this district once held. **Broad Street**, built on filled-in land in 1807, is still home to several Federal-style mercantile buildings designed by Bulfinch. Back on State Street, get a look at the elaborate cast-iron façade of the **Richards Building**, at no. 114, a clipper ship company's office in the 1850s, and the **Cunard Building**, at no. 126, its ceremonious ornamental anchors a reflection of Boston's status as North American terminus of the first transatlantic steamship mail service.

State Street, called King Street in colonial days, is indeed about the most stately commercial thoroughfare in America. It once extended far into Boston Harbor, where

THE CUSTOM HOUSE DISTRICT

Long Wharf now is, and was almost from its inception the focal point of Boston's maritime prosperity. With all the trading activity came a thriving banking and insurance industry and an accompanying collection of rather staid office buildings. A modern exception is the opulent **Fleet Bank** headquarters at no. 75, a medium-sized skyscraper crowned with 3600 square feet of gold leaf, and a lobby six stories high decked out in marble, mahogany and bronze.

FANEUIL HALL

Map 3, H2. Daily 9am–5pm; free. State Ⓣ.

Located between the Financial District and the North End, the **Faneuil Hall Marketplace** is the kind of active, bustling public gathering ground that's none too common in Boston, popular with locals and tourists alike. Built as a market during colonial times to house the city's growing mercantile industry, it declined during the nineteenth century and, like the area around it, was pretty much defunct until the 1960s, when it was quite successfully redeveloped as a restaurant and shopping mall.

Much-hyped Faneuil Hall doesn't appear particularly majestic from the outside; it's simply a small, four-story brick building topped with a Georgian spire, hardly the grandiose auditorium one might imagine would have housed the Revolutionary war meetings that earned its "Cradle of Liberty" sobriquet. Early Faneuil Hall housed an open-air market on its first floor and a space for political meetings on its second, a juxtaposition that inspired local poet Francis Hatch to pen the lines, "Here orators in ages past / Have mounted their attacks, / Undaunted by the proximity / Of sausage on the racks." Faneuil Hall was where revolutionary firebrands such as Samuel Adams and

James Otis whipped up popular support for independence by protesting British tax legislation. The first floor now houses a panoply of tourist shops which make for a less than dignified memorial; you'll also find an information desk and a post office. The second floor is more impressive: the auditorium has been preserved to reflect modifications made by Charles Bulfinch in 1805, however its focal point is a massive – and rather preposterous – canvas depicting an imagined scene in which Daniel Webster speaks in Faneuil Hall as a range of luminaries from Washington to de Tocqueville look on.

> **During the War of 1812, folks in Beantown who were suspected of being spies were asked what flew atop Faneuil Hall as a weathervane. Those who knew it was a grasshopper were trusted as true Bostonians; those who didn't were regarded with suspicion, and occasionally decapitated.**

Immediately in front of Faneuil Hall is **Dock Square**, so named for its original location directly on Boston's waterfront; carvings in the pavement indicate the location of Boston's shoreline in 1630. The square's center is dominated by a statue of Samuel Adams, interesting mostly for its over-the-top caption: "A Statesman, fearless and incorruptible."

QUINCY MARKET

Map 3, I2. Mon–Sat 10am–9pm, Sun noon–6pm; free. State Ⓣ.
The markets just behind Faneuil Hall – three parallel oblong structures that house restaurants, shops and office buildings – were built in the early eighteenth century to contain the trade that had quickly outgrown its space in the

hall. The center building, known as **Quincy Market**, holds a superextended corridor lined with stands vending a variety of decent though pricey take-out treats – the mother of mall food courts. To either side of Quincy Market are **North and South Markets**, which hold restaurants and popular chain clothing stores, as well as curiosity shops where narrow specialization is the running gimmick (one sells only purple objects, another nothing but vests). You'll also find the usual complement of street musicians, fire-jugglers and mimes, weather permitting. There's not much to distinguish it from any other shopping complex, although there are several good restaurants, and the surrounding nightlife, with one of the few concentrations of bars in the downtown area, is among Boston's best. Sitting on a bench in the carnivalesque heart of it all on a summer day, eating scrod while the mobs of townies and tourists mill about is a slightly absurd but quintessential Boston experience.

BLACKSTONE BLOCK AND THE HOLOCAUST MEMORIAL

Map 3, H1.

From Faneuil Hall, traverse the dim, narrow corridor known as **Scott's Alley** up to Creek Square, where you enter **Blackstone Block**, an area so far bypassed by urban renewal and as such a reasonably authentic remnant of central Boston's original architectural character. Its uneven cobblestoned streets and low brick buildings have remained largely untouched since the 1650s.

Nearby on Union Street jut six tall hollow glass pillars erected as a **memorial** to victims of the Holocaust. Built to resemble smokestacks, the columns are etched with quotes and facts about the Holocaust, with an unusual degree of attention to its non-Jewish victims. Steam rises from grates beneath each of the pillars to accentuate their symbolism; the effect is particularly striking at night. The brief walk makes for a sobering contrast to the self-congratulatory tone of the Freedom Trail.

GOVERNMENT CENTER

Map 3, G2–H3.

Most visitors pass through **Government Center** during their time in Boston, as it's an essential travel hub located in the midst of downtown – and passing through is just about all there is to do in this sea of towering gray government buildings which stands on the former site of **Scollay Square**, once Boston's most notorious den of porn halls and tattoo parlors. As part of a city-wide face-lift, Scollay was razed in the early 1960s, eliminating all traces of its salacious past and, along with it, most of its lively character; indeed, the only thing that remains from that time is the steaming tea kettle sign just across from the Government Center Ⓣ stop. The area is now overlaid with concrete, and two monolithic edifices tower above: **Boston City Hall,** at the east side of the plaza, and the **John F. Kennedy Federal Building**, on the north. Unless the workings of bureaucracy get you going, the only conceivable reason to stop here is to go to the **visitors center** on the fourth floor of City Hall, which has the usual array of travel information, and some aberrantly clean public restrooms.

THE WATERFRONT

Map 3, K1–L7.

The series of wharves occupying the harborside stretch below Christopher Columbus Park, Boston's **Waterfront** is still a fairly active area, though no longer the city's focal point, as it was as recently as the mid-1800s. The city's decline as a port left the Waterfront with no real function, and the construction of the elevated central artery in the 1950s physically separated it from the rest of the city. Today, the Waterfront thrives, but mainly on tourism, with stands selling tacky T-shirts, furry lobsters and the like. Nevertheless, strolling around the wharves on a sunny day affords an unbeatable view of Boston Harbor, and a pleasant respite from the masses that can clog Faneuil Hall and the Common.

Long Wharf

Map 3, L1.

Long Wharf is the best place to head for, the district's main drag since its construction in 1710. Summer is its most active season, when the wharf is dotted with stands vending kitschy souvenirs and surprisingly excellent ice cream. This is also the main point of departure for harbor cruises, whale watching, and ferries to Cape Cod.

Walk out to the end of Long Wharf for an excellent vantage point on **Boston Harbor**. Since the city is surrounded by other land masses, you'll only see a series of peninsulas and islands, which are generally smoky and grinding with industry. It's perhaps most enjoyable – and still relatively safe – at night, when even the freighters appear graceful against the moonlit water.

New England Aquarium

Map 3, L2. Mon–Tues & Fri 9am–6pm, Wed–Thurs 9am–8pm, Sat–Sun and holidays 9am–7pm; weekdays $10.50; weekends $12. Aquarium Ⓣ.

Next door to Long Wharf is the **New England Aquarium,** at Central Wharf – the Waterfront's main draw

The Harborwalk

The **Harborwalk** was conceived as a way to recall Boston's history as a major commercial port, days that seem ever more in the past, especially considering the Harbor's notorious recent reputation for pollution. While the sights along the walk don't have the historical all-star quality of those on the Freedom Trail, and some of the facts would have to be spruced up to even be considered mundane, it's still a picturesque stroll, usually running along the water, that provides a historical perspective on the Waterfront not otherwise readily evident. The Harborwalk starts at the corner of State Street and Merchant's Row, proceeds along the wharves, and ends up on the Congress Street bridge at the Boston Tea Party museum. Visitors' center maps can guide you along, and blue plaques along the way illustrate the relevance of the various stopping points.

and, like many of Boston's attractions, aimed at kids, though enjoyable for anyone as long as you don't expect too much. It doesn't win points for atmosphere: the interior is plain, dank, and reeks vaguely, though not surprisingly, of fish. The opening display is one of the best: a backlit tank swarming with translucent jellyfish. Less beautiful but more engaging are the penguins on the bottom floor. Be sure to play with the device that allows you to maneuver a point of light around the bottom of the pool; the guileless waterfowl will mistake the light for a fish and follow it around obediently. In the center of the aquarium's spiral walkway is its single most impressive collection of marine life: a three-story cylindrical tank with moray eels, great white sharks, and a range of other sea exotica that swim by in unsettling proximity.

THE HARBORWALK

The Boston Tea Party

The first major act of rebellion preceding the Revolutionary War, the **Boston Tea Party** was far greater in significance than it was in duration. On December 20, 1773, a long-standing dispute between the British government and its colonial subjects, involving a tea tax, came to a dramatic head. At nightfall, an angry mob of about 1000, which had been whipped into an anti-British frenzy by Samuel Adams at Old South Meeting House, converged on Griffin's Wharf. Around a hundred of them, some dressed in Indian garb, boarded three brigs and threw their cargo of tea overboard. The partiers disposed of 342 chests of tea each weighing 360 pounds – enough to make 24 million cups, and worth more than one million dollars by today's standards. While it had the semblance of spontaneity, the event was in fact planned beforehand, and the mob was careful not to damage anything but the offending cargo. In any case, the Boston Tea Party transformed protest into revolution; even Governor Hutchinson agreed that afterwards, war was the only recourse. The ensuing British sanctions, colloquially referred to as the "Intolerable Acts," and the colonists' continued resistance, further inflamed the tension between the crown and its colonies, which eventually exploded at Lexington and Concord several months later.

Boston Tea Party Ship and Museum

Map 3, K7. March–Nov daily 9am–5pm; $7, students $3.50. South Station Ⓣ.

Out of the brief but seminal events of the Boston Tea Party, the curators have forged the **Boston Tea Party Ship and Museum** by combining history with a sense of

irreverence. Displays range from the expected (......
tory) to the wildly tangential (shipbuilding, the ....
ture of tea), and the whole affair takes place on a ....
the original ship floating off the Congress Street bri....
Fort Point Channel. While the exhibits won't challe....
your mind, they're fun in a hokey way: the information...
video is set to the dubious 1970s anthem "A Fifth of
Beethoven," and you can grab a cup of complimentary hot
tea on your way out.

Spirited recreations of the Tea Party are held on occasion
here, but don't be taken in: the Congress Street bridge was
not the real site of the Boston Tea Party. It actually took
place on what is today dry land, near the intersection of
Atlantic and Congress streets. Indeed, at the **Harbor
Plaza**, at 470 Atlantic, there's a commemorative plaque
engraved with a spirited but silly patriotic poem expressing
outrage at "King George's trivial but tyrannical tax of 3p.
per pound."

Children's Museum

Map 3, L7. Tues–Sun 10am–5pm (Fri until 9pm); $7, kids $6, Fri
5–9pm $1. South Station Ⓣ.

Across the Congress Street bridge is the **Children's
Museum**, at 300 Congress St, which comprises five floors of
deceptively educational exhibits, designed basically to trick
kids into learning about a huge array of topics, from kine-
matics to the history of popular culture. The key here is
interactivity; the displays are meant to be touched rather than
observed. There is, for instance, the climbing maze-cum-
sculpture in the central shaft that no one over fourteen could
possibly get into. Others are amusing even for adults, particularly the features on Japanese youth culture, though it's really
not worth the admission price unless you're there with kids.

CHILDREN'S MUSEUM |

5pm (Fri until 9pm); $7, children $5,
Station Ⓣ.

's Museum is another treat for the
um, two floors of displays aimed
history and capabilities of com-
e a blast here, especially with the
n can play, though there's less of
stuck waiting for the wee ones,
either head to the engaging artificial intelligence display or
take a stroll through the museum's proudest attraction, the
Walk-Through Computer, which allows visitors to experience a PC from the vantage point of a microchip.

SEAPORT DISTRICT

The **Seaport District** loosely refers to a harborside area
across the Northern Avenue bridge from Boston, accessible
by a free shuttle from the South Station Ⓣ, where businesses
have recently banded together in an attempt to forge an
attractive identity. The only real draw here, however, is the
excellent range of restaurants near Boston's **Fish Pier**.
There are also a number of odoriferous **lobster whole-
salers** on the Fish Pier and along Northern Avenue. If
you're in the area and want some crustaceans, brave the harrowing sights and smells of these seafood warehouses to
avoid paying standard market price.

CHINATOWN AND AROUND

Map 3, F8–I8.

Boston's colorful and authentic **Chinatown** lies wedged
into just a few square blocks between the Financial and

Theater districts, but it makes up in activity what it lacks in size. Lean against a pagoda-topped payphone on the corner of **Beach and Tyler streets** anytime and watch the way life here revolves around the food trade. By day, merchants barter in Mandarin and Cantonese over the going price of produce; by night, Bostonians arrive in droves to nosh in Chinatown's restaurants. Continue walking down either of these streets – the neighborhood's two liveliest thorough-fares – and you'll pass most of the restaurants, bakeries and markets, in whose windows you'll see the usual comple-ment of roast ducks hanging from hooks and aquariums filled with future seafood dinners.

**For our recommendations on the best restaurants
in Chinatown, see p.190.**

The prosperity of Boston's Chinatown has increased dra-matically in recent years, so much so that the district is expanding to the north, taking up some of the land that lies between it and Downtown Crossing. Despite this growth, the heart of Chinatown contains little in the way of sights and the atmosphere is best enjoyed by wandering around with no particular destination in mind.

There are a few important landmarks, such as the impres-sive **Chinatown Gate,** a three-story red-and-gilt monolith guarded by four Fu dogs at the intersection of Hudson and Beach streets, a gift from Taiwan in honor of Chinatown's centennial. Adjacent **Tian An Men Park** provides a place to rest, but it's poorly kept, generally littered with trash and inhabited by fearsomely aggressive pigeons.

Chinatown is at its most vibrant during various festivals, none more so than the **Chinese New Year** (late Jan–early Feb), when frequent parades of papier-mâché dragons fill the streets and the acrid smell of firecrackers permeates the

CHINATOWN AND AROUND

air. During the **Festival of the August Moon,** not surprisingly held in August, there's a bustling street fair. Call the *Chinese Merchants' Association* for more information (✆482-3972).

Combat zone

Around Washington Street, between Essex and Kneeland, you can still see some vestiges of the old red-light district enigmatically called the **Combat Zone** – not quite as dangerous as it sounds. It was designated by the city as an "adult entertainment zone" in the 1960s after Old Scollay Square was demolished to make room for Government Center, and nowadays it keeps up a few X-rated theaters and bookshops, enhanced by some low-key drug dealing and prostitution, all of which provides some Bostonians with an antidote to the city's much-maligned stuffier side. It doesn't look like the visible reminders will be around much longer, especially with Chinatown's encroachment; indeed, the former *Naked I* adult theater, at 417 Washington St, now stands as Chinatown's first *McDonald's,* decked out with green pagodas as well as golden arches. Back on the stodgier side is the plaque at the corner of Essex and Washington that marks the site where the **Liberty Tree** stood. This oak, planted in 1646, was a favored meeting point of the Sons of Liberty; the British chopped it down in 1775.

Leather District

Just east of Chinatown are six square blocks, bounded by Kneeland, Atlantic, Essex and Lincoln streets, that designate the **Leather District**. It takes its name from the days when the shoe industry was a mainstay of the New England economy, and the leather needed to make the shoes was shipped through the warehouses here. Since then, the Financial District – with which it is frequently lumped – has horned in, and the leather industry has pretty much dried up. The distinction between the Financial and Leather districts is actually quite sharp, and most evident where High Street transitions into South Street, the Leather District's main drag. Gleaming modern skyscrapers are replaced by stout brick warehouses, and the place of suited bankers is taken by a melange of merchants and gallery owners. Some of the edifices still have their leather warehouse signs on them. Check out the *Boston Hide & Leather Co* at 15 East St, and the *Fur and Leather Services Outlet* at 717 Atlantic – but don't expect too much going on behind the façades.

Otherwise, the Leather District has little to offer of historical interest, but the area is gradually picking itself up, its abundance of cheap warehouse space attracting a number of **art galleries** and the trendy punters that go with them, making it the capital of Boston's modest contemporary arts scene. For a list of galleries, see p.266.

THEATER DISTRICT

Map 3, D8–E9.

Just south of Boston Common is the slightly seedy **Theater District**, the chief attractions of which are the flamboyant theaters that lend the area its name, such as the Wilbur, Colonial and Majestic – though not surprisingly you'll have to get play tickets in order to inspect the grand old interiors (see p.243). The Colonial anchors so-called **Piano Row**, a section of Boylston Street between Charles and Tremont that was the center of American piano manufacturing and music publishing in the nineteenth and early twentieth centuries, and still has a few piano shops. Of greater interest,

Banned in Boston

Boston's Puritan founders would be horrified to find that an area called the **Theater District** even exists. Their ingrained allergy to fun resulted in theatrical performances actually being outlawed in Boston until 1792, and in 1878, the Watch & Ward Society was formed to organize boycotts against indecent books and plays. Still the shows went on, and in 1894 vaudeville was born at the lavish (now extinct) B.F. Keith Theater. Burlesque soon followed, prompting the city licensing division in 1905 to deny performances that didn't meet their neo-Puritan codes, thus the phrase "Banned in Boston." As recently as 1970, a production of *Hair* was banned for a month due to its desecration of the American flag.

Yet Boston still managed to become the premier theater try-out town that it is today; the high production costs on Broadway dictated that the hits be sifted from the misses at an early stage. During the 1920s – the heyday of theater in the city – there were as many as forty playhouses in this small neighborhood. But the rise of film meant the fall of theater, and after brief stints as movie halls many of the grand buildings slid into disrepair and eventual abandonment, including the Art Deco **Paramount**, the sadly crumbling **Opera House** – formerly the Savoy – and the **Modern Theater**, all on lower Washington Street. Others have fared better: the old **Metropolitan Theater**, a movie house of palatial proportions, survives as the glittering **Wang Center**, home of the Boston Ballet; and the **Colonial** is still the little grand dame of Boston theater. The **Majestic Theater**, with its soaring Rococo ceiling and neo-Classical friezes, was restored after Emerson College bought it in 1983 and it's now the main stage for the Boston Lyric Opera and Dance Umbrella.

though, are the trendy restaurants and clubs in the immediate vicinity, many of which are tucked into Charles and Stuart streets around the mammoth **Massachusetts Transportation Building**, and cater to the theater-going crowd.

THEATER DISTRICT

THE NORTH END

The **North End** is a small yet densely populated neighborhood whose narrow streets are chock-a-block with Italian bakeries and restaurants, and also hold some of Boston's most storied sights. Bordered by Boston Harbor and separated from downtown by the elevated Fitzgerald Expressway (I-93), it may seem an inaccessible district at first, and indeed the protracted dismantling of I-93 can make access a challenge, but you can avoid the hassle – and get a much better sense of the area's attractiveness – by entering from the waterfront Christopher Columbus Park, then taking Richmond Street past quiet North Square to **Hanover Street**, the North End's main drag. Once there, you can cover the must-sees fairly quickly – the **Old North Church**, **Paul Revere House** and **Copp's Hill Burying Ground** – but to soak up the street life and appreciate the variety of the North End's cafés and the like, plan on more than one visit.

The North End's detached quality goes back to colonial times, when it was actually an island, later to be joined by short bridges to the main part of town, known then as the South End. This physical separation bred antagonism that culminated every 5 November in Pope's Day, when North and South Enders paraded effigies of the Pope through their neighborhoods and then attempted to capture the other's pontiff on Boston Common. If the North Enders won, they would burn the thing atop Copp's Hill (see pp.52–53). Though landfill eventually ended the district's physical isolation, the North End remained very much a place apart. It became the residence of choice for the wealthy merchant class: Massachusetts Bay Colony governors Hutchinson and Phips had roomy houses here, as did the notoriously Puritanical Mather family. But most of the British Loyalists who called the area home fled to Nova Scotia after the Revolution, hastening de-gentrification. Irish immigrants poured in after the potato famine of 1840; John F. Fitzgerald, JFK's grandfather, was born on Ferry Street, and the late president's mother, Rose, on nearby Garden Street.

The Irish were just the first of several immigrant groups to colonize the North End, displaced by Eastern European Jews in the 1850s, and Southern Italians in the early twentieth century. The latter have for the most part stayed put, and the North End is still Boston's most authentically Italian neighborhood. This flavor is most pronounced during the eight annual summer *festas*, during which members of private charity clubs parade figurines of their patron saints (usually the same as those of their home towns in Italy) through the narrow streets. The processions, complete with marching bands, stop every few feet to let people pin dollar bills to the streamers attached to the statues.

Thanks to the local mafia, still alive if not flourishing, crime (of the nonorganized kind) has long been held at bay here; and when the Central Artery tore through it in 1954 the North End was effectively cut off even more. This safety, along with comparatively low rents, has acted as a magnet for yuppies, who colonized the waterfront side of the neighborhood and are now making inroads into rehabilitated tenements. You can still see laundry dangling from upper-story windows and grandmothers chattering in

Italian in front of their apartment buildings, but it's perhaps only a matter of time before gentrification wins out.

....

**The area covered by this chapter is shown
in detail on color map 4.**

....

HANOVER STREET

Map 4, C6–F3.

Hanover Street has long been the main connection between the North End and the rest of Boston, and it is along here – and its small side streets like Parmenter and Richmond (actually a continuation of each other on either side of Hanover) – that many of the area's trattorias, cafés and bakeries are located. It's also where you'll find, in its first few blocks, perhaps Boston's most authentically European flavor, though when a *CVS* drugstore opened here in 1996, it marked the first chain store intruder on the street – and probably not the last. The classic Italian spots remain, including *Mike's Pastry*, at no. 300, where President Clinton has been known to put back a few *cannollis* when in the area. The quieter side of the North End reasserts itself on the short blocks north of the Paul Revere Mall – about midpoint on the street – but even these are home to an increasing number of restaurants, geared as much to locals as tourists.

NORTH SQUARE

Map 4, D6–E6.

The little triangular wedge of cobblestones and gaslights known as **North Square**, one block east of Hanover between Prince and Richmond streets, is among the most historic and attractive pockets of Boston, although its actual center is cordoned off by a heavy chain. Here the eateries recede in deference to the **Paul Revere House**, the oldest residential address in the city, at 19 North Square (daily

Paul the Revered

It wasn't until decades after his death that **Paul Revere** achieved fame for his fifteen-mile journey to Lexington to warn John Hancock and Sam Adams of the impending British march inland to seize colonial munitions – and that thanks to a fanciful poem by Henry Wadsworth Longfellow, which failed to note that another patriot, **William Dawes**, made the trip as well. Its opening line, "Listen, my children, and you shall hear/Of the midnight ride of Paul Revere" is as familiar to American schoolchildren as the Pledge of Allegiance. But during his lifetime, this jack-of-all-trades was principally known for his abilities as a silversmith – with a side business in false teeth – and as a propagandist for the patriot's cause, not so much as a legendary messenger.

Revere's engraving of the Boston Massacre did much to turn public opinion against the Tories, and he went so far as to stage an exhibition of similar engravings at his North End home one year after the incident. He also rode on horseback to carry news of the Boston Tea Party to New York and Philadelphia, only hours after participating in the event. In December 1774, four months before the legendary ride to Lexington, Revere rode to Portsmouth, New Hampshire to notify locals of the British intent to shore up fortifications there, precipitating the first organized American assault on a royal fortress flying the king's flag. After the Revolution he engraved the first American currency; more profitable was his bell and cannon foundry in the present-day town of – not coincidentally – Revere, just north of Boston. He died in 1818 at the age of 83, and rests among his Revolutionary peers in Old Granary Burying Ground (see p. 16).

PAUL REVERE

9.30am–4.15pm, until 5.15pm April 15–Oct 31; $2.50). The small two-story post-and-beam structure, which dates from about 1680, stands on the site of the considerably grander home of Puritan heavyweight Increase Mather, father of Cotton – that one burned down in the Great Fire of 1676. A North Ender for most of his life, Revere lived here from 1770 to 1800 (except for much of 1775, when he hid out from the British in Watertown), during which time he sired his six-teen-strong brood. The building was restored in 1908 to reflect its seventeenth-century appearance; prior to that it served variously as a grocery store, tenement and cigar factory.

Though the house is more impressive for its longevity than appearance, from the outside the second-story over-hang and leaded windows provide quite a contrast to the red brick buildings around it. On the inside, the first-floor "hall," or living room, resembles a hunting lodge with its low ceiling and enormous fireplace. Examples of Revere's self-made silver wares upstairs merit a look, as does a small but evocative exhibit about the mythologizing of Revere's horseback ride to warn patriots that the British were com-ing. Fragments of gaudy wallpaper, once considered quite fashionable, adorn the walls throughout the house.

North Street itself was first called Anne's Street, some-what of a red-light district in the early nineteenth century. It is home to an unusual, obscure relic, too: the **oldest sign in Boston**. If you look at the building on the corner of North and Richmond streets, you'll see a sign with the intials "W, T, S" affixed to the third floor, a reference to the owners of an inn that stood here in 1694.

A small courtyard, the focus of which is a glass-encased 900-pound bell that Revere cast, separates the Paul Revere House from the **Pierce-Hichborn House** (tours by appointment ℂ523-2338; $2.50), a simple Georgian-style house built in 1710, making it the oldest surviving *brick* house in Boston.

Moses Pierce, a glazier, built the house, and it later belonged later to Paul Revere's shipbuilding cousin, Nathaniel Hichborn – thus its present name. Though Hichborn was considerably wealthier than his more famous cousin, you'd never guess it from the interior: typical colonial American, sparsely furnished with some very unremarkable period tables, chairs and a few decorative lamps and cabinetry.

ST STEPHEN'S CHURCH AND PAUL REVERE MALL

At Hanover's intersection with Clark Street is **St Stephen's Church** (Map 4, F4), the only still-standing church in Boston built by Charles Bulfinch and one with a striking three-story recessed brick arch entrance. Originally called New North Church, it received its new name in 1862 to keep up with the increasingly Catholic population of the North End; you'd never guess it today, but the whole building was moved back sixteen feet when Hanover Street was widened in 1870. Its other claim to fame is that Rose Kennedy's funeral ceremony was held here in 1995.

Just across Hanover, the famous bronze **statue** of Paul Revere on his borrowed horse marks the edge of the **Paul Revere Mall** (Map 4, E4). Sometimes called the Prado, this much-needed urban space was carved out of a chunk of apartment blocks in 1933 and runs back to tiny **Unity Street** – home of the small red brick **Clough House**, at no. 21, built by the mason who helped lay the brick of the Old North Church.

OLD NORTH CHURCH

Map 4, E3. Daily 9am-5pm; free. Haymarket Ⓣ.

Were it not for **Old North Church**, 93 Salem St, as a sign affixed to a collection box just inside its entrance reads, "You

ST. STEPHEN'S CHURCH AND PAUL REVERE MALL

49

Might be Making Donations in Pound Notes." Few places in Boston have as emblematic a quality as the simple yet noble Christ Church (as Old North is officially called), rising unobstructed above the monotonous blocks of red brick apartments around it. Built in 1723, and inspired by St Andrew's-by-the-Wardrobe in Blackfriars, London, it's the oldest church in Boston, easily recognized by its gleaming 191ft **steeple**, which is actually a replica – hurricanes toppled both the original in 1804 and its first replacement in 1954 (the weathervane, however, is the colonial original). What secured its place in history were the two lanterns that church sexton Robert Newman is said to have hung inside it on the night of April 18, 1775, to signal the movement of British forces "by sea" from Boston Common, which then bordered the Charles River. Some historians speculate that the lanterns were actually hung from another church, also called Old North, which occupied the North Square spot where the **Sacred Heart Italian Church** now stands, at no. 12; that irate Tories burned it for firewood in 1776 adds fuel to the theory. What is certain is that Paul Revere had already learned of the impending British advance and was riding to Lexington by the time the lanterns were in place – he simply needed Newman's help to alert Charlestown in case his mission was thwarted. As it turned out, both he and fellow patriot William Dawes were detained by British patrols, but each managed to continue his ride.

The eight bells inside the belfry, which is unfortunately not open to the public, were the first cast for the British Empire in North America and, ironically, have tolled the death of every US President. The interior itself is spotlessly white and well-lit thanks to the Palladian windows behind the pulpit. Twelve bricks from a prison cell in Boston, England, where an early group of Pilgrims was incarcerated, are set into the vestibule wall; just past them is an unusually lifelike bust of George Washington. The four cherubim near the organ are eighteenth-century relics that were looted from a French vessel. You can check your watch by the clock at the rear – it's the oldest one still ticking in an American public building, made in 1726. Wander among the high box pews: no. 62 belonged to General Thomas Gage, commander-in-chief of the British army in North America; descendants of Paul Revere still lay claim to no. 54. The timber on which the pews rest is supported by 37 basement level brick crypts. One of the 1100 bodies encased therein is that of John Pitcairn, the British major killed in the Battle of Bunker Hill. His remains were tagged for Westminster Abbey, but didn't quite make it.

Some of Old North's greatest charms are actually outside the church, notably the diminutive **Washington Memorial Garden**, the brick walls of which are bedecked with plaques commemorating one thing or another; more inviting and secluded is the unnamed **pocket garden** behind it. The quirky **souvenir shop** on the opposite side of the church is worth a stop if only for a look at some of its not-for-sale items, such as a vial of Boston Tea Party tea and the bellringers' contract that Paul Revere signed as a mere lad in 1750.

SALEM AND PRINCE STREETS

While the Old North Church is **Salem Street**'s star attraction, in the lower blocks between Prince and Cross streets, Salem is arguably the North End's most colorful artery. The change in atmosphere when venturing here from the commercialized Quincy Market and bland Government Center couldn't be more striking – as soon as you traverse Cross Street (which snakes alongside the elevated expressway), the agreeable onslaught of Italian grocers, aromatic *pasticcerias* and cafés begins. Salem Street itself is so narrow that the red brick buildings seem to lean into one another; light traffic makes it a common practice to walk right down the middle of the street. The Naples-esque bustle ends rather abruptly at the intersection with Prince; from here on up the street is primarily residential.

Serpentine **Prince Street** cuts through the heart of the North End on an east-west axis, linking Salem and Hanover streets. At no. 76 is the 24-hour **Bova's Bakery**, which in addition to purveying a good range of sweet treats is a major supplier of bread to North End restaurants. Nearer Hanover Street is **St Leonard's Church** supposedly the first Italian church in New England. The garish interior is a marked contrast to the simplicity of most other Boston churches, while the so-called "Peace Garden" in front, with its prosaic plantings and tacky statuary, is in a sense vintage North End.

COPP'S HILL BURYING GROUND

Map 4, D2. Daily dawn–dusk.

Up Hull Street from Old North Church, **Copp's Hill Burying Ground**, with its eerily tilting slate tombstones and stunning harbor views, makes up in atmosphere what it lacks in the way of illustrious deceased. The first burial here, on the highest ground in the North End, took place in 1659. Among the 10,000 interred are 1000 blacks, who lived in the exotically named district of New Guinea, a long vanished colonial enclave of blacks (free and slave) at the foot of the hill. The most famous gravesite here is that of the Mather family, just inside the wrought-iron gates on the northern Charter Street side. Increase Mather and son Cotton – the latter a Salem Witch Trial judge – were big players in Boston's early days of Puritan theocracy, a fact not at all reflected in the rather diminutive, if appropriately plain, brick vault tomb. Robert Newman, who hung Paul Revere's lanterns in the Old North Church, is buried near the western rim of the plot.

You'll notice that many gravestones have chunks missing, the consequence of British soldiers using them for target practice during the 1775 Siege of Boston. The grave of one Captain Daniel Malcolm, toward the left end of the third row of gravestones as you enter the grounds, bears particularly strong evidence of this: three musketball marks scar his epitaph, which refers to him as a "true son of liberty" and "enemy of oppression." Though unusally quiet today, the granite **Copp's Hill Terrace**, separated from the burial ground by Charter Street, was the place from which British cannon bombarded Charlestown during the Battle of Bunker Hill. In 1919, a 2.3-million-gallon tank of molasses exploded nearby, creating a syrupy tidal wave fifteen feet high that engulfed entire buildings and drowned 21 people along with a score of horses. Old North Enders – the kind you'll see playing bocci in the little park at the bottom of the terrace – claim you can still catch a whiff of the stuff on an exceptionally hot day.

CHARLESTOWN

Charlestown, across Boston Harbor via Charlestown Bridge from the North End, is a largely Irish working-class neighborhood that's quite isolated from the city, despite its annexation more than a century ago. Its historic core of quiet streets and elegant rowhouses is now all but surrounded by elevated highways and construction projects, though you won't have to worry much about the inelegant surroundings if you arrive on one of the trolley tours – or even better, by the short $1 ferry trip from Long Wharf. That deposits you right at the Charlestown Navy Yard, where the area's big draw, the **USS Constitution**, is berthed.

The earliest Puritan settlers had high hopes for developing Charlestown when they arrived in 1629, but an unsuitable water supply pushed them over to the Shawmut Peninsula, which they promptly renamed Boston (see p.301). Charlestown grew slowly after that, and had to be completely rebuilt after the British burned it down with a vengeance in 1775. The mid-1800s witnessed the arrival of the so-called "lace-curtain Irish," somewhat better off than their North End brethren, and the district remains an Irish one at heart. The longtime locals, known as "townies," have acquired a reputation for being standoffish, due to instances such as their resistance to school desegregation in the 1970s.

The neighborhood was long a haven for criminals – if a bank was robbed in Boston, police would simply wait out on the Charlestown Bridge for their quarry to come home – and a "code of silence" still keeps locals from turning in known criminals to the authorities. Recent years have seen urban professionals practically overtake the Federal- and Colonial-style townhomes south of the **Bunker Hill Monument** – Charlestown's other big sight – much to the chagrin of the townies. The rest of the neighborhood is fairly nondescript and even somewhat dodgy in parts.

> **The area covered by this chapter is shown in detail on color map 5.**

THE USS CONSTITUTION ("OLD IRONSIDES") AND CHARLESTOWN NAVY YARD

Map 5, F4. Daily 9.30am–sunset; free.

The sprawling **Charlestown Navy Yard** was one of the first and busiest US naval shipyards – riveting together an astounding 46 destroyer escorts in 1943 alone – though it owes most of its present-day liveliness to being home to the frigate **USS Constitution**, at Constitution Wharf. In 1974 the yard became part of the Boston National Historical Park after President Nixon decommissioned it, and since then it has been ambitiously repurposed as marinas, upscale condos and offices. But its focal point remains the USS Constitution, the oldest commissioned warship afloat in the world. When in 1997 "Old Ironsides" went on her first unassisted sail in 116 years, news coverage was international in scale, a measure of the public's fondness for the symbolic flagship of the US Navy. Launched two centuries ago to safeguard American merchant vessels from Barbary pirates and the French and

THE USS CONSTITUTION

British navies, she earned her nickname during the War of 1812, when cannonballs fired from the British *HMS Guerrière* bounced off the hull (the "iron sides" were actually hewn from live oak, a particularly sturdy wood from the southeastern US), leading to the first and most dramatic naval conquest of that war. The ship went on to clinch victory in more than forty battles before it was retired from service in 1830.

As tall as a twenty-story building and three hundred feet long from bowsprit to back end, she is an impressive sight from any angle, if not quite what she seems – while authentic enough in appearance, roughly ninety percent of the ship has been reconstructed. Even after extensive renovations, Old Ironsides is too frail to support sails for any extended period of time, and the only voyages it makes with any regularity are annual Fourth of July turnarounds in Boston Harbor. But it's still an active commissioned ship, meaning the guides are certified US Navy sailors. Though there's often a line, especially in the summer, it's worth the wait to get a close-up view of the elaborate rigging and to amble about the main deck – and scuttle down the nearly vertical stairways to a deck below, where you'll find two long rows of cannons.

Housed in a substantial granite building a short walk from Old Ironsides and across from Pier 1, the **USS Constitution Museum** (daily 9am–5pm; $4) is worth visiting before you board the ship. Its excellent exhibits help contexualize the vessel and its unparalleled role in American maritime history. One especially evocative display consists of curios which sailors acquired during a two-year round-the-world diplomatic mission begun in 1844, creatively arranged under a forest of faux palm fronds. Among the souvenirs are wooden carved toys from Zanzibar, a chameleon from Madagascar, preserved in a glass jar, and a Malayasian model ship made of cloves. The highlight upstairs is an infectiously fun wooden "deck," replete with sail and spinning helm, that rocks back and forth according to where you throw your weight. There's also a portion of the keel and frames of the Constitution and interactive exhibits that re-create sea battles from the War of 1812.

Berthed in between Old Ironsides and the ferry to Long Wharf is the hulking gray mass of the World War II destroyer **USS Cassin Young** (daily 10am–5pm; free). You're free to stride about the expansive main deck and check out some of the cramped chambers below, but it's mostly of interest to WWII history buffs. Several similar destroyers were built in Charlestown, but Cassin Young itself was made in San Pedro, California. At the northern perimeter of the Navy Yard is the **Ropewalk building.** For years "ropewalkers" made all the cordage for the US Navy in this narrow, quarter-mile-long granite building, the only one of its kind still standing in the country, though unfortunately it's not open to the public. The **Bunker Hill Pavilion** sits near the point where the Freedom Trail dips under an elevated road to continue toward the Bunker Hill Monument (see p.60). Inside, a thirty-minute program entitled *Whites of Their Eyes* attempts to re-create the famous battle with blinking lights and voiceovers that pass for "multimedia."

CITY SQUARE, MAIN STREET AND WINTHORP SQUARE

Toward Charlestown's center, there's a wealth of eighteenth- and nineteenth-century townhouses, many of which you'll pass on your way from the Navy Yard to the Bunker Hill Monument. John Harvard, the young English minister whose library and funds launched Harvard University after his death, lived in Charlestown and left a legacy of street names here: directly behind **City Square** (Map 5, D5) – a traffic circle anchored by one of Boston's most popular restaurants, *Olives* – Harvard Street curves through the small **Town Hill** district, site of Charlestown's first settled community. You'll also find Harvard Mall and adjacent Harvard Square (not to be confused with the one in Cambridge), both lined with well-preserved homes. The wooden 1795 house of **Deacon John Larkin**, who lent Paul Revere his horse for the ride to Lexington (and never got it back) is at 55 Main St, on the eastern edge of Town Hill.

Just up Main Street is the atmospheric **Warren Tavern**, at no. 105, a small three-story wooden structure built soon after the British burned Charlestown in the Battle of Bunker Hill, and named for Dr. Joseph Warren, killed in combat. From the tavern, crooked Devens Street to the south (called Crooked Lane in 1640) and Cordis Street to the north are packed with historic, private houses; the most imposing is the Greek Revival Swallow mansion at **33 Cordis St**. West on Main Street, the landmark **Savings Bank Building**, with its steep mansard roof and Victorian Gothic ornamentation, looms above the street-level convenience stores. Further west is the **Phipps Street Burying Ground**, which dates from 1630. While many Revolutionary soldiers are buried here, it's not part of the Freedom Trail – perhaps even more of a reason to make the detour.

Double back and head up Monument Avenue, toward the Bunker Hill Monument. The red-brick townhouses which you'll pass are some of the most eagerly-sought residences in town. Nearby is **Winthrop Square** (Map 5, E3), Charlestown's unofficial common, just south of the monument. The prim rowhouses overlooking it form another upscale enclave. Appropriately enough, the common started out as a military training field – a series of bronze tablets at its northeastern edge lists the men killed just up the slope in the Battle of Bunker Hill.

The Battle of Bunker Hill

The Revolutionary War was at its bloodiest on the hot June day when British and colonial forces clashed in Charlestown. In the wake of the battles at Lexington and Concord two months before, the British had assumed full control of Boston, while the patriots had the upper hand in the surrounding counties. The British, under the command of generals Thomas Gage and "Gentleman Johnny" Burgoyne, intended to sweep the countryside clean of "rebellious rascals." Americans intercepted the plans and fortified **Breed's Hill** with a thousand-plus citizen-soldiers, who streamed in on the night of June 16, 1775. The next morning, more reinforcements came to take up positions while the British, preparing for a three-day military foray in the country, set about baking bread for the journey.

Spotting the Yankee fort, the Redcoats, each carrying 125 pounds of food and supplies, rowed across the harbor to take the rebel-held town. On the patriots' side, Colonel William Prescott issued his order to his troops that they not fire "'til you see the whites of their eyes," such was their limited store of gunpowder. When the enemy's approach was deemed near enough, the patriots opened fire; though vastly outnumbered, they successfully repelled two full-fledged assaults. Some British units lost more than ninety percent of their men, and what few officers survived had to push their men forward with their swords to make them fight on. By the third British assault, the Redcoats had shed their gear, reinforcements had arrived and the Americans' supply of gunpowder was dwindling – as were their chances of clinching victory. The rebels continued to fight with stones and musket butts; meanwhile, British cannon fire from Copp's Hill in the North End was turning Charlestown into an inferno. Despite the eventual American loss, the battle did much to persuade the patriots – and the British, who lost nearly half their men who fought in this battle – that continued armed resistance made independence inevitable.

BUNKER HILL MONUMENT

Map 5, E1. Daily 9am–4.30pm; free.

Commemorating the Battle of Bunker Hill – and the final stop on the Freedom Trail – is the gray, dagger-like **Bunker Hill Monument**, a towering obelisk that probably stirs more passion for its name confusion than anything else. Around midnight on June 16, 1775, revolutionary troops began fortifying what they presumed to be Bunker Hill; at dawn they realized they were actually atop Breed's Hill, only a short distance away. Even though the battle was fought (and the memorial built on) Breed's Hill, the misnomer stuck. The tower is centrally positioned in **Monument Square** and fronted by a statue of Colonel William Prescott; at its base is a lodge that houses some decent dioramas of the battle. Inside, 294 steps wind up the 221-ft granite shaft to the top; hardy climbers will be rewarded with sweeping views of Boston, the Harbor and surrounding towns – and, to the northwest, the stone spire of the **St Francis de Sales Church**, which stands atop the real Bunker Hill.

BEACON HILL AND
THE WEST END

Beacon Hill, a dignified stack of red brick rising over the north side of Boston Common, is the Boston of wealth and privilege, one-time home to numerous historical and literary figures – including John Hancock, John Quincy Adams, Louisa May Alcott, and Oliver Wendell Holmes – and still the address of choice for the city's elite. Its narrow, hilly byways are lit with gaslamps and lined with quaint, nineteenth-century-style townhouses, all part of an enforced preservation that prohibits modern buildings, architectural innovations, or anything else to disturb the carefully cultivated atmosphere of urban gentility.

It was not always this way. In Colonial times, Beacon Hill was the most prominent of three peaks known as the Trimountain which formed Boston's geological backbone. The sunny south slope was developed into prime real estate and quickly settled by the city's political and economic powers, while the north slope was closer in spirit to the **West End**, a tumbledown port district populated by free blacks and immigrants; indeed, the north slope was home to so much salacious activity that outraged Brahmins termed it "Mount Whoredom." During the twentieth century, this social divide has been almost entirely eradicated, though it can still be seen in the somewhat shabbier homes north of Pinckney Street and in the tendency of members of polite society to refer to the south slope as "the good side." Still, both sides have much to offer, if of very different character: on the south slope, there's the grandiose **Massachusetts State House**, attractive boulevards like **Charles Street** and the **Beacon Street Promenade**, and the residences of past and present luminaries. More down-to-earth are the north slope's **Black Freedom Trail** sites, such as the **African Meeting House**, and some vestiges of the old West End.

**Most of the area covered by this chapter
is shown in detail on color map 3.**

BEACON STREET

Map 3, B6–E5.

Running along the south slope of Beacon Hill above the Common, **Beacon Street** was described as Boston's "sunny street for the sifted few" by Oliver Wendell Holmes in the late nineteenth century. This lofty character remains today; the row of stately brick townhouses, fronted by ornate iron grillwork, presides regally over the area. The story behind the **purple panes** in some of their windows – most visibly nos. 63 and 64 – evinces the street's long association with Boston wealth and privilege. When the panes were installed in some of the first Beacon Street mansions, they turned purple upon exposure to the sun, due to an excess of manganese in the glass. At first, their owners perceived the purple panes as nothing more than an irritating accident, but due to their prevalence in the windows of

Boston's most prestigious houses, they eventually came to be perceived as the definitive Beacon Hill status symbol by subsequent generations – in fact, some residents have gone so far as to shade their windows purple in imitation.

At 84 Beacon St is the Bull and Finch Pub, inspiration for the TV sitcom *Cheers*, a fact the bar doesn't let you forget; see our listing on p.219.

Across from no. 50, on the **Beacon Street Promenade** that edges Boston Common, is the **Founder's Monument**, commemorating Boston's first white settler, William Blackstone. The stone bas-relief depicts an apocryphal transaction in which the peculiar loner Blackstone, who had acquired much of present-day Boston from the Shawmut Indians, sold most of his acreage in 1630 to a group of Puritans from Charlestown who were seeking more hospitable land.

Further up the Promenade is the majestic monument honoring **Robert Gould Shaw and the 54th Massachusetts Regiment**. The memorial commemmorates America's first all-black company to fight in the Civil War, who were led by Shaw, scion of a monied Boston Brahmin clan. Isolated from the rest of the Union army, given the worst of the military's resources, and saddled with menial or terribly dangerous assignments, the regiment performed its service bravely; most of its members, including Shaw, were killed in a failed attempt to take Fort Wagner from the Confederates. Augustus Saint-Gaudens' 1897 high-relief bronze sculpture depicts the 54th's farewell march down Beacon Street, and the names of the soldiers who died in action are listed on its reverse side (though these were belatedly added in 1982). Robert Lowell won a Pulitzer Prize for his poem, *For the Union Dead*, about this monument; the regiment's story was depicted in the film *Glory*.

BEACON STREET

MASSACHUSETTS STATE HOUSE

Map 3, E4. Mon–Fri 10am–4pm, last tour at 3.15pm; free. Park Street Ⓣ.

Across from the Shaw Memorial rises the large gilt dome of the Charles Bulfinch-designed **Massachusetts State House**, at Beacon and Park streets, the scale and grandeur of which recall the heady spirit of the then-newly independent America in which it was built. Just three stories high, it seems taller sitting at the confluence of the steep grade of Park and Beacon streets. In fact, it was originally much smaller. Of the current structure, only the central section was part of Bulfinch's original design; the huge wings jutting out toward the street on either side and the section extending up Bowdoin Street behind the State House were all added much later. An all-star team of Revolution-era luminaries contributed to its construction: built on land donated by John Hancock, its cornerstone was laid by Samuel Adams and the copper for its dome was rolled in Paul Revere's foundry (though it was covered over with gold leaf in the 1870s). Its front lawn is dotted with statuary honoring favorite sons such as Henry Cabot Lodge and JFK. More interesting is the likeness of Mary Dyer, which overlooks the spot on Boston Common where she was hanged for adhering to her Quaker faith.

Once inside the labyrinthine interior, make your way up one flight and proceed to the central hallway, the only section of any real interest to visitorrs and the easiest one to navigate. The central hallway's second floor is littered with statues and murals celebrating even the most obscure Massachusetts statesmen and historical events, though the best section is the sober and impressive **Hall of Flags**, a circular room surrounded by tall columns of Siena marble, displaying original flags carried by Massachusetts soldiers into battle and lit by a vaulted stained-glass window bearing the state seal. On the third floor, the carved wooden fish known as the **Sacred Cod** hangs above the Senate chambers. The senators take this symbol of maritime prosperity so seriously that when it was stolen by Harvard pranksters in the 1930s, they shut down the government until it was recovered. Tours given by nervous, barely post-pubescent volunteers start from **Doric Hall**, on the second floor, but you'd do as well to grab a free map and show yourself around.

Behind the State House, on Bowdoin Street, lies pleasant, grassy **Ashburton Park**, centered on a pillar that is a replica of a 1789 Bulfinch work. The column indicates the hill's original summit, which was sixty feet higher and topped by a 65-ft post with the makeshift warning light – constructed from an iron pot filled with combustibles – that gave Beacon Hill its name.

Charles Bulfinch

America's foremost architect of the late eighteenth and early nineteenth centuries, **Charles Bulfinch** developed a distinctive style somewhere between Federal and Classical that remains one of Boston's most recognizable architectural motifs. Mixing Neoclassical training with New England practicality, Bulfinch built residences characterized by their rectilinear brick structure and pillared porticoes – examples remain throughout Beacon Hill, most notably at **87 Mt Vernon St** and **45 Beacon St**. While most of his work was residential, Bulfinch made his name with the design of various government buildings, such as the 1805 renovation of Faneuil Hall and, more significantly, the Massachusetts State House, whose dome influenced the design of state capitols nationwide.

CHARLES BULFINCH

NICHOLS HOUSE

Map 3, D4. May–Oct Tues–Sat noon–5pm, Nov–Dec & Feb–April Mon, Wed & Sat noon–4.15pm; $4. Park Street Ⓣ.

Behind the State House and up the slope of Mt Vernon Street, at no. 55, is the only Beacon Hill residence open regularly to the public, the **Nichols House**, yet another Bulfinch design, and most recently the home of eccentric spinster Rose Standish Nichols, who counted among her allegiances Fabian Socialism and the International Society of Pen Pals. Miss Rose, as she is known to posterity, lived in the house until her death in the early 1960s, and left it to the public as a museum rather than bequeathing it to her greedy relatives. Crowded with a patchwork of post-Victorian period pieces, the interior isn't too gripping unless you have an abiding interest in antique furnishings, though there are some striking Asian tapestries and an original self-portrait by John Singleton Copley. The thirty-minute guided tours are painfully thorough, but worth putting up with to get some perspective on the interior life of overstuffed leisure led by Beacon Hill's monied elite.

LOUISBURG SQUARE AND AROUND

Map 3, C4–C5.

Farther up the slope, between Mt Vernon and Pinckney streets, is **Louisburg Square**, the geographic and spiritual heart of Beacon Hill. The central lawn, surrounded by wrought-iron fencing and flanked by statues of Columbus and Aristides the Just, is owned by local residents, making it the city's only private square. On either side of this oblong green space are rows of stately brick townhouses, though the square's distinction is due less to its architectural character than to its long history of illustrious residents and the sense of elite civic parochialism that has made this Boston's most coveted address. Among those to call the area home were novelist Louisa May Alcott and members of the illustrious Vanderbilt family; today, Senator John Kerry and his wife, ketchup heiress Teresa Heinz, own a townhouse here, reportedly purchased for a cool $2 million.

Just below Louisburg Square, between Willow and West Cedar streets, is **Acorn Street**, a narrow byway that still has the cobblestones from its construction in the early nineteenth century. Barely wide enough for a car to pass through, it was originally built as a minor byway to be lined with servants' residences, and locals cling to it as the epitome of Beacon Hill quaint. In the 1960s, residents permitted the city to tear up the street to install sewer pipes only after exacting the promise that every cobblestone would be replaced in its original location. One more block down is **Chestnut Street**, which features some of the nicest private homes in the region.

....

The 's' in Louisburg is not silent, as any Hill resident will tell you should you ask about "Louie-burg Square."

....

North of Louisburg Square runs **Pinckney Street**, once the sharp division between the opulent south and ramshackle north sections of Beacon Hill. The area's original developers planned it that way, arranging it so that only the back entrances and stables of estates could abut Pinckney. As recently as the 1920s, resident Robert Lowell expressed shock at the proximity of the area to shadier districts, claiming that while he lived only fifty yards from Louisburg Square, he was nevertheless "perched on the outer rim of the hub of decency." The distinction is no longer so sharp, and now Pinckney is merely another of Beacon Hill's picturesque streets, though its location at the crest of the hill makes for great views; on a clear day, you can see across the Charles River to Cambridge, and all over the West End from its intersection with Anderson Street.

CHARLES AND MT VERNON STREETS

Just west of the square is **Charles Street**, the commercial center of Beacon Hill, lined with scores of restaurants, antique shops and pricey specialty boutiques. A jaunt just off Charles down **Mt Vernon Street** along the flat of the hill brings you past some of Beacon Hill's most beautiful buildings, though you can't go into any of them. The Federal-style **Charles Street Meeting House** (Map 3, B5), at the corner of the two streets, was, true to its name, a hotbed of political activity in the nineteenth century, but it's been repurposed as an office building. Farther along, at River and Mt Vernon, is the old **Boston Fire Department** building, which was recently refurbished and made into the elaborate residence for the 1996 season of *The Real World*, an MTV docudrama that places young hipsters into a stylish apartment and watches them at close hand. At Mt Vernon's intersection with Brimmer Street, you'll find the beautiful, vegetation-enshrouded Victorian Gothic **Church of the Advent** (Map 3, A5).

THE ESPLANADE

Map 3, A1–A6.

Connected to Charles Street at its north end by a footbridge and spanning nine miles along the Charles River, the **Esplanade** is yet another of Boston's well-manicured public spaces, with the requisite playgrounds, landscaped hills, lakes and bridges. The nicest stretch runs alongside Beacon Hill – and continues into Back Bay – providing a unique and picturesque way to appreciate the Hill from a distance, while also serving as a hotspot for the city's pretty young things. On summer days the Esplanade is swarming with well-toned singles scoping and flirting during jogs and rollerblading sessions. Just below the Longfellow Bridge is a **public boathouse**, the point of departure for sailing excursions on the Charles (April–Oct; two-day visitor's pass $50; ©523-1038).

The white half-dome rising from the riverbank along the Esplanade is the **Hatch Shell**, a public performance space best known for its Fourth of July celebration, which features a free concert by the Boston Pops, a pared-down version of the Boston Symphony Orchestra. The popularity of this event has caused it to become terribly overcrowded, but the other summer happenings at the Shell, such as free movies and jazz concerts, occur almost nightly and are far more mellow. Call ©727-1300 for schedules and upcoming events.

AFRICAN MEETING HOUSE

Map 3, D3. Mon–Fri 10am–4pm, Sat noon–4pm; donation requested. Park Street Ⓣ.

The north side of slope, across Pinckney Street, is keyed by **Smith Court**, once the center of Boston's substantial pre-Civil War black community when the north slope was still a low-rent district, and now home to a few crucial stops on Boston's Black Heritage Trail (see below). Free blacks, who were denied access to participation in Boston's civic and religious life, worshipped and held political meetings in what became known as the **African Meeting House**, at 8 Smith Court. Informally called the Black Faneuil Hall, the meeting house grew into a center for abolitionist activism: in 1832, William Lloyd Garrison founded the New England Anti-Slavery Society here. Today, it houses the **Museum of Afro-American History**, which, considering its site, is rather a disappointment. You won't find much in the way of displays; there's only a rotating exhibit on the first floor, usually themed on contemporary African-American art, and meeting house on the second, restored to look like the church it once was. Well-informed rangers lead **free tours** and add much to contextualize what you actually see.

At the end of Smith Court, you can wander down **Holmes Alley**, a path that was part of the old Underground Railroad used to protect escaped slaves, who would duck into the doors along the narrow alley, left open by sympathizers to the cause. The **Abiel Smith School**, back on Joy Street, was the first public educational institution established for black schoolchildren in Boston. Today, it houses the Museum of Afro-American History's gift shop, which vends a decent array of literature and historical material.

The Black Heritage Trail

Massachusetts was the first state to declare slavery illegal, in 1783, partly as a result of black participation in the Revolutionary War, and a large community of free blacks and escaped slaves swiftly sprung up in the North End and Beacon Hill. Very few blacks live in either place nowadays, but the **Black Heritage Trail** traces Beacon Hill's key role in local black history – and is the only major historical site in America devoted to pre-Civil War African-American history and culture. Another in the line of Boston's self-guided walking tours, the trail begins at **Smith Court**, site of the **African Meeting House** and **Abiel Smith School**, and winds around Beacon Hill, passing the memorial for the **54th Massachusetts Regiment** as well as schools, other institutions, and residences ranging from the small cream clapboard houses of Smith Court to the imposing **Lewis and Harriet Hayden House** at 66 Phillips St.

THE WEST END

North of Cambridge Street, the tidy rows of townhouses transition into a more urban spread of office buildings and old brick structures, signaling the start of the **West End**. Once Boston's main port of entry for immigrants, this area was populated by a broad mix of ethnic groups as well as transient sailors who brought with them a rough-and-tumble sex-and-tattoo industry. The eventual drift of Boston's ethnic populations to southern districts, along with 1960s urban renewal, however, has effaced the district's once-lively character.

A vestige of the old West End remains in the small tangle of byways – namely Friend, Portland and Canal streets – behind the high-rise buildings of **Massachusetts General Hospital**, where you'll see urban warehouses interspersed with numerous Irish bars, some of which, such as *Irish Embassy* and *McGann's*, possess an authenticity that makes them well worth a visit (see "Drinking," pp.218–220). These bars swell to a fever pitch after Celtic basketball and Bruin hockey games at the nearby **FleetCenter**, 150 Causeway St (tours daily at 11am, 1pm and 3pm; $5), the slick, corporate-named arena built next to the legendary, but decrepit, Boston Garden.

For information about tickets to sports events at the FleetCenter, see p.278.

Back along Cambridge Street, at no. 141, the brick **Harrison Gray Otis House** (Wed–Sat 11am–5pm, tours hourly; $4), originally built for the wealthy Otis family in 1796, sits incongruously among mini-malls and office buildings. Its first two floors have been painstakingly restored – from the bright wallpaper right down to the silverware sets – in the often loud hues of the Federal style.

THE WEST END

Museum of Science

Daily 9am–5pm (Fri until 9pm); $8. Science Park Ⓣ.

Situated on a bridge over the Charles, Boston's **Museum of Science** consists of several floors of interactive, though patchy and often well-worn, exhibits illustrating basic principles of natural and physical science. Still, there's enough here to entertain kids for most of the day, and this doesn't mean it's off-limits to adults, who will probably get an equal kick out of the place.

The best exhibit is the Theater of Electricity in the Blue Wing, a darkened room full of optical illusions and glowing displays on the presence of electricity in everyday life. Containing the world's largest Van de Graaf generator, the theater puts on daily electricity shows in which simulated lightning bolts flash and crackle around the space. More cerebral is Mathematica, also in the Blue Wing, in which randomly dropped balls fall neatly into a bell curve to demonstrate the notion of probability, and a series of steel spheres orbit around each other in a funnel to replicate the Galilean motion of planets. Check out, too, The Big Dig on the lower level, where videos and interactive displays provide an engaging chronicle of Boston's Sisyphean attempt to put the unsightly elevated highway I-93 underground.

....

For information on events in the Hayden Planetarium or Omni Theater, call Ⓒ523-6664.

....

The museum also holds the **Charles Hayden Planetarium** and the **Mugar Omni Theater**, though neither has too much to recommend it. The planetarium hosts talks and presentations throughout the day – free with museum admission – but it's better known for its laser shows, usually set to a soundtrack of classic rock and shown before an audience of precocious children and drug-addled teens. The Omni Theater's enormous domed IMAX screen and state-of-the-art sound system provide enough sensory impact to make up for the generally vapid content of the films.

MUSEUM OF SCIENCE

BACK BAY AND THE SOUTH END

Back Bay, a meticulously planned neighborhood where elegant, angular tree-lined streets form a pedestrian-friendly area that looks much as it did in the nineteenth century, right down to the original gaslights and brick sidewalks, is Boston at its most cosmopolitan. A youthful population helps offset stodginess and keeps the district, which begins at the **Public Garden**, buzzing with chic eateries, trendy shops and the aura of affluence that goes along with both. Its other main draw is its trove of Gilded Age rowhouses, specifically their exquisite architectural details; there really is no end to the fanciful bay windows and ornamental turrets. On its southern border, the sprawl of the **South End** offers another impressive, if less opulent, collection of Victorian architecture, alongside some of Boston's more inventive restaurants.

Both neighborhoods were fashioned in response to a shortage of living space in Boston, a problem still somewhat unresolved. In the case of Back Bay, an increasingly cramped Beacon Hill prompted developers to revisit a failed dam project on the Charles River, which had made a swamp of much of the area. With visionary architect and urban planner **Arthur Gilman** at the helm of a huge land-fill project, the sludge began to be reclaimed in 1857. Taking his cue from the grand boulevards of Paris, Gilman decided on an orderly street pattern extending east to west from the Public Garden, itself sculpted from swampland two decades before. By 1890, the cramped peninsula of old Boston was flanked by 450 new acres, on which stood a range of churches, townhouses and schools. You'll notice that, with a few exceptions, the brownstones get fancier the farther from the Garden you go, a result of architects and those who employed them trying to one-up each other. It was no surprise when Back Bay quickly became one of Boston's most sought-after addresses, although that subsided somewhat during the Great Depression, when single families were unable to afford the houses. Developers converted many of the spaces into apartments, often gutting the interiors in the process; other properties were purchased by colleges and universities. More recently gentrification has set in, and the demand for whole houses has led to developers actually knocking out many of the apartment walls their predecessors erected.

Whatever may have happened on the inside, by law the exteriors of most buildings remain unaltered, although visually that's as far as you usually get. Still, many apartments retain their old wood ornamentation and Victorian embellishments, contributing to the high rents that in turn feed the consumer-driven culture on Newbury Street, which with its hundreds of shops, designer hair salons and tiny gourmet eateries is a far cry from the traditional image of Boston. The district has its share of urban problems, from homeless people trawling for designer garbage to bad traffic jams, a shortage of parking space and a rat problem. But the pervasive grace of the bowfronts and wrought iron terraces provides at least an illusion of safety and serenity.

Starting with the side closest to the Charles River, the east-west thoroughfares of Back Bay are **Beacon** and **Marlborough** streets, **Commonwealth Avenue**, and **Newbury** and **Boylston** streets. These are transsected by eight shorter streets, so fastidiously laid out that not only are their names in alphabetical order, but trisyllables are deliberately intercut by disyllables: Arlington, Berkeley, Clarendon, Dartmouth, Exeter, Fairfield, Gloucester and Hereford, until you get to Massachusetts Avenue. Generally, the grandest townhouses are found on Beacon Street and Commonwealth Avenue, though Marlborough, in between the two, is more atmospheric; Boylston and Newbury are the main commercial drags. In the middle of it all is a small green space, **Copley Square**, surrounded by the area's main sights: Trinity Church, the imposing Boston Public Library and the city's classic skyscraper, the John Hancock Tower.

Most of the area covered by this chapter is shown in detail on color map 6.

THE PUBLIC GARDEN

Map 3, B6–C8.

The value of property in Boston goes up the closer its proximity to the lovingly maintained **Public Garden**, a 24-acre park first earmarked for public use in 1859. Of the garden's 125 types of trees, many identified by little brass placards, most impressive are the weeping willows which ring the picturesque manmade **lagoon**. Here you can take a fifteen-minute ride in one of six **Swan Boats** ($1.50), which trace gracious figure-eights in the oversized puddle. The campy pedal-powered conveyances, inspired by a scene in Wagner's opera *Lohengrin*, have been around since 1877 – long enough to become a Boston institution. The boats carry up to twenty passengers at a time, and in the height of summer there is often a line to hop on board – instead of waiting, you can get just as good a perspective on the park from the tiny **suspension bridge** that crosses the lagoon.

The park's other big family draw also happens to be fowl-related: a cluster of inexplicably popular bronze birds collectively called **Mrs Mallard and Her Eight Ducklings**. Toddlers have a habit of mounting the things whether they're supposed to or not; parents seem to think it's cute. The sculptures were installed in 1987 to commemorate Robert McClosky's 1941 children's tale *Make Way for Ducklings*, set in the Public Garden. Of the many small statues and monuments throughout the park, the oldest and oddest is the thirty-foot-tall **Good Samaritan** monument, a granite and red marble column that is a tribute to, of all things, the anesthetic qualities of ether. Controversy as to which of two Boston men invented the wonder drug led Oliver Wendell Holmes to christen it the "Either Monument." A dignified equestrian statue of **George Washington**, installed in 1869 and the first of its kind, watches over the Garden's Commonwealth Avenue entrance.

COMMONWEALTH AVENUE

Map 6, E3–L3.

Commonwealth Avenue, the 220-foot-wide showcase street of Back Bay, was modeled after similar Parisian thoroughfares, and its tree-lined, 100-foot-wide median forms the first link in Frederick Law Olmsted's so-called **Emerald Necklace**, which begins at Boston Common and extends all the way to the Arnold Arboretum, in Jamaica Plain. This mall is peppered with several elegantly placed **statues**, though with the exception of a particularly dashing execution of Revolutionary War soldier John Glover – who helped Washington cross the Delaware in 1776 – between Berkeley and Clarendon streets, few of these hold any interest. "Comm Ave," as locals ignobly call it, is at its prettiest in early May, when the magnolia and dogwood trees are in full bloom, showering the brownstone steps with their fragrant pink buds.

The **Baylies Mansion**, at no. 5, now houses the Boston Center for Adult Education, so feel free to slip inside for a look at the opulent ballroom Baylies built expressly for his daughter's coming-out (in the old-fashioned sense) party. You'll have to be content to see the **Ames-Webster Mansion**, a few blocks down at 306 Dartmouth St, from the outside. Built in 1872 for US congressman and railroad tycoon Frederick Ames, it features a two-story conservatory, central tower and imposing chimney. Still further down Commonwealth, at no. 314, is the **Burrage House**, a fanciful synthesis of Vanderbilt-style mansion and the French château of Chenonceaux. The exterior of this 1899 urban palace is a riot of gargoyles and sundry carved cherubim; inside it's less riotous – it serves as a retirement home.

First Baptist Church of Boston

Map 6, K3. Mon–Fri 10am–4pm. Arlington Ⓣ.

Rising above the avenue, at no. 110, is the landmark belfry of the **First Baptist Church of Boston**, designed by architect H. H. Richardson in 1872 for a Unitarian congregation, though at bill-paying time only a Baptist group were able to pony up the necessary funds. The puddingstone exterior is topped off by a 176-ft **bell tower**, which is covered by four gorgeous friezes by Frédéric-Auguste Bartholdi, of Statue of Liberty fame – a product of his friendship with Richardson that developed at the Ecole des

Beaux Arts in Paris. More interesting than what the tableaux depict (baptism, communion, marriage and death) are some of the illustrious stone-etched visages: those of Emerson, Longfellow, Hawthorne and Lincoln. Trumpeting angels protrude from each corner, inspiring its inglorious nickname, "Church of the Holy Bean Blowers."

Richardson's lofty plans for the interior never materialized, again for lack of money, but its high ceiling, exposed timbers and Norman-style rose windows are still worth a peek if you happen by when someone's in the church office. Ring the bell on the Commonwealth Avenue side and hope for the best.

NEWBURY AND BOYLSTON STREETS

Newbury Street takes in eight blocks of alternately traditional and eclectic boutiques, art galleries and designer spas, all tucked into Victorian-era brownstones. It's an atmospheric place to shop, though the encroachment of big chain stores like *Gap* and *NikeTown* have eroded some of its charm. Wealthy foreign students have colonized cafés like *29 Newbury* and *Emporio Armani Express*, but despite the occasional nod to pretentiousness, the strip's overall mood is surprisingly inviting. And not all is shopping: Newbury and neighboring **Boylston Street** are home to most of the old schools and churches built in the Back Bay area.

In fact, right on the corner of Boylston and Arlington streets is Back Bay's first building, the **Arlington Street Church** (Map 6, L4; Mon–Fri 10am–5pm), a minor Italianesque masterpiece whose construction in 1861 started a trend that resulted in many downtown congregations relocating to posher quarters in Back Bay. Arthur Gilman, chief planner of Back Bay, designed the clay-colored, squat structure, marked by a host of Tiffany stained glass windows, added from 1895 to 1930. A history of progressive rhetoric has also earned it some

NEWBURY AND BOYLSTON STREETS

note: abolitionist minister William Ellery Channing intoned against slavery here just a year before the Civil War erupted, and the church was a favored venue of peace activists during the Vietnam War; nowadays there's an active gay congregation. A block down is the prison-like **New England Mutual Life building**, with some national chain stores on the first floor that do little for its character. However, it's worth nipping inside to have a look at the **murals**, which depict such historic regional events as John Winthrop sailing from Old to New England aboard the *Arbella*, Paul Revere sounding his famous alarm, and the Declaration of Independence being read in Boston for the first time.

Back on the first block of Newbury Street itself, sandwiched between the hair salons and upscale retail stores, is the **Emmanuel Church of Boston**, an unassuming rural Gothic Revival building. Of greater interest is the full-blown Gothic Revival **Church of the Covenant** (Map 6, K3), further down the street on the same side. Most passersby are too intent on window shopping to notice the soaring steeple, so look up before checking out the interior, famous – like its neighbor, the Arlington Street Church – for its Tiffany stained-glass windows, some of which are thirty feet high. It's a nice setting for such things as chamber music performances – the Boston Pro Arte Chamber Orchestra was founded here – and the church's chapel houses one of Boston's biggest contemporary art spaces in the form of the Gallery NAGA; pop in to see the latest paintings, sculptures or photographs on exhibit.

For the best stores on Newbury Street, see "Shopping," p.253.

Designed as an architect's house, the medieval flight-of-fancy at **109 Newbury St** is arguably more arresting for its two donjon towers than the Cole-Haan footwear inside. A block down at 275 Dartmouth is the *Rodier Paris* boutique, but again the burnt sienna-colored building with mock battlements hunkered over it steals the show: originally the **Hotel Victoria** in 1886, it looks like a combination Venetian-Moorish castle, not a bad place to have your in-town condo. A block west, on the exposed side of no. 159, is the **Newbury Street Mural**, a fanciful tribute to a hodgepodge of notables from Sam Adams to Sammy Davis, Jr. A key to who's who is affixed to the parking attendant's booth in the lot next to it.

Newbury gets progressively funkier after Exeter Street; the shoppers are more often students and locals than wealthy ladies venturing in from the suburbs. This is where you'll find Boston's most original fashion boutiques and alternative record stores, in addition to several decent restaurants with popular summer sidewalk terraces. On the final block, between Hereford Street and Massachusetts Avenue, a span of nineteenth-century **stables** has been converted to commercial space; check out the cavernous *Patagonia* shop at no. 346. Looming over Massachusetts Avenue, the colossal *Tower Records*, at no. 350, is probably the biggest student magnet of all.

Housed in a Romanesque-style police and fire station built in 1886, half of which Back Bay's firefighters still call home, the **Institute of Contemporary Art**, 955 Boylston St (Map 6, G4; Wed–Sun noon–5pm, Thurs until 9pm; $5.25, free Thurs 5-9pm), around the corner from Tower Records, is Boston's main venue for modern art and such has no permanent collections. Instead, there are rotating exhibits and installations of mixed success.

BEACON AND MARLBOROUGH STREETS

As a continuation of Beacon Hill's stately main thorough-fare, **Beacon Street** was long the province of blueblood

Bostonians. It is the Back Bay street closest to the Charles River, yet its buildings turn their back to it, principally because in the nineteenth century the river was a stinking mess. On the first block of the Back Bay portion of Beacon, at no. 137, is the only house museum in the neighborhood, the **Gibson House Museum** (Map 6, L2; Wed–Sun 1–3pm, tours hourly; $3). Built in 1860, this standard-issue Back Bay townhouse has been more or less preserved as it was, with an almost complete lack of sunlight and a host of Victoriana that includes a still-functioning dumbwaiter, antique globes and writing paraphernalia (one of the Gibsons was apparently a travel writer), and gilt-framed photos of long-gone relatives of the long-gone Bostonian Catherine Hammond Gibson. Notable among the various chinoiserie is a sequined pink velvet cat house, or, if you prefer the Gibsons' term, "pet pagoda." At the far end of Beacon Street, the rundown exterior of **Crossroads Ale House**, at no. 405, a major-league student haunt, may be familiar to some thanks to the TV series *Boston Common*. The turreted **Charlesgate building** at no. 535, a former hotel, has been nicknamed "The Witch's Castle" by the Emerson College students who now call it home.

Sandwiched between Beacon Street and Commonwealth Avenue is quiet **Marlborough Street**, which with its brick sidewalks and vintage gaslights is one of the most prized residential locales in Boston, after Louisburg Square in Beacon Hill and the first few blocks of Commonwealth Avenue. Even though the townhouses here tend to be smaller than elsewhere in Back Bay, they display a surprising range of stylistic variation, especially on the blocks between Clarendon and Fairfield streets. The final block, which links Massachusetts Avenue to Charlesgate East, is the only street in Back Bay proper that curves.

COPLEY SQUARE AND AROUND

Map 6, J4.

Bounded by Boylston, Clarendon, Dartmouth and St James streets, **Copley Square** is the busy commercial center of Back Bay. Various design schemes have come and gone since the square was first filled in the 1870s; the present one is a remnant from 1984, a nondescript central grassy expanse and a strange fountain with two stone obelisks on the Boylston Street side. A farmers' market occasionally materializes on the side opposite the *Copley Plaza Hotel*. Fortunately, the periphery holds more interest than the space it surrounds.

Trinity Church

Map 6, K4. Daily 8am–6pm. Copley Ⓣ.

In his meticulous attention to detail – from the polychromatic masonry on the outside to the rather generic stained glass windows within – Boston architect H.H. Richardson seemed to overlook the big picture for his 1877 **Trinity Church**, 206 Clarendon St, which as one 1923 guidebook averred "is not beautiful" – despite the reaction of the critics at the time, who dubbed it a masterpiece of Romanesque Revivalism. The hulking exterior is a bit easier on the eye when approached from Clarendon Street instead of Dartmouth, the usual view; gazing up at the chunky centered tower from behind affords an unusual, even dizzying perspective. From here, you'll also have an easier time of finding the church's cloister and hidden garden, one of Back Bay's more enchanting quiet spots. Skip the rather spartan interior, which feels more empty than awe-inspiring. Indeed, the most interesting aspect of Trinity Church is probably its juxtaposition to the John Hancock Tower (see p.85), in whose mirrored panes it's reflected.

COPLEY SQUARE, TRINITY CHURCH

The church rests rather precariously on 4500 submerged wood pilings – before the advent of modern construction techniques the only way for buildings to stay put in the very moist depths of Back Bay.

Boston Public Library

Map 6, I4. Mon–Thurs 9am–9pm, Fri–Sat 9am–5pm, Sun 1–5pm. Copley Ⓣ.

A decidedly secular building anchors the end of Copley Square opposite Trinity Church, in the form of the **Boston Public Library** – the largest public research library in New England, and the first one in America to actually permit the borrowing of books. McKim, Mead & White, the leading architectural firm of its day, built the Italian Renaissance Revival structure in 1852; the visibility of its Dartmouth Street entrance is heightened by the presence of the landmark spiky yet sinuous lanterns that overhang it. The massive inner bronze doors were designed by Daniel Chester French (sculptor of the Lincoln Memorial in Washington DC); inside them, a musketeer-like statue of Sir Henry Vane stands guard. An early Governor of the Massachusetts Bay Colony, he believed, as the inscription relates, that "God, law and parliament" were superior to the king, which couldn't have helped his case much when his free-thinking head got the chop in 1662.

Beyond the marble grand staircase and beneath the extensively coffered ceilings are a series of **murals**, most impressive of which is a diaphanous depiction of the nine Muses; to its right stands a statue of a smiling naked woman holding a baby in one hand and a bunch of grapes in the other, a replica of an original bacchante which, due to neo-Puritan prudishness, never graced the library's inner courtyard as intended. Just right of that is the gloomy **Abbey**

Room, named for Edwin Abbey's murals depicting the Holy Grail legend, and where Bostonians took delivery of their books. Most of these were kept in the imposing **Bates Reading Room**, which with its 218-foot-long sweep, 50-foot-high barrel-vaulted ceiling, dark oak paneling and incomparable calm, hasn't changed much since its debut more than a century ago. Tranquility also reigns in the library's open-air central **courtyard**, modeled after that of the Palazzo della Chancelleria in Rome.

New Old South Church

Map 6, J4. Mon–Fri 9am–5pm. Copley ⓣ.

Just opposite the Boston Public Library, on the corner 'of Boylston and Dartmouth streets, is one of Boston's most attractive buildings – the **New Old South Church**, 645 Boylston St, a name to which there is actually some logic: the congregation in residence at downtown's Old South Meeting House (and church) outgrew it and decamped here in 1875. You need not be a student of architecture to be won over by the Italian Gothic design, most pronounced in the ornate, 220-foot bell tower – a 1937 addition – and copper-roof lantern, replete with metallic gargoyles in the shape of dragons. The dramatic zebra-striped archways on the Dartmouth Street side are unfortunately partially obscured by the entrance to the Copley ⓣ station. It's not just to be admired from the outside either: its interior is an alluring assemblage of dark woods set against a forest green backdrop, coupled with fifteenth-century English-style stained-glass windows.

John Hancock Tower and Observatory

Map 6, K4. Mon–Sat 9am–11pm, Sun 10am–11pm; $4.25. Copley ⓣ.

At 62 stories, the **John Hancock Tower**, at 200

NEW OLD SOUTH CHURCH

Clarendon St, is the tallest building in America north of New York City, and in a way Boston's signature skyscraper – first loathed, now loved, and taking on startlingly different appearances depending on your vantage point. In Back Bay, the characteristically angular edifice is often barely perceptible, due to designer I. M. Pei's deft understatement in deference to adjacent Trinity Church and the old brownstones nearby. From Beacon Hill, however, it appears broad-shouldered and stocky; from the South End, taller than it really is; from across the Charles River, like a crisp metallic wafer. One of the best views is, in fact, from the **Harvard/Mass Ave Bridge**, with the clouds reflected in the tower's lofty, fully-mirrored coat. You'd never guess that soon after its 1976 construction, dozens of windowpanes popped out, showering Copley Square with glass.

The sixtieth floor **observatory** affords the expected stunning views – on a clear day you can see New Hampshire – but most interesting is the opportunity to see Boston splayed out below. A twenty-foot-tall topographical model eases comprehension, as does a miniature sound-and-light exhibit called "Boston 1775." Next door to the tower is the *old* Hancock Tower, which cuts a distinguished profile in the skyline with its truncated step-top pyramid roof. It is locally famous for the neon weather beacon on top: solid blue, clear view; flashing blue, clouds are due; solid red, rain ahead; flashing red, snow instead, except in summer – Red Sox game cancelled.

PRUDENTIAL TOWER AND AROUND

Map 6, H5.

Not even the darkest winter night can cloak the ugliness of the **Prudential Tower**, at 800 Boylston St, just west of Copley Square. This 52-story gray intruder to the Back Bay skyline is one of the more unfortunate by-products of the urban renewal craze that gripped Boston and most other American cities in the 1960s – though it did succeed in replacing the Boston & Albany rail yards, a blighted border between Back Bay and the South End. Today its chief attraction is its fiftieth-floor **Skywalk** (daily 10am-10pm; $4), not quite as high as the nearby John Hancock Observatory, but offering the only 360-degree aerial view of Boston. On a clear day you can discern Cape Cod across the waters of Massachusetts Bay. If you're hungry (or just thirsty) you can avoid the admission charge by ascending two more floors to the *Top of the Hub* restaurant, though your bill will more than make up for it. The crowded ground-floor **Shops at Prudential Center** is about as generic a mall as they come, and adjoins the hulking mass of the equally bland **Hynes Convention Center**.

People gazing down at Boston from the top of the Prudential Tower are often surprised to see a 224-foot tall Renaissance Revival basilica vying for attention amidst the urban outcroppings lapping at its base. This rather artificial-looking structure is the central feature of the world headquarters of the sprawling **First Church of Christ, Scientist**, at 75 Huntington Ave. With seating for 3000 (and an enormous pipe organ), it dwarfs the earlier, prettier Romanesque **Christian Science Mother Church** just behind it, built in 1894. The nice thing about wandering round the central plaza, a huge concrete block hammered out by I. M. Pei in the early 1970s, is that no one tries to convert you. In fact there may be no better place in Boston to contemplate the excesses of religion than around the center's 670-foot-long red granite-trimmed **reflecting pool** (which somehow cools water from the complex's air conditioning system).

The highlight of a visit here, though, is the unique **Mapparium** (Mon–Sat 10am–4pm; free), tucked into the

PRUDENTIAL TOWER AND AROUND

grand Art Deco lobby of the Christian Science Publishing building (headquarters of the *Christian Science Monitor*), close to Massachusetts Avenue. This is an inverted, stained-glass globe, the thirty-foot diameter of which you can cross on a bridge of glass. The technicolor hues of the six hundred-plus glass panels, illuminated from the outside, reveal the geopolitical reality of the world in the early 1930s, when the globe was constructed, as evidenced by names such as Siam, Baluchistan and Transjordan. Intended to symbolize the worldwide reach of the Christian Science movement, the Mapparium has perhaps a more immediate payoff, courtesy of its glass design: whisper "What's Tanganyika called today?" at one end of the bridge and someone on the opposite end will hear it clear as a bell – and perhaps proffer an answer.

Right around Christian Science Center, before Back Bay fades into the less posh Fenway, are a few small but alluring residential blocks, such as **St Germain Street**, with its bricked sidewalks, cast-iron streetlamps and renovated three-story brownstones. South of the plaza is the equally idyllic **St Botolph Street**, outside Back Bay proper but architecturally in the same vein, though less showy. The narrow ribbon of the **Southwest Corridor Park**, the next block south, separates Back Bay from the northern reaches of the South End.

BAY VILLAGE

Back near the Public Garden is **Bay Village**, a small atmospheric satellite of Back Bay and one of the oldest sections of Boston, bounded by Arlington, Church, Fayette and Stuart streets. This warren of gaslights and tiny brick houses has managed to escape the trolley tours that make other parts of the city feel like a theme park;

it's also increasingly popular with Boston's gay population, and is something of an extension to the nearby
South End. The obvious streets to explore – spreading
out as they do in the shadow of the area's landmark
Boston Park Plaza Hotel – are Piedmont, Winchester
and Church, but lightly trafficked Melrose and Fayette
streets, footsteps beyond them, are also worth inspection.
Bay Village wakes up after the sun sets, when men of all
ages zero in on spots like the *Napoleon Club* and the
Luxor, two of the most popular gay clubs in Boston.
Others looking for action head for the district's southern
and eastern reaches, where prostitution has long plagued
the neighborhood; campaigns to push the flesh-peddlers
out have not amounted to much.

....

See p.250 for listings of Bay Village's gay clubs.

....

Until the 1960s, Bay Village was simply called the
Church Street district; the street still exists, the church it
was named for is gone, and its new name is in honor of
tiny Bay Street. The overall resemblance to Beacon Hill is
no accident; many of the artisans who pieced that district
together built their own, smaller houses here throughout
the 1820s and 1830s. A few decades later, water displaced
from the filling in of Back Bay threatened to turn the district back into a swamp, but Yankee practicality resulted in
the lifting of hundreds of houses and shops onto wooden
pilings fully eighteen feet above the water level. Backyards
were raised only twelve feet, and when the water receded
many building owners designed sunken gardens. You can
still see some of these in the alleys behind slender Melrose
and Fayette streets, but one of the most unusual remnants
from the nineteenth century is the **fortress** at the intersection of Arlington and Stuart streets and Columbus

BAY VILLAGE

89

Avenue, complete with drawbridge and fake moat, that was built as an armory for the **First Corps of Cadets**, a private military organization. It's been relegated to use as an exhibition hall and convention facility for the Park Plaza Hotel.

Bay Village's proximity to the theater district made it a prime location for **speakeasies** in the 1920s, not to mention a natural spot for actors and impresarios to take up residence; indeed, the building at **48-50 Melrose Street** originally housed a movie studio. Around the corner from it is the site of the **Cocoanut Grove Fire** of 1942, in which 490 people perished in a nightclub because the exit doors were locked.

THE SOUTH END

Map 6.

Though it lacks obvious tourist attractions, the **South End**, separated from Back Bay by the Copley Place shopping complex, merits a look for its wealth of Victorian architecture and its generally upbeat streetlife, which is in certain respects the most happening in town. There are large black and gay communities here, and the latter has ushered in several trendy cafés and restaurants, most clustered on **Tremont Street** and on gentrified pockets of **Columbus Avenue**. Still, despite the tendency of Boston realtors to promote the South End as the ultimate up-and-coming area, the more affluent zones here run up against some pretty destitute ones. For a long time anything south of Tremont Street was considered off limits; today, the border has been pushed further to Shawmut Avenue, though you should still be careful wherever you're walking and don't hesitate to take a cab if you're heading to one of the South End's many excellent restaurants at night.

For listings of South End restaurants, see p.206.

Like Back Bay, the South End was originally a marshland that now sits on landfill. Though the mud-to-mansion process kicked off in 1834 – predating Back Bay – the area really took shape between 1850 and 1875, when the new land was auctioned off. Quaint slivers like **Union Park Square** were created to attract wealthy buyers, and the neighborhood emerged in piecemeal fashion, unlike the grids of Back Bay. Towards the turn of the century, the South End went into prolonged decline, as the *nouveau riche* headed for Back Bay, displaced by an immigrant population. Over the past thirty years, however, things have again picked up, with brownstones here available on the cheap – though with this new era of gentrification, prices are skyrocketing.

The Golden Triangle and Union Park Square

Not a model of geometric precision, the so-called **Golden Triangle** was named by South End realtors to describe a gentrified zone, loosely bounded by Columbus Avenue and Tremont and Dartmouth streets, that is almost always modified by the term "quaint" – though for once the tag fits. Walk along quiet Chandler and Appleton streets and the appeal is obvious – refurbished bowfronted rowhouses that would be at home in London's Mayfair, and with a community feel all but absent in surrounding areas.

Its heart is the intersection of Tremont Street – actually the southernmost edge of the triangle – and **Clarendon Street**, an upmarket crossing home to some of the trendiest restaurants in Boston, such as the acclaimed *Hamersly's Bistro*, at 553 Tremont St. Next door is the domed **Cyclorama Building**, at no. 539 (Map 6, K7), built in

1884 to house an enormous circular painting of the Battle of Gettysburg (since moved to Gettysburg itself), and now housing the **Boston Center for the Arts**. If the ornate kiosk in front of it looks a trifle oversized, that's because it was designed as the cupola for a building close by. The world-renowned **Boston Ballet** practices in a postmodern brick building at 19 Clarendon St (call ©695-6950 to schedule a studio tour). Also close by is another attractive space, **Union Park Square** (Map 6, K8), that you can walk around, although not through. The elliptical park, lined by well-preserved Victorian rowhouses and accented with fountains and formal plantings, is inaccessible, encircled by a wrought-iron fence; you'll have to make do with noting its carefully planned elegance from there.

KENMORE SQUARE, THE FENWAY AND BROOKLINE

A t the western edge of Back Bay, the decorous brownstones and smart shops fade into the more casual **Kenmore Square** and **Fenway** districts, both removed from the tourist circuit but good fun nonetheless, with a student vibe and some of the city's more notable cultural institutions. The Fenway spreads out beneath Kenmore Square like an elongated kite, taking in a disparate array of sights ranging from **Fenway Park**, where the star-crossed Red Sox play, to some of Boston's finest cultural institutions: **Symphony Hall**, the **Museum of Fine Arts** and the **Isabella Stewart Gardner Museum**. Further west and more residential is the suburb of **Brookline**, which feels like just another sleepy part of the city, though one in which you're unlikely to find yourself spending too much time.

KENMORE SQUARE

Map 6, C2.

Kenmore Square, at the junction of Commonwealth Avenue and Beacon Street, is the primary location of **Boston University** and the unofficial playground for its students. Back Bay's Commonwealth Avenue Mall leads right into this lively stretch of youth-oriented bars, record stores and casual restaurants that cater to the late-night cravings of local students – as such the Square is considerably more alive when school's in session. Many of the buildings on its north side have been snapped up by BU, such as the bustling six-story *Barnes & Noble* bookstore, 660 Beacon St, on top of which is perched the monumental **Citgo Sign**, Kenmore's most noticeable landmark. This sixty-square-foot neon advertisement, a pulsing red triangle that is the oil company's logo, has been a popular symbol of Boston since it was placed here in 1965.

You can cross the Brookline Avenue bridge over the Mass Turnpike to the block-long **Lansdowne Street**, an unlovely but perennially popular stretch of show-your-ID bars and nightclubs, most popular of which are *Avalon* and *Mama Kin*, the latter partially owned by Aerosmith and taking its name from one of their songs. There's little point in coming here during daylight hours, as it really only wakes up at midnight.

BOSTON UNIVERSITY

Map 6, Map 7.

Boston University, one of the country's biggest private schools, has its main campus alongside the Charles River, on the narrow stretch of land between Commonwealth Avenue and Storrow Drive. Though it boasts a few Nobel-prize winners, such as Derek Walcott and Elie Wiesel, the school is more interesting for its inventive reuse of old buildings, such as the dormitory **Myles Standish Hall**, at 610 Beacon St, a scaled-down version of New York's Flatiron Building that once was a hotel where notables like Babe Ruth camped out. One of its rooms also served as the fictional trysting place of Willy Loman in *Death of a Salesman*. **Shelton Hall**, behind it on Bay State Road, is another hostelry-turned-student dorm where playwright Eugene O'Neill rather undramatically made his long day's journey into night.

Bay State Road was the westernmost extension of Back Bay, evidenced by its wealth of turn-of-the-century brownstones, most of which now house BU graduate institutes and smaller residence halls. An ornate High Georgian Revival mansion at no. 149 houses the office of the university president. The street ends at **The Castle**, an ivy-covered Tudor mansion now used for university functions. Just beyond is one of BU's few green spaces, the **Warren Alpert Mall** and its so-called "BU Beach," a sliver of lawn that's been purposefully upswept at the edge to shield busy Storrow Drive from view.

Continuing the theme back on Commonwealth is the domed **Morse Auditorium**, formerly a synagogue; behind the adjacent College of Communication is the **Sony Nickelodeon**, surprisingly the only art house movie theater in Boston (there are others in Cambridge). One long block down is the closest thing the BU campus has to a center, **Marsh Plaza**, with its Gothic Revival chapel and memorial to Martin Luther King, Jr, a graduate here. Further out, Commonwealth Avenue leads into **Allston-Brighton**, a largely nondescript area home to a mix of students and Russian immigrants.

FENWAY PARK

Map 6, B3. Tours April–Oct Mon–Fri 10am, 11am and 1pm; $5. Kenmore Ⓣ.

The Curse of the Bambino

In 1903, Boston (then nicknamed the "Pilgrims") became the first team to represent the American League in baseball's World Series, upsetting the heavily favored Pittsburgh Pirates to claim the championship; their continued financial success allowed them to build a new stadium, **Fenway Park**, in 1912. During their first year there, Boston won the Series again, and repeated the feat in 1915, 1916 and 1918, led in the latter years by the young pitcher **George Herman "Babe" Ruth**, who also demonstrated an eye-opening penchant for hitting home runs.

The team was poised to become a dynasty, when its owner, Harry Frazee, began a firesale of the team to finance a Broadway play that was to star his ingenue girlfriend. Most of the players were sold at bargain prices, including Ruth, who went to the New York Yankees, which of course went on to become the most successful franchise in professional sports history, with the Babe and all his home run records at the forefront – indeed, Yankee Stadium is often referred to as "The House That Ruth Built." On the other hand, Frazee's play, *No, No, Nanette*, flopped. So did his Red Sox team – the 1918 World Series was the last they won. Their long periods of mediocrity have been punctuated by even more disappointing seasons in which they came agonizingly close to the championship, only to snatch defeat from the jaws of certain victory: in 1978, a late-season collapse was capped off when the Yankees' light-hitting shortstop Bucky Dent slugged a three-run homer to beat the Sox in a one-game playoff; in 1986, the Sox were one strike away from clinching the World Series against the New York Mets when a series of miscues, including the infamous grounder that rolled through the legs of first-baseman Bill Buckner, brought about another crushing loss. These Red Sox failures have become fodder for the long-suffering fans, who refer to "The Curse of the Bambino" (referring to the Babe); Boston sportswriter Dan Shaughnessy even penned a 1991 book by that same name. The myth must have something to it – the Red Sox have publicly denied its existence.

Baseball is treated with reverence in Boston, so it's appropriate that it is played here in what may be the country's most storied stadium, **Fenway Park**, at 24 Yawkey Way, whose giant 37ft-tall left-field wall, aka the "Green Monster," is an enduring symbol of the quirks of early ballparks. Fenway Park was constructed in 1912 in a tiny, asymmetrical space wedge just off Brookline Avenue, resulting in its famously awkward dimensions – also included in which are an abnormally short right-field line (302 ft) and a fence that doesn't at all approximate the smooth arc of most outfields. That the left-field wall was built so high makes up for some of the short distances in the park and also gives Red Sox' leftfielders a distinct advantage over their counterparts – it takes some time before one gets accustomed to the whimsical caroms a ball hit off there might take. You can take tours of the stadium, where greats like Ted Williams, Carl Yazstremski and even Babe Ruth roamed about, but your best bet is to come see a game, really a must for any baseball fan and still a reasonable draw for anyone remotely curious. The season runs from April to October, and tickets are quite reasonable, especially if you sit in the bleachers. For more information, see p.277.

THE BACK BAY FENS AND SYMPHONY HALL

Map 6.

The Fenway's defining element is the **Back Bay Fens**, a snakelike segment of Frederick Law Olmsted's Emerald

The Emerald Necklace

The string of urban parks that stretches through Boston's southern districts, known as the **Emerald Necklace**, grew out of a project conceived in the 1870s, when landscape architect **Frederick Law Olmsted** was commissioned to create for Boston a series of urban parks, as he had done in New York and Chicago. A Romantic naturalist in the tradition of Rousseau and Wordsworth, Olmsted conceived of nature as a way to escape the ills wrought by society, and considered his urban parks a means for city-dwellers to escape the clamor of their everyday life. He converted much of Boston's remaining open space, which was often disease-ridden marshland, into a series of fabulous, manicured parks beginning with the **Back Bay Fens**, including the **Riverway** along the Boston-Brookline border, and proceeding through **Jamaica Pond** and the **Arnold Arboretum** to Roxbury's **Franklin Park** (see "Southern Districts," p.108). While Olmsted's original skein of parks was limited to these, further development linked the Fens, via the Commonwealth Avenue Mall, to the Public Garden and Boston Common, all of which now function as part of the Necklace, and which make it all the more impressive in scale, although the Necklace's sense of pristine natural wonder has slipped in the century since their creation – the more southerly links in the chain, starting with Fens, have grown shaggy and are unsafe at night.

The **Boston Park Rangers** (daily 9am–5pm; ©635-7383) organize free walking tours covering each of the Necklace's segments from Boston Common to Franklin Park.

Necklace that rather uninspiringly takes over where theprim Commonwealth Avenue Mall leaves off. The Fens were fashioned from marsh and mud in 1879, a fact reflected in the name of the waterway that still runs through them today

– the **Muddy River**. This narrow channel is crossed in its northernmost part by a medievalesque puddingstone bridge designed by H.H. Richardson, East of Agassiz Road, which roughly splits the Fens in two, local residents maintain small garden plots, one of the better uses of the landscape, though the area also makes an agreeable backdrop for some of Boston's smaller colleges, such as **Simmons** and **Emmanuel**, as well as the **Harvard Medical School**.

The renowned **Berklee College of Music** makes its home on the busy stretch of Massachusetts Avenue south of Boylston Street, an area with several appropriately budget-friendly eateries. Looming a few short blocks south, **Symphony Hall**, where the Boston Symphony Orchestra plays, anchors the corner of Massachusetts and Huntington avenues. The inside of the 1900 McKim, Mead and White design, modeled after the no longer extant Neues Gewandhaus in Leipzig, Germany, resembles an oversized cube, apparently just the right shape to lend it its perfect acoustics. The big English Baroque-style building across the street is **Horticultural Hall**, headquarters of the Massachusetts Horticultural Society, while **Jordan Hall**, venue of the New England Conservatory of Music's chamber music concerts, is a few blocks down on Huntington, at nos. 290-294. The modern campus of **Northeastern University** spreads out on both sides of the avenue about a half-mile further south. There's not much to see here, though; it's largely a commuter campus, and as such lacks the collegiate atmosphere of Boston's more happening universities.

MUSEUM OF FINE ARTS

Map 6, B7–C7. Tues, Thurs–Fri & Sun 10am–4.45pm, Wed until 9.45pm, Sat until 5.45pm; West Wing also open Thurs & Fri until 9.45pm; $10. Museum Ⓣ. *http://www.mfa.org.*

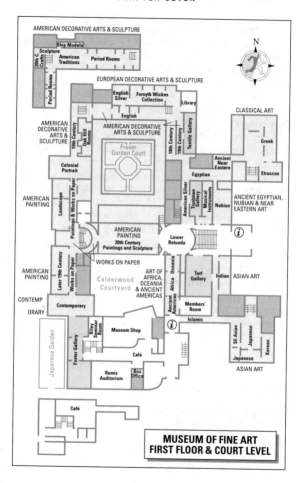

MUSEUM OF FINE ARTS

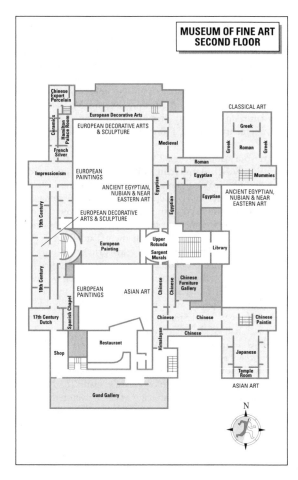

Rather inconveniently located in the south Fenway but well worth the trip out, is New England's premier art space, the **Museum of Fine Arts**, at 465 Huntington Ave. It originated in the 1850s as an adjunct of the Boston Athenæum when that organization decided to focus more exclusively on local history rather than art. The collection was given public imprimatur and funding by the Massachusetts Legislature in 1870, and after moving around at the end of the nineteenth century, found its permanent home here in 1906.

Start your tour with the Evans Wing on the first floor, a marvelously rich **American collection** that features works from the two major figures of the Colonial period: Gilbert Stuart's nationalistic *Washington at Dorchester Heights*, along with his portrait of Washington that appears on the one-dollar bill, and a number of John Singleton Copley portraits of Revolutionary figures, among them Paul Revere, John Hancock, and Sam Adams, and his gruesome narrative *Watson and the Shark*. Romantic naturalist landscapes from the first half of the nineteenth century – such as Albert Bierstadt's quietly majestic *Buffalo Crossing* – dominate several rooms, mixed in with representations of popular culture, such as William Sidney Mount's *The Bone Player*. From the latter half of the century there are several seascapes by Winslow Homer, Whistler's morose *Nocturne in Blue and Silver: the Lagoon*, and works from the Boston school, notably Childe Hassan's gauzy *Boston Common at Twilight* and John Singer Sargent's provocatively spare *The Daughters of Edward Darley Boit*. A scattering of early-twentieth-century American work rounds out the wing, with Edward Hopper's uncharacteristically hopeful *Room in Brooklyn* and Maurice Prendergast's sentimental renderings of genteel life, *Sunset* and *Eight Bathers*. Don't miss the **American Decorative Arts**, either: a gloriously nostalgic assemblage of coffee urns, elaborately styled oak furnishings and reconstructed living rooms with period furniture.

The second-floor **European** wing begins with Dutch paintings from the Northern Renaissance, featuring two outstanding Rembrandts, *Artist in his Studio* and *Old Man in Prayer*, and follows with several rooms of grandiose Rococo and Romantic work from the eighteenth and early nineteenth centuries, most interestingly Pannini's self-referential *Picture Gallery with Views of Modern Rome*, Jean-Baptiste Greuze's erotic *Young Woman in White Hat*, and John Martin's epic *The Seventh Plague of Egypt*. The culmination of the wing is the late nineteenth-century collection, which begins with works by the Realist Jean-Francois Millet, whose *Man Turning over the Soil* and *The Sower* exhibit the stark use of color and interest in common subjects that characterized later French artists. Early Impressionists are well-represented by Manet's *Execution of Emperor Maximilian* and Cezanne's *Uncle Dominique*. The Impressionist room also contains Monet's heavily abstracted *Grainstack (Snow Effect)* and *Rouen Cathedral (Morning Effect)*; Degas figures prominently with his madding *Pagans and Degas' Father* and a bronze cast of the famous *Little Dancer*, and there are several land- and cityscapes from Renoir and Pissarro. The room's highlight, however, is its selection of Post-Impressionist art, best of which are Van Gogh's richly hued *Enclosed Field with Ploughman* and *Houses at Auvers* and Gauguin's vibrant narrative of Tahitian life, *Where do we come from? What are we? Where are we going?*

A series of MFA-sponsored digs at Giza have made its **Egyptian collection** the standout of a fine collection of **Ancient art**. Best among pieces that range from prehistoric pots to artifacts from the Roman period are several statues of King Mercerinus and Queen Kha-Merer-Nebty, a colossal head of Ramses II, and two fully reconstructed burial chambers of Old Kingdom royalty. While rather modest by comparison, the Nubian collection is nevertheless the largest of its kind outside Africa. Most of the pieces, such as the *Granite Sphinx of a Nubian King*, are funerary and actually quite similar to their Egyptian contemporaries. Not nearly as well-represented, the Classical section is worth a glance mostly for its numerous Grecian urns, a fine Cycladic *Female Figure*, and several Etruscan sarcophagi with elaborately wrought narrative bas-reliefs.

Less visited are the **Asian galleries**, though they're among the best of their kind in the world. A marvelous array of Japanese pieces stands out, including ornamental munitions that date back to the thirteenth century, the largest assemblage of Japanese Buddhist art outside Japan, and the woodblock print cityscapes of Ando Hiroshige, whose sharply delineated chromatic schemes influenced Van Gogh, Gauguin and Whistler. An excellent cross-section of illustrations from the Mughal Dynasty highlights the Indian collection, and there are also a number of fine Buddhist sculptures, particularly a sinuous *Ganesha* and the voluptuous *Fertility Goddess (Yakshi)*. In the Chinese section, don't leave before checking out the scrolls, decorated with spare naturalist abstractions as well as finely detailed graphic narratives, and the life-size statue of *Guanyin, Bodhisattva of Compassion*, one of the best-preserved pieces from the twelfth-century Jin Dynasty.

THE ISABELLA STEWART GARDNER MUSEUM

Map 6, A7. Tues–Sun 11am–5pm; $9, students $5. Museum Ⓣ.

Less broad in its collection, but more distinctive and idiosyncratic than the MFA, is its neighbor, the **Isabella Stewart Gardner Museum**, at 280 The Fenway. Eccentric Boston socialite Gardner collected and arranged more than 2500 objects in the four-story Fenway building she designed herself, making this the only ma, museum in the country that is entirely the creation of a single individual. It's a hodgepodge of works from around the globe, presented without much attention to period or style; Gardner's goal was to foster the love of art rather than its study, and she wanted the setting of her pieces to "fire the imagination." Your imagination does get quite a workout – there's art everywhere you look, with many of the objects are unlabeled, placed in corners or above doorways, for an effect that is occasionally chaotic, but always striking and at times quite effective.

The Gardner is best known for its spectacular central **courtyard**, styled after a fifteenth-century Venetian palace, where flowering plants and trees bloom year-round amid statuary and fountains. However, the museum's greatest success is the **Spanish Cloister**, a long, narrow corridor which perfectly frames John Singer Sargent's ecstatic representation of Spanish dance, *El Jaleo*, and also contains fine seventeenth-century Mexican tiles and Roman statuary and sarcophagi. Gardner had an affinity for altars, and the collection boasts several, cobbled together from various religious artifacts. Most notable of these is her **Chapel**, on the third floor, which incorporates sixteenth-century Italian choirstalls and stained glass from Milan and Soissons cathedrals, as well as assorted religious figurines, candlesticks and crucifixes, all surrounding Paul-Cesar Helleu's moody representation of the *Interior of the Abbey Church of Saint-Denis*. Another dramatic concentration of these surrounds the third-floor stairwell, and includes a medieval stone carving of the beheading of John the Baptist, the particularly agonized *Dead Christ* from twelfth-century Spain, and Giovanni Minelli's maudlin altar painting, the *Lamentation*.

THE ISABELLA STEWART GARDNER MUSEUM

BROOKLINE Court

...ese and Raphael Rooms comprise
Italian Renaissance and Baroque work,
famous *Europa*, Botticelli's *Tragedy of*
...velli's Mannerist *St George and the Dragon*.
... a first-rate array of seventeenth-century
...opean works was debilitated by a 1990 art
... n two Rembrandts and a Vermeer were among
ten ca... ...s stolen. But the majority of works in the
Dutch Room remain, most notably an early *Self-Portrait*
by Rembrandt and Rubens' austere *Thomas Howard, Earl of
Arundel*.

BROOKLINE

Map 2.

The leafy, affluent town of **Brookline**, south of Boston
University and west of the Fenway, appears as if it's just
another well-maintained Boston neighborhood, though in
fact it's a distinct municipality. It holds some vaguely divert-
ing attractions, most oriented around bustling **Coolidge
Corner**, at the intersection of Beacon and Harvard streets,
though it's unlikely any of them will bring you out this way
unless you're an avid fan of Massachusetts politicians.

....

**To reach Brookline, take the Green Line's C
branch to Coolidge Corner or D branch
to Brookline Village.**

....

Perhaps the biggest draw at Coolidge Corner is the
Coolidge Corner Theater, at 290 Harvard St, a refurbished art house cinema; with plenty of students living in
the area it maintains itself quite well. A short ways west up
Harvard Street is a plethora of Jewish delis and bakeries, the
best of which is *Kupel's*, at no. 421, with its excellent

BROOKLINE

bagels. Close by is the **John F. Kennedy National Historic Site**, at 83 Beals St (Wed–Sun 10am–4.30pm; $2), the outwardly unremarkable house where JFK was born on May 29, 1917. The inside is rather plain, too, though a narrated voiceover by the late President's mother, Rose, adds some spice to the roped-off rooms. Brookline also happens to be where a more recent presidential aspirant, former Massachusetts governor **Michael Dukakis**, was born; strangely this, too, has failed to put Brookline on the map.

Along Brookline's southern fringe is the **Frederick Law Olmsted National Historic Site**, at 99 Warren St (Fri–Sun 10am–4.30pm; free), the Olmsted family home that provides a retrospective on his life and work and is located, unsurprisingly, in idyllic grounds.

SOUTHERN DISTRICTS

The parts of Boston that most visitors see – Downtown, Beacon Hill, Back Bay, the North End – actually only cover a small proportion of the city's geography. To the south lies a vast spread of residential neighborhoods known collectively to Bostonians as the **Southern Districts**, including **South Boston**, **Dorchester**, **Roxbury** and **Jamaica Plain**, which count just a handful of highlights among them, most notably Jamaica Plain's **Arnold Arboretum** and Dorchester's **John F. Kennedy Museum and Library**. These were once rural areas, dotted with the swish summer resort homes of Boston's monied elite, but population growth in the late nineteenth century pushed middle- and working-class families here from the increasingly crowded downtown area. Three-story row houses soon replaced the mansions, and the moniker "streetcar suburbs" was coined as a catch-all for the newly redefined neighborhoods. In the years immediately following World War II, each was hit to varying degrees by economic decline, and the middle class moved farther afield, leaving the districts to the mostly immigrant and blue-collar communities that remain today.

The areas covered by this chapter can be
seen on color map 2.

SOUTH BOSTON

Across Fort Point Channel from downtown and east into
Boston Harbor lies **South Boston**, affectionately referred to
as "Southie" by its large Irish-American population.
Originally a peninsula separated from Boston proper by
waterways, it was connected to the city in 1805, and throughout the nineteenth century expanded geographically, via land-
fill, and in population, thanks to a steady influx of Irish immigrants. South Boston remained staunchly blue-collar and Irish
until just after World War II, when it was particularly hard hit
by recession, and its makeup began to change; and, despite
some economic revival of late, especially in the shipbuilding
industry, it is better known today for the tensions between its
old-timers and the newer communities of African-Americans
and gays that have moved into the area. Indeed, radical gay
activists Act Up! met with staunch resistance when they petitioned in 1994 to march in Southie's annual St. Patrick's Day;
the battle went to the Supreme Court, which upheld the
exclusion. South Bostonians showed a different side in a less
publicized incident shortly afterward, when the Ku Klux Klan
marched in the area and were met with jeers and protests
from local residents.

The area's Celtic heritage is quite evident on the main
commercial boulevard, **Broadway**, where seemingly every
laundromat, convenience store, even Chinese restaurant, has
a sign plastered with shamrocks. You'll also find an unsur-
prising profusion of Irish bars and pubs along West
Broadway that make up in enthusiasm for the mother
country what they lack in authenticity. *The Blackthorn*, at
no. 471, comes closest to the real feel of an Irish pub.

SOUTH BOSTON

Castle Island and Fort Independence

Map 2, K5. Island open daily dawn–dusk, fort open Sat–Sun noon–3.30pm; free. Broadway Ⓣ, then bus #9 or #11.

South Boston narrows to an end in Boston Harbor on a strip of land called **Castle Island**, off the end of William J. Day Boulevard, a favorite leisure spot for Southie residents and, in fact, many Bostonians. The island is covered by parks and beaches, though you wouldn't want to swim here, since Boston Harbor's waters, while cleaner than in the past, are far from non-toxic – and they're freezing to boot. However, the views of downtown and the harbor are spectacular, best appreciated along the walkway known as the "Sugar Bowl," which follows along a narrow peninsula that curls out into the water.

The island's lone snack bar, *Sullivan's*, is a local institution, with tasty seafood and grill fare.

Fort Independence, a stout granite edifice just north of the island, was one of the earliest redoubts in the Americas, originally established in 1634, though it has been rebuilt several times since. Today, what remains is a skeleton of its 1801 version, and its slate-gray walls aren't much to look at from the outside, though the ranger-led weekend tours provide some decent history and folklore about the dank interior corridors. One such story recalls a prisoner held here in the early 1800s for killing another man in a duel. One night, the victim's friends supposedly broke into the prison and chained the assassin into an alcove, then built a brick wall around him and left him to die. A young lawyer in the area by the name of Edgar Allan Poe apparently heard the rumor; he used it as the basis for his story, "The Cask of Amontillado."

DORCHESTER

Occupying the southeast corner of Boston beneath South Boston is **Dorchester**, originally built on the narrow neck of land that connected Boston to the mainland, and now a fairly unlovely and uninteresting lower- and middle-class residential neighborhood. North Dorchester was from its earliest days a center of trade and remains focused on industry and commerce today, while South Dorchester has seen more turbulence over the years – it went from coveted spot for elite country homes into the "streetcar suburb" pattern of the Southern Districts, until post WWII, when the middle class left, property values plummeted, and crime and unemployment rose. Today, both parts of Dorchester are home to a broad ethnic mix, notably Irish, Haitians, Vietnamese, Caribbeans and African-Americans. Save for the **John F. Kennedy Museum and Library**, there's not much to see, and parts – especially in South Dorchester – are downright unsafe.

Dorchester Heights Monument

Map 2, I6. Grounds open daily, monument closed. Broadway Ⓣ to #11 bus (G St stop).

At the convergence of South Boston and Dorchester rises the incline of **Dorchester Heights**, a neighborhood of three-story rowhouses whose northernmost point, **Thomas Park**, is crowned by a stone obelisk **monument** commemorating George Washington's bloodless purge of the Brits from Boston. After the Continental Army had held the British under siege in the city for just over a year, Washington wanted to put an end to the whole thing. On March 4, 1776, he amassed all the artillery he could get his hands on and placed it on the towering peak of Dorchester

DORCHESTER

Heights, so the tired Redcoats could get a good look at the patriots' firepower. Intimidated, they swiftly left Boston – for good.

The park is generally empty, pristinely kept, and still commands the same sweeping views of Boston and its southern communities that it did during the Revolutionary War. Unfortunately, the monument is permanently closed to the public, and it's all quite a bit out of the way from any other major points of interest.

John F. Kennedy Museum and Library

Map 2, J7. Daily 9am–5pm; $6. JFK/UMass Ⓣ; free shuttle from the station to the museum every twenty minutes.

As with all presidential museums, the **John F. Kennedy Museum and Library**, at Columbia Point, is faced with the difficult task of extolling a president's – and local icon's – virtues while maintaining a veneer of scholarly objectivity, a task it performs with mixed results. But if the museum comes up a bit short in that respect, it still stands out by providing a fascinating glimpse into the culture of a recent era, while being spectacularly sited in an I.M. Pei-designed building overlooking Boston Harbor. The library, meanwhile, is not open to the public, only to researchers with specific requests, and holds JFK's papers from his brief stint in the Oval Office.

The presentation opens with a well-done eighteen-minute film covering Kennedy's political career through the 1960 Democratic National Covention, narrated by voiceovers by Kennedy himself. The remaining displays cover the presidential campaign of 1960 and the highlights of the brief Kennedy administration. The campaign exhibits are most interesting for their television and radio ads, which illustrate the squeaky-clean self-image America possessed at that time. Several features on JFK and the media unabashedly play up the contrast between Kennedy's telegenic charisma and Richard Nixon's jowly surliness and correctly cite this as a key factor in JFK's victory over Tricky Dick. The section on the Kennedy administration is more serious, highlighted by a 22-minute film on the Cuban Missile Crisis that well evokes the tension of the event, if exaggerating Kennedy's heroics. And for Jackie O. fanatics, there's an exhibit which traces her life from early debutante days to her status as First Lady-cum-popular icon.

> **Oddly enough, the museum is also the repository for Ernest Hemingway's original manuscripts. Call ©929-4523 for an appointment to see them.**

The final section of the museum is perhaps its best: a roomy glass-enclosed space overlooking the harbor, with modest inscriptions bearing some of Kennedy's more memorable quotations – affecting enough to move even the most jaded JFK critic.

ROXBURY

Roxbury has a reputation as Boston's worst neighborhood, a designation that for the most part still holds true, although it was once one of the city's most coveted addresses and today holds the **Franklin Park Zoo**, in yet another of Olmsted's green spaces. Occupying most of south-central Boston below the South End and between Dorchester and Jamaica Plain, Roxbury had its heyday in the seventeenth and eighteenth centuries, when it was rural land where the wealthy built sumptuous country houses. It wasn't really until the 1950s that the area hit hard times, but the urban blight has left its scars, despite the revitalization of the past decade and an ongoing attempt to restore some of the impressive, if neglected, properties. It has nowhere near the danger level of slums in cities like LA or New York, but visitors still may feel unwelcome or unsafe in parts, especially at night.

Roxbury's commercial center is **Dudley Square**, the intersection of Dudley and Washington streets, which is little more than the usual mix of shops and convenience stores. If you're in the area, you may want to check out the **Dillaway-Thomas House**, at 183 Roxbury St (Wed–Fri 10am–4pm, Sat–Sun noon–5pm; donation requested), a structure built in 1750 and used as a fort in the Revolutionary War, located between Dudley Square and the Roxbury Crossing Ⓣ stop. Its first floor is remarkably well-preserved, featuring many details of its original construction, like the hardwood floors, while the upstairs has rotating exhibits of African- and African-American-themed art. Further south, the **Museum of the National Center for Afro-American Artists**, at 300 Walnut Ave (Tues–Sun 1–5pm; $4), housed in the Victorian Gothic "Oak Bend" mansion, has a decent collection of African-American visual art from throughout the twentieth century, highlighted by some richly textured woodcuts by Wilmer Jennings and Hale Woodruff, as well as Roy DeCarava's photogravuras of jazz and blues greats.

Franklin Park Zoo

Map 2, F8. April–Oct Mon–Fri 10am–5pm, Sat & Sun 10am–6pm, Nov–March daily 10am–4pm; $6. Forest Hills Ⓣ.

The **Franklin Park Zoo**, located at 1 Franklin Park Rd in Franklin Park – the southernmost link in the Emerald Necklace – has little besides its backdrop to distinguish it from any other zoo, and is perhaps only a must-see if you're traveling with kids. It does boast a decent array of exotic fauna, much of which is contained in the African Tropical Forest, an impressively re-created savanna that's the largest indoor open-space zoo design in North America, and houses gorillas, monkeys and pygmy hippos. The **Children's Zoo** allows kids to pet and feed rhinos and the like, while Bird's World is a charming relic from the days of Edwardian zoo design: a huge, ornate wrought-iron cage you can walk through while birds fly overhead.

Franklin Park itself was one of Olmsted's proudest accomplishments when it was completed, due to the sheer size of the place, and its scale is indeed astounding – 527 acres of green space, with countless trails for hikers, bikers, and walkers leading through the hills and thickly forested areas. That's about it, as much of the park has unfortunately become overgrown from years of halfhearted upkeep. It's quite easy to get lost among all the greenery and forget that you're in the middle of a city, though this is perhaps not such a hot idea – the park borders some of Boston's more dangerous areas, and can feel quite threatening, especially at night.

JAMAICA PLAIN

Diminutive **Jamaica Plain** – "JP" in local parlance – is one of Boston's more successfully integrated neighborhoods, with a good mix of students and working-class families crowded into its cheap apartments. Located between Roxbury and the section of the Emerald Necklace known as the Muddy River Improvement, the area's activity centers around, appropriately, **Centre Street**, which holds some inventive, and remarkably inexpensive, cafés and restaurants (see p.209). Otherwise, head straight for JP's star attraction, the Arnold Arboretum, on its southwestern edge.

Arnold Arboretum

Map 2, D8. Daily dawn–dusk; $1 donation requested. Forest Hills Ⓣ.

The 265-acre **Arnold Arboretum**, at 125 Arborway, is the most spectacular link in the Emerald Necklace and the only real must-see sight in all the Southern Districts. Its collection of trees, vines, shrubs and flowers has benefited from more than 100 years of both careful grooming and ample funding, and is now one of the finest in North America. The plants are arranged along a series of paths populated by runners and dog-walkers as well as serious botanists, though it certainly doesn't require any expert knowledge to enjoy the grounds.

The array of Asian species – the best in the world outside Asia – is highlighted by the **Larz Anderson Bonsai Collection**, and is brilliantly concentrated along the Chinese Path, a walkway near the center of the park. Although the staff does an impressive job of keeping the grounds looking fabulous year-round, it's best to visit in spring, when crabapples, lilacs and magnolias complement the greenery with dazzling chromatic schemes. "Lilac Sunday," the third Sunday in May, sees the Arboretum at its most vibrant (and busiest), when its collection of lilacs – the second largest in the US – is in full bloom. One of the best ways to appreciate the scope of the place is to make your way to the top of **Bussey Hill** in the Arboretum's center, where you can overlook the grounds in their impressive entirety and, on a clear day, catch a great view of downtown Boston as well.

CAMBRIDGE

Past and present stand comfortably opposed in **Cambridge** – just across the Charles River from Boston, but a world apart in atmosphere and attitude. A walk down most any street takes you past plaques and monuments honoring literati and revolutionaries who lived and worked in the area as early as the seventeenth century. But along its colonial-period brick sidewalks and narrow, crooked roads, Cambridge vibrates with a vital present: starched businesspeople bustle past disaffected punks; clean-cut college students coexist beside a growing homeless population; and busloads of tourists look on as street people purvey goods and perform music. In fact, many residents tend to forget the world beyond the Charles River, and the Puritan parochialism of its founders has turned into a different breed of exclusivity, touched with civic and intellectual elitism. Simultaneously insular and outward-looking, Cambridge's exhilarating mix of Colonial past and urban present, its diversity of residents and activities, and the sense of sheer energy that pervades its classrooms and coffeehouses make it an essential stopover while traveling in the Boston area.

The shape of Cambridge resembles a bow tie, or a butterfly. On its southern border is the sinuous Charles River, with Boston on the opposite bank, while the concave northern side is shared with the large, mostly residential town of Somerville. The city is loosely organized around a series of squares – in fact confluences of streets that are the focus of each area's commercial activity. By far the most important of these is **Harvard Square**, center of the eponymous university, and the top draw for Cambridge's visitors. The area around it is home to the city's main sights, particularly the stretch of Colonial mansions in **Old Cambridge**. The squares of **Central and East Cambridge** are more down-to-earth. Blue-collar **Central Square** is less touristy but no less urban than its collegiate counterpart: here you can eat at *McDonald's* (a rarity in Cambridge), and enjoy the city's best blues bars and rock music shows. Farther east along the Charles is **Kendall Square**, home to a cluster of technology companies and also the beginning of East Cambridge, a mostly Hispanic working-class district. The only part of this area that really warrants a visit is the **Massachusetts Institute of Technology** (MIT), one of the world's premier science and research institutions and home to some peculiar architecture and an excellent museum. Tiny **Inman Square**, nearby Central, has some of the city's best restaurants, but little else to recommend it. Finally, above Harvard stretch the ragged boundaries of **Northwest Cambridge**, a diverse residential area that takes in both posh Huron Avenue and the housing projects of the Alewife Brook Parkway.

The area covered by this chapter is shown in detail on color map 7.

Some history

Cambridge began inauspiciously in 1630, when a group of English immigrants from Charlestown founded New Towne village on the narrow, swampy banks of the Charles

River. These Puritans hoped New Towne would become an ideal religious community; to that end, they founded a college in 1636 for the purpose of training clergy. Two years later, the college took its name in honor of a local minister, John Harvard, who bequeathed his library and half his estate to the nascent institution. New Towne was eventually renamed Cambridge in honor of the English university where many of its figureheads were educated, and became one of the largest publishing centers in the New World after the importation of the printing press in the seventeenth century. Its printing industry and university established Cambridge as an important center of intellectual activity and political thought. This status became entrenched over the course of the United States' turbulent early history, particularly during the late eighteenth century, when the Cambridge population grew sharply divided · between the numerous artisans and farmers who sympathized with the Revolution and the minority of monied Tories. When fighting began, the Tories were driven from their mansions on modern-day Brattle Street (then called "Tory Row"), and their place was taken by Cambridge intelligentsia and prominent Revolutionaries.

The area remained unincorporated until 1846, when the Massachusetts Legislature granted a city charter linking Old Cambridge (the Harvard Square area) and industrial East Cambridge as a single municipality. Initially, there was friction between these two very different parts of Cambridge; in 1855, citizens from each area unsuccessfully petitioned for the two regions to be granted separate civic status. The failure of these efforts was followed by a thaw in relations which has resulted in a more cohesive community, though each area retains a distinctive character. The late nineteenth and early twentieth century brought substantial growth to the town. A large immigrant population was drawn to opportunity in the industrial and commercial sectors of East Cambridge, while academics increasingly sought out Harvard, whose reputation had continued to swell, and the Massachusetts Institute of Technology, which moved here from Boston in 1916. The district's political leanings are less liberal today than in the 1960s, when Cambridge earned the name "Moscow on the Charles" due to its unabashedly Red character, but the fact that nearly half of its 93,000 residents are university affiliates ensures that it will remain one of America's most opinionated cities.

Finding your way around Cambridge

Spanning a square mile centered around the Harvard Ⓣ station, **Harvard Square** and **Harvard University** make up the cultural and academic heart of Cambridge. This is where people converge to check out Ivy League academia, historical monuments, a lively coffeehouse-and-bookstore scene, and a disgruntled counterculture; few go away disappointed. The area itself is roughly divided into the Square, which radiates out from the Ⓣ stop along Massachusetts Avenue, JFK Street and Brattle Street; and the University, roughly coterminous with Harvard Yard. Its geographic area is small in comparison with the entirety of Cambridge, but this is one part of town you shouldn't miss. Next to the University District is **Old Cambridge –** the clean, impeccably kept colonial heartland of the city.

Grittier than neighboring Harvard Square, **Central and East Cambridge** lack any semblance of pretension, having both grown up around industry rather than academia. They were originally settled in the 1640s, not as separate communities from Boston, but as agrarian adjuncts, to be used primarily for raising crops and livestock. Eventually, these areas evolved into Cambridge's industrial quarters, their skylines serried with smoke-stacks; in the nineteenth century, large numbers of immigrants streamed in to find opportunity in the emerging manufacturing center. Today, East Cambridge in particular is renowned for its technology and research industry, evident in the many computer and software companies that call it home and in the presence of the Massachusetts Institute of Technology.

Northwest Cambridge is an ill-defined corner of Cambridge, a catch-all term for some of the places not identified with the city's more happening districts – and as such it is easily missed. There's some good shopping and decent restaurants, but it's mostly geared toward residents rather than travelers.

HARVARD SQUARE

Map 7, D5.

The Harvard ⓣ station marks **Harvard Square's** ground zero, where musicians perform and a moody youth brigade stews in the shadow of Yard buildings. When you exit the station, take a pass through the adjacent sunken area known as **The Pit,** a triage center for fashion victims of alternative culture. Disgruntled teens spend entire days sitting here admiring each other's green hair and body piercings while the homeless (and some of the teens) hustle for change and other handouts. This is also the focal point of the **street music scene**, where folk diva Tracy Chapman (a graduate from nearby Tufts University, in Somerville) got her start, and it's at its most frenetic and fascinating on Friday and Saturday nights and Sunday afternoons, when all the elements converge – crowds mill about; evangelical demonstrators engage in shouting matches with angry youths; and magicians, acrobats and bands perform on every corner.

OLD BURYING-GROUND AND DAWES PARK

Map 7, D4.

North of Harvard Square along Massachusetts Avenue lies one of Cambridge's first cemeteries, the **Old Burying-Ground**, whose style and grounds have scarcely changed since the seventeenth century. The epitaphs have an archaic ring to them ("Here lyes..."), and the stone grave markers, some of which date to the middle of the seventeenth century, are adorned in a style between Puritan austerity and medieval superstition: inscriptions praise the simple piety of the staunchly Christian deceased, but are surrounded by death's-heads carved to ward off evil spirits. Its most famous occupants include several of Harvard's first presidents as well as two black veterans of the Revolutionary War, Cato Stedman and Neptune Frost. Be sure to check out the **milestone** at the northeast corner of the cemetery, just inside the gate, whose two-and-a-half centuries-old inscription is still readily visible. Originally set to mark the then-daunting distance of eight miles to Boston, the letters A. I. identify the stone's maker, Abraham Ireland. You're supposed to apply to the sexton of Christ Church for entry, but if the gate at the path behind the church is open (as it frequently is), you can enter so long as you're respectful of the grounds.

> **Cambridge's street signs give evidence of the city's early layout, with each road's original name and its year of inception printed below the current tag. For example, Garden Street was created as the Watertown Path in 1630.**

A triangular wedge of concrete squeezed into the intersection of Massachusetts Avenue and Garden Street, **Dawes Park** is named for the patriot who rode to alert residents that the British were marching on Lexington and Concord on April 19, 1775 – the *other* one that is, William Dawes. While Longfellow opted to commemorate Paul Revere's midnight ride instead, as have all history classes, the citizens of Cambridge and other areas north of Boston must have appreciated poor Dawes' contribution just as much. Bronze hoofmarks in the sidewalk mark the event, and several placards behind the pathway provide information on the history of the Harvard Square/Old Cambridge area. Though calling this island in the midst of a crowded intersection a "park" is rather a stretch, it's still a conveniently located place to remember a forgotten part of an historical event and get an introduction to Cambridge's past as well.

CAMBRIDGE COMMON

Map 7, C4.

Cambridge Common, a roughly square patch of green space located between Massachusetts Avenue, Garden Street and Waterhouse Street, has been a site for recreation and community events since Cambridge's earliest settlers first used it as a cow pasture. Tourists flock to the Common for its historical interest, but native Cantabridgians congregate in its wide green spaces for frisbee and sunbathing – although after dusk it can be a lonelier, and more dicey, place altogether. Single pedestrians, especially women, should avoid cutting across the area during this time.

Early Harvard commencements took place here, as did public debates and training exercises for the local militia. You can retrace the old **Charlestown–Watertown path**, along which Redcoats beat a sheepish retreat during the Revolutionary War, and which still transects the park from east to west. A broad range of **statuary** dots the southeast corner of the park, and you can't miss the towering monument to Lincoln and other Civil War dead, which all but overshadows the recently added tableau of two emaciated figures nearby, wrought as an unsettling memorial to the Irish Potato Famine.

The most prominent feature on the Common is, however, the revered **Washington Elm,** under which it's claimed George Washington took command of the Continental Army. The elm is at the southern side of the park, near the intersection of Garden Street and Appian Way, and is accompanied by a predictable wealth of commemorative objects: a cannon captured from the British when they evacuated Boston, a statue of Washington standing in the shade of the beloved tree, and monuments to two Polish army captains hired to lead Revolutionary forces – excessive rewards, really, for mercenaries. What the memorials don't tell you is that the city of Cambridge cut down the original Washington Elm in 1946 when it began to obstruct traffic; it stood at the Common's southwest corner, near the intersection of Mason and Garden streets. The present tree is only the offspring of that tree, raised from one of its branches. To further confuse the issue, the Daughters of the American Revolution erected a monument commemorating the south*east* corner of the park as the spot where Washington did his historic thing. And recently, American historians have adduced evidence strongly suggesting that Washington never commissioned the troops on the Common at all, but rather in Wadsworth House at Harvard Yard.

RADCLIFFE YARD

Map 7, C5.

Just across Garden Street from Cambridge Common is a less crowded park, **Radcliffe Yard**, originally the center of Radcliffe College, established in 1878 to give women access to (then exclusively male) Harvard. The two colleges merged in the 1970s, and since then Radcliffe has functioned primarily as a resource center for women in higher education. Much of its funding now goes to beautifying the Yard, and the results show. It's a picturesque, impeccably preserved quadrangle, dotted with fountains and pathways, and enclosed by brick buildings and Ionic columns – on sunny days a great place to bring a picnic lunch or a book.

JFK STREET

Map 7, D5–D6.

The stretch of JFK Street below Harvard Square holds more of the city's many public spaces, certainly the least of which is **Winthrop Square,** site of the original New Towne marketplace and since converted into a bedraggled park. Cross the park and walk down Winthrop Street to the right to get a sense of the sloping topography and narrow street design of early Cambridge. Just to the right of the nightclub *House of Blues* is a **stone wall** that was built along the original shoreline of the Charles River.

John F. Kennedy Park, where JFK Street meets Memorial Drive, was only finished in the late 1980s, making it an infant among Harvard Square's venerable spaces, though certainly not the first pious shrine to the university's favorite modern son. Unlike most other area parks, this one is cleaner, more spacious, and relatively tramp-free. The **memorial** to Kennedy in its center is unusual and worth a look; it's a low granite pyramid surrounded by a moat, covered constantly but imperceptibly by a thin film of flowing water.

HARVARD HOUSES

Harvard's fancy upperclassmen's residences, most of which are nested in the area east of JFK Street and south of

Harvard Yard, are a visible – and rather ostentatious – remnant of the university's elite past. Nearest the Yard, at 46 Plympton St, is **Adams House.** Once a haven for the Harvard avant-garde, Adams' counterculture has grown feeble, though its subterranean tunnels, decorated with residents' graffiti, give a taste of its once-subversive character. Just south of Adams juts the graceful, blue-topped bell tower of **Lowell House,** at 2 Holyoke Place, which boasts one of Harvard's most beautiful courtyards, surrounded by a compound of sober brick dormitories and fastidiously manicured grounds. Further west on the banks of the Charles rises the purple spire of **Eliot House,** a community that remains a bastion of social privilege despite Harvard's attempts to shed this image. To the east along Memorial Drive lies **Dunster House,** whose red Georgian top is a favorite subject of Cambridge's tourist brochures. Alongside Adams, it has long been considered a center for radical culture, though its character is not wilting so rapidly – Dunster's riverside courtyard was recently rated by *Spy* magazine as one of the top ten places in the country to have sex.

HARVARD YARD AND AROUND

Map 7, D8.

The transition between Harvard Square and **Harvard Yard** is brief and dramatic: in a matter of only several feet, the noise and crowds give way to grassy spaces and towering oaks. Its narrow, haphazard footpaths are constantly trafficked by preoccupied students and camera-clicking tour groups. The Yard is where Harvard myth and reality converge – the grandeur of Ivy League aura besieged by the visitor traffic of an amusement park.

The most common entrance is the one directly across from Harvard Square proper, which leads by

Massachusetts Hall (holding the office of the university president) to the **Old Yard,** a large, rectangular area enclosed by freshman dormitories that has been around since 1636, when it was created as a grazing field for university livestock. In front of stark, symmetrical, slate-gray University Hall is the Yard's trademark icon, the **John Harvard statue,** around which chipper student guides inform tour groups of the oft-told story of the statue's three lies (it misdates the college's founding; erroneously identifies John Harvard as the college's founder; and isn't really a likeness of John Harvard at all). While it's a popular spot for visitors to take pictures, male students at the college covet the statue as a site of public urination; it's a badge of honor around here – and as a result, there are about twenty surveillance cameras trained on the statue.

Along the northwest border of the Yard is stout **Hollis Hall**, the dormitory where Henry David Thoreau lived as an undergraduate. The architectural contrast between modest Hollis, which dates from 1762, and its grandiose southern neighbor, **Matthews Hall**, built around a hundred years later, mirrors Harvard's transition from a quiet training ground for ministers to a wealthy, cosmopolitan university. The **indentations** in Hollis' front steps also hold some historical interest: students used to warm their rooms by heating cannonballs; come time to leave their quarters for the summer, they would dispose of the cannonballs by dropping them from their windows rather than having to carry them down the stairs.

Relentlessly cheerful students lead free tours of the Yard weekdays at 10am and 2pm, from Holyoke Center, 1350 Massachusetts Ave.

To the east of the Old Yard lie the grander buildings of the **New Yard**, where a vast set of steps leads up to the

HARVARD YARD AND AROUND

enormous pillars of **Widener Library**. Named after Harvard grad and Titanic victim Harry Elkins Widener, whose mother paid for the project, it's the center of the largest private library collection in the US. Through the entrance and up one flight of stairs is the Widener Memorial Room, flanked by two melodramatic murals by John Singer Sargent. Some of the library's most valuable volumes are displayed here, including a first folio of Shakespeare and a Gutenberg Bible. At the opposite side of the New Yard is **Memorial Church**, whose narrow, white spire strikes a balancing note to the heavy pillared front of Widener; its towering steeple is a classic postcard image of Harvard Yard.

The immense structure just north of the Yard is Harvard's **Science Center**; the big lecture halls on the first floor are the locations of Harvard's most popular classes. Stop by most weekday mornings and you can sit in lectures by popular bigwig professors including Stephen Jay Gould and Milton Friedman. A popular myth has it that the Center was designed to look like a camera, since one of its main benefactors was Polaroid magnate Edwin Land, though any likeness is purely accidental.

North past the Science Center, and just behind the physical science labs, lies the main quad of the famed **Harvard Law School**, focusing on the stern gray pillars of **Langdell Hall**, the imposing edifice on its western border. Above Langdell's entrance is a Latin inscription encapsulating the Western ideal of the Rule of Law, tinctured with a unusual degree of religiosity: *"Non sub homine, sed sub deo et lege"* ("Not under man, but under God and law"). Inside is the newly renovated **Harvard Law Library**, where you can practically smell the stress in the air. On the far left and right sides are the Root Room and the Treasure Room, respectively, which occasionally display a rotating series of Harvard Law's more interesting possessions concerning the history of Anglo-American jurisprudence. The library is officially reserved for Harvard students, but you can apply for visitor privileges at the front desk.

East of the Science Center are the pointed arches and flying buttresses of **Memorial Hall**, built to commemorate the Harvard students who died during the Civil War. Its central vaulted **narthex** is sober and atmospheric; light filtering through the stained-glass windows illuminates inscriptions of the many soldiers' names.

It's hard to miss the conspicuously modern **Carpenter Center** as you walk past Memorial Hall and down Quincy Street, a slab of slate-gray granite amidst Harvard's everpresent brick motif. Completed in 1963 as a center for the study of visual art at Harvard, the Carpenter Center is the only building in America designed by the French architect Le Corbusier, and its jarring difference from its surroundings has drawn a great deal of criticism from staunch Harvard traditionalists, although it's a striking and reasonably functional space. Be sure to traverse its trademark feature, a **walkway** that leads through the center of the building, meant to reflect the path worn by students on the lot on which the center was constructed. The lower floors of the building frequently house student art exhibits, which are free and open to the public.

HARVARD UNIVERSITY MUSEUMS

Harvard's **museums** have benefited from years of scholarly attention and rich donors' ample gifts. Largely underappreciated and underattended by most visitors, not to mention the students themselves, the collections are easily some of the finest in New England.

William Hayes Fogg Art Museum

Map 7, E8. Mon–Sat 10am–5pm, Sun 1–5pm; $5, students $4.

Housed on two floors which surround a lovely mock six-teenth-century Italian courtyard, the collections of the **William Hayes Fogg Art Museum**, at 32 Quincy St, showcase the highlights of Harvard's substantial collection of Western art. Much of the first floor is devoted to Medieval and Renaissance material, mainly religious art with the usual complement of suffering Christs. This part of the collection is best for a series of capitals salvaged from the French cathedral of Moutiers-Saint-Jean, which combine a Romanesque predilection for Classical design with Medieval didactic narrative. The rest of the first floor is devoted to portraiture of the seventeenth and eighteenth centuries, featuring two Rubens and a Rembrandt, though it's more notable for a fine display of lesser-known Neapolitan Baroque works, particularly the grotesque *Martyrdom of Saint Sebastian* by Battistello and Francesco Fracazano's robust *Drunken Silenus*. The remainder is rather stale, though the work of local John Singleton Copley figures prominently, and Cavaletto's extraordinarily precise *View of the Piazza San Marco* is not to be missed.

....

A ticket to the Fogg is also good for entry to the Sackler and Busch-Reisinger museums

....

The second floor includes several spaces for rotating exhibits, while its permanent holdings are strongest in Impressionism and Modernism, especially the late nine-teenth century French contingent of Degas, Monet, Manet, Pissarro and Cezanne. You'll also see Picasso's *Mother and Child,* famously exemplary of his blue period, a sickly *Self-Portrait, dedicated to Paul Gauguin* by Van Gogh, and

Toulouse-Lautrec's queasy *Hangover*. But what distinguishes this upper floor is its focus on American counterparts to these largely European trends in art during the late nineteenth and early twentieth century. There is a range of fine John Singer Sargent portraits and a pair of Whistler's moody *Nocturnes,* though the standout is Sheeler's *Upper Deck,* a representation of technology that ingeniously manages to combine realism and abstraction.

Busch-Reisinger Museum

Map 7, E8. Mon–Sat 10am–5pm, Sun 1–5pm; $5, students $4.

Secreted away at the rear of the Fogg's second floor is the entrance to Werner Otto Hall, home of the rich – though somewhat harrowing – **Busch-Reisinger Museum**, concentrating exclusively on the German Expressionists and the work of the Bauhaus, and, despite its small size, one of the world's finest collections of its kind. The gallery starts off with fin-de-siecle art, including Klimt's *Rue de Rivoli* and *Pear Tree*, a pair of meditations on constructed and natural environments. The Bauhaus standouts are Moholy-Nagy's sculpture-machine *Light-Space Modulator* and Feininger's angular *Bird Cloud*. But the gallery's highlight is its Expressionist portraiture, which includes Kirchner's sardonic *Self-Portrait with a Cat* and Beckmann's nauseated *Self-Portrait in a Tuxedo*.

Arthur M. Sackler Museum

Map 7, E8. Mon–Sat 10am–5pm, Sun 1–5pm. $5, students $4.

Right out of the Fogg and dead ahead is the five-floor Arthur M. Sackler Building, 485 Broadway, the first, second and fourth floors of which comprise the **Sackler Museum**, dedicated to the art of Classical, Asian and

Islamic cultures. The museum's holdings far outstrip its available space, which is why the first floor is devoted to rotating exhibits. Islamic and Asian art are the themes of the second floor, featuring illustrations from Muslim texts and Chinese landscapes from the past several centuries. The fourth floor is best for its excellent array of sensuous Buddhist sculptures from ancient China, India and Southeast Asia. You'll also see a solid display of Classical work – standing out from the usual Greek vases and sculpture are intelligent studies on the coins of Alexander the Great and seals from ancient Babylonia.

Harvard Semitic Museum

Map 7, E7. Mon–Fri 10am–4pm, Sun 1–4pm; free.

North past the Sackler is Divinity Avenue, on which another series of museums begins, led by the **Harvard Semitic Museum**, at no. 6, whose informative and impeccably presented displays chronicle Harvard's century-old excavations in the near east. Pieces range from Egyptian tombs to Babylonian cuneiform, but what makes the collection distinctive is that it focuses nearly as much on the process and methodology of the digs as on their results. For some reason, the Semitic isn't officially part of the consortium known as the Harvard Museums of Cultural and Natural History, so you don't even have to pay admission to see its excellent collection.

Peabody Museum of Archeology and Ethnology

Map 7, E7. Mon–Sat 9am–5pm, Sun 1–5pm. $5, students $4.

What officially begins the Harvard Museums of Cultural and Natural History, and the most prominent in that group, is the **Peabody Museum of Archeology and Ethnology**, 11

Divinity Ave, which displays materials culled from Harvard's anthropological and archeological expeditions. The strength of the museum lies in its collection of pieces from Mesoamerica, ranging from digs in the pueblos of the southwestern United States to artifacts from Incan civilizations. The anthropological material centers mainly on indigenous cultures of America, and includes a special program about the Ju/wa bushmen of the Kalahari desert. The displays are extensive and informative, covering the history, art, traditions and lifestyles of native peoples from around the world, though the wax dummies in traditional garb and the miniature dioramas can't help but seem hokey and out of place.

One ticket covers entry to the Peabody, Comparative Zoology, Mineralogical and Geological and Botanical museums. All are free between 9am and noon on Saturdays.

Mineralogical and Geological Museum

Map 7, D7. Mon–Sat 9am–5pm, Sun 1–5pm. $5, students $4.

Harvard's **Mineralogical and Geological Museum**, another of the University's very specialized museums, is, basically, a bunch of rocks. If you don't know much about geology, this probably won't do too much for you. On the other hand, it's reputed to be one of the world's finest mineral collections, and most of the gems are aesthetically as well as academically interesting.

Botanical Museum

Map 7, D7. Mon–Sat 9am–5pm, Sun 1–5pm. $5, students $4.

Right next door, and similarly narrow in scope, is the **Botanical Museum**, at 26 Oxford St. You may think this collection is only of interest to botanists, and much of it may well be, but it's still worth a pass to take in the stunning *Ware Collection of Glass Models of Plants*. This project began in 1887 and terminated almost fifty years later in 1936, leaving the museum with an absolutely unique and visually awesome collection of flower models constructed to the last detail, entirely from glass. Only seeing the display can do it justice. Go there.

Museum of Comparative Zoology

Map 7, D7. Mon–Sat 9am–5pm, Sun 1–5pm. $5, students $4.

Housed in the same building as the Botanical Museum, but lacking a similar knockout centerpiece, the **Museum of Comparative Zoology** is really just the tip of the iceberg of the university's collection of zoological materials, most of which is inaccessible to visitors. Among the rote displays of stuffed dead animals, however, are some fascinating insects preserved in amber and impressive arrays of fossils and ants.

OLD CAMBRIDGE: UPPER BRATTLE STREET

Map 7, A5–D5.

After the outbreak of the American Revolution, Cambridge's bourgeois majority ran the Tories out of town, leaving their sumptuous houses to be used as the quarters of the Continental Army. What was then called Tory Row is modern-day **Brattle Street**, the main drag of the **Old Cambridge** district, a tree-lined neighborhood of stately mansions, behind expansive, impeccably kept lawns.

The **Brattle House**, at 42 Brattle St, just off Harvard Square, fails to reflect the unabashedly extravagant lifestyle of its former resident, William Brattle. It doesn't appear nearly as grand as it once did, dwarfed as it is by surrounding office buildings, nor is it open to the public – no great loss since it now only houses offices. Down the street and to the right, tiny **Farwell Street** features several modest Federal-style houses dating to the early nineteenth century and is the best (and only remaining) example of the square's residential character before it became a teeming center of activity.

The city has labeled every sight of conceivable interest with an explanatory blue oval plaque. Call the Cambridge Historical Commission ©547-4252 for the exhaustive list.

A sign on the corner of Brattle and Story streets commemorates the site of a tree which once stood near the **Dexter Pratt House,** home of the village blacksmith celebrated by Longfellow in a popular poem that began, "Under a spreading chestnut tree / The village smithy stands, / the smith a mighty man is he, / With large and sinewy hands; / And the muscles of his brawny arms / Are strong as iron bands." In 1876, the chestnut was cut down, despite Longfellow's vigorous opposition, because it was spreading into the path of passing traffic. The city of Cambridge fashioned a chair out of the felled tree, presented it to Longfellow as a birthday present, who then composed a mawkish poem about the whole affair ("From My Easy Chair"), and all was forgiven. These days the house has a more humdrum role, home to the *Blacksmith House* bakery, producers of some of the finest scones in greater Boston – which may be the most exciting thing about the place. Beyond the Pratt House, at the intersection of Mason and Brattle streets, the advent of a tree-lined neighborhood of elite mansions signals the edge of Old Cambridge proper.

OLD CAMBRIDGE: UPPER BRATTLE STREET

Longfellow House

Map 7, B5. Wed–Sat 10am–4.30pm, tours every hour; $2.
Harvard Ⓣ.

One house you can visit is the **Vassal-Craigie-Longfellow House**, 105 Brattle St, the best-known and most popular of the Brattle Street mansions, where the poet Henry Wadsworth Longfellow lived while serving as a professor at Harvard. It was erected for Royalist John Vassal in 1759, who promptly vacated it on the eve of the Revolutionary War. During the war, it was inhabited by George Washington and used as his headquarters during the siege of Boston, and it wasn't until 1843 that it became home to Longfellow, who moved in as a boarder; when he married the wealthy Fanny Appleton, her father purchased the house for them as a wedding gift. Longfellow lived here until his death in 1882, and the house is preserved in an attempt to portray it as it was during his residence. It's a solid, if somewhat strenuously presented, example of Brattle Street's opulence during the last century. The halls and walls are festooned with Longfellow's furniture and art collection: most surprising is the wealth of nineteenth-century pieces from the Far East, amassed by Longfellow's renegade son Charlie on his world travels. His other son, Ernie, stayed at home, trying – and failing – to make a name for himself as a landscape painter; a number of his unremarkable works also adorn the walls of the house, along with a copy of Gilbert Stuart's famous portrait of George Washington, done by his daughter, Jane Stuart.

Hooper-Lee-Nichols House

Map 7, A5. Tues & Thurs 2–5pm; $2. Harvard Ⓣ.

The second of the Brattle Street mansions open to the public, half a mile west of the Longfellow House and well worth the trip if you've got the stamina, is the **Hooper-Lee-Nichols House**, at no. 159, one of the two oldest residences in Cambridge and the best example of the character of life and style of housing design during Cambridge's Colonial period. The house is particularly unusual for its various architectural incarnations. It began as a stout, post-medieval farmhouse, and underwent various renovations until it became the Georgian mansion it is today. Knowledgeable tour guides open secret panels to reveal centuries-old wallpaper and original foundations; otherwise, you'll see rooms predictably restored with period writing tables, canopy beds and rag dolls.

> The Hooper-Lee-Nichols house is officially open Tuesdays and Thursdays 2-5pm, but that doesn't mean someone will be waiting out front for you. Knock vigorously on the front door.

Mt Auburn Cemetery

Map 7, A8–A9. Harvard Ⓣ to Watertown bus #71.

At the terminus of Brattle Street is the **Mt Auburn Cemetery**, whose 170 acres of grounds are more like a beautifully kept municipal park than a necropolis. You'll see just as many people here for a picnic or a stroll as you will those who have come to honor the deceased. The best way to get a sense of the cemetery's scope is to ascend the **tower** that lies smack in its center – from here, you can see not only the entire grounds but, on a clear day, all of downtown Boston. Of course, like most cemeteries in the Boston area, Mt Auburn also has its share of dead luminaries, most notably Winslow Homer and Isabella Stewart Gardner; ask the folks in the main office for a map of famous graves if you're interested. You could spend a day walking the grounds; bring a lunch or a book and allow at least a few hours.

CENTRAL SQUARE

Map 7, H5.

Central Square, as you might expect, is located roughly in the geographical center of Cambridge, and is appropriately the city's civic center as well, home to its most important government buildings. It's an interesting mix of cultural and industrial Cambridge, a working-class area with an ethnically diverse population and little of the hype that surrounds other parts of town. There's nothing as such to see, but it's a good place to shop and eat, and is home to some of the best nightlife in Cambridge. The Gothic quarters of **City Hall**, 795 Mass Ave (Mon–Fri 8.30am–5pm), house Cambridge's municipal bureaucracy and act as an occasional venue for town meetings or public events, but little else stands out here.

INMAN SQUARE

Map 7, G2.

Overshadowed by Cambridge's busier districts, **Inman Square** marks a quiet stretch directly north of Central Square, centered around the confluence of Cambridge, Beacon and Prospect streets. There's little of interest here either, just a pleasant, mostly residential neighborhood where much of Cambridge's working-class Portuguese-speaking population resides. What does make Inman worth a visit, along with its ethnic markets, is its broad range of excellent restaurants, where you can enjoy some of Cambridge's finest food without breaking the bank. If you're in the area, check out Inman's lone landmark, the charmingly inexpert **Cambridge Firemen's Mural**, at the corner of Cambridge and Antrim streets, a work of public art commissioned to honor local men in red.

EAST CAMBRIDGE AND KENDALL SQUARE

Map 7, L1–L3.

East Cambridge is split into two main areas of activity, though neither has especially much to recommend it unless you're into checking out the corporate headquarters of software companies that pepper them. In the northernmost region, there's the **CambridgeSide Galleria** (see "Shopping," p.267), a gargantuan shopping multiplex, where mall rats mingle in the neon-lit food court. There are some good shops of the slightly upscale ilk, such as *J. Crew* and *Banana Republic*, though the **New England Sports Museum**, which once called the Galleria home, has recently packed up and left.

Further inland, **Kendall Square** grew from the ashes of the post-industrial desolation of East Cambridge in the Sixties and Seventies to become a glittering testament to the economic revival that sparked Massachusetts in the Eighties. Technology and its profits built the square, and it shows. By day, Kendall bustles with wealthy eggheads lunching in chic eateries; at night, the business crowd goes home and the place becomes largely deserted. The exception to this is the **Kendall Square Cinema**, which draws large crowds to see some of the best art and second-run movies in the area (see "Film," p.247).

MASSACHUSETTS INSTITUTE OF TECHNOLOGY

Map 7, J7–L4.

Occupying 153.8 acres alongside the Charles, the **Massachusetts Institute of Technology** (MIT) provides an intellectual counterweight to the otherwise working-class character of East Cambridge. Originally established in Allston in 1865, MIT moved to this more auspicious campus across the river in 1916 and has since risen to international prominence as a major center for theoretical and practical research in the sciences. Both NASA and the Department of Defense pour funds into MIT in exchange for research and development assistance from the university's best minds.

The campus buildings and geography reflect the quirky, nerdy character of the institute, emphasizing function and peppering it with a peculiar notion of form. Everything is obsessively numbered and coded: you can go to E15 (the Weisner Building) for a lecture in 4.103 (advanced computer-assisted design), which, of course, gets you no closer towards a degree in 17 (political science). Behind the massive pillars that guard the entrance of the **Rogers Building**, at 77 Massachusetts Ave, you'll find a labyrinth of corridors through which students can traverse the entire east campus without ever going outside – known to Techies as the **Infinite Corridor**. Atop the Rogers Building is MIT's best-known architectural icon, a massive gilt hemisphere called the **Great Dome**. Just inside the entrance to Rogers, you'll find the **MIT Information Center** (Mon-Fri 9am-5pm), which dispenses free campus maps and advice.

MIT has drawn the attention of some of the major architects of the twentieth century, who have used the university's progressiveness as a testing ground for some of their more experimental works. Two of these are located in the courtyard across Massachusetts Avenue from the Rogers Building. The **Kresge Auditorium**, designed by Finnish architect Eero Saarinen, resembles a large tent, though its real claim to fame is that it puzzlingly rests on three, rather than four, corners. In the same courtyard is the **MIT Chapel**, also the work of Saarinen. Shaped like a stocky cylinder and topped with abstract sculpture crafted from paper-thin metals, it's undoubtedly the city's least traditional religious space. The I. M. Pei-designed **Weisner Building** is home to the **List Visual Art Center** (Tues–Sun noon–6pm; free), which displays student works, often heavily influenced by science and involving a great deal of computer design, and more technologically impressive than visually appealing.

Of perhaps more interest, down Massachusetts Ave at no. 265, is the **MIT Museum** (Tues–Fri 10am–5pm, Sat–Sun noon–5pm; $3, students and seniors $1.) The museum has two main permanent displays, the *Hologram Museum* and the *Hall of Hacks*, the latter of which provides a retrospective on the various pranks ("hacks") pulled by techies. Among other things, the madcap funsters have placed a fake cow and a real MIT police car atop the Great Dome, and have wreaked havoc at the annual Harvard-Yale football game by landing a massive weather balloon in the middle of the gridiron. Both shows alone warrant a visit, though there are excellent rotating exhibits as well.

PORTER SQUARE

Map 7, A1.

If Northwest Cambridge has a center, it's **Porter Square**, located a mile north of Harvard Square along Massachusetts Avenue. The walk from Harvard will take you past some of Cambridge's chicest eateries and boutiques, while Porter Square itself is hard to miss – look for the forty-foot red kinetic **sculpture** right outside the subway stop. Just before this gargantuan mobile is the **Porter Exchange**, a mall of mostly unimpressive shops, save for an obscure hallway lined with tiny **Japanese food outlets**. They're not really restaurants, just bars with several seats where the food is so authentic you'll have to point to the menu for your order, unless you speak the language.

STRAWBERRY HILL

In the lowest corner of Northwest Cambridge, just to the east of the Fresh Pond reservoir, slopes the gently grade of **Strawberry Hill**, whose main street, Huron Avenue, runs up and around it. This slice of upper-middle class suburbia is serene and arboreal, one with a charming array of apothecaries and specialty shops. The *Huron Spa*, for example, still functions as a soda fountain where you can get vanilla cokes and the like; and *Bryn Mawr Book Shop*, at 373 Huron Ave, has bookshelves that open onto the street for passers-by to investigate.

DAY-TRIPS

There's enough of interest in Boston itself to keep you going for several days at the very least. However, the city lies at the center of an extremely historic part of the United States and there's plenty to see and do within a short distance – not to mention further afield. Perhaps the best inland **day-trip** you can make within a 25-mile radius of Boston is to the Revolutionary battlegrounds of **Lexington** and **Concord**. Otherwise, the city's central position along the Massachusetts coast makes it an excellent base for visiting the many quaint and historic towns that line the **North Shore**. **Salem** is the first place of interest, though nearby **Marblehead** is pretty enough to merit a wander too; after that, you can continue on to the somewhat more rustic **Gloucester** and **Rockport**, worthwhile if you have the time and are interested in the faded glories of the New England fishing trade. The quickest way up here is by taking Route 1, although Route 1A, along the coast, is more scenic. Buses run up this way too, operated both by the MBTA and by independent tour companies (see p.9). On the **South Shore**, **Plymouth** is the main tourist draw, and in summer a ferry from Boston puts **Provincetown**, the exuberant old fishing village at the tip of Cape Cod, within easy reach.

LEXINGTON AND CONCORD

The sedate towns of **Lexington** and **Concord**, almost always mentioned in the same breath, trade in on their notoriety as the locations of the first armed confrontation with the British. Lexington is today mostly suburban, while Concord, five miles east, is even sleepier, though it has a bit more character. Most of Concord and Lexington's historical quarters have been incorporated into the **Minute Man National Park**, which takes in the Lexington Battle Green, the North Bridge area in Concord, and much of Battle Road, the route the British followed on their retreat from the latter back to Boston. The Battles of Lexington and Concord are evoked in a piecemeal but relentless fashion throughout, with scale models, remnant musketry and the odd preserved bullet hole. The Park also includes the Old Manse and The Wayside, two rambling old Concord houses with bookish pasts, though some other "literary" sites, such as Walden Pond in Concord, are just beyond its boundaries.

Lexington

The main thing to see in **Lexington** itself is the grassy **Battle Green**, one of the few public places where the American flag flies 24 hours a day. The land serves as Lexington's town common and is fronted by Henry Kitson's famous statue of *The Minute Man*. This musket-bearing figure of Captain John Parker was not dedicated until 1900, but it stands on boulders dislodged from the stone walls behind which the colonial militia fired at the British opponents on April 19, 1775. The **visitors center** (daily: Jan–April 10am–3pm; May–Oct 9am–5pm; Nov–Dec 10am–4pm) on the eastern periphery of the Green has a diorama that shows the detail of the battle, while in the **Buckman Tavern**, facing the Green, a British bullet hole has been preserved in an inner door near the restored first-floor tap room. A couple of blocks north, at 36 Hancock St, a plaque affixed to the **Hancock-Clarke House** solemnly reminds that this is where "Samuel Adams and John Hancock were sleeping when aroused by Paul Revere." Otherwise, exhibits on the free first floor include the drum on which William Diamond beat the signal for the Minute Men to converge and the pistols that British Major John Pitcairn lost on the retreat from Concord. Less interesting is the small wooden **Munroe Tavern** a bit removed from the town center at 1332 Massachusetts Ave: it served as a field hospital for British soldiers, but for a mere one and one-half hours.

The Buckman Tavern, Hancock-Clarke House and Munroe Tavern are all open Mon–Sat 9am–5pm, Sun 1–5pm; each costs $4.

Concord

One of the few sizeable inland towns of New England at the time of the Revolution, **Concord** retains a pleasant country town atmosphere. Start your wanderings at the **Colonial Inn**, near the corner of Main and Monument streets, a rambling old hostelry with a traditional dining room and tavern that served as a makeshift Revolutionary hospital during the war. Outside of its history, it's also a good place to stop for an ale or a hearty lunch. From the top of **Hill Burying Ground**, just west of the Colonial Inn, you can survey Concord, as did Pitcairn when the Americans amassed on the far side of North Bridge. A few blocks behind it on Route 62 is **Sleepy Hollow**

LEXINGTON AND CONCORD

Cemetery, where Concord literati Emerson, Hawthorne, Thoreau and Lousia May Alcott are interred atop the grave-yard's "Author's Ridge"; signs point the way.

The most hyped spot in Concord is around **North Bridge**, site of the first effective armed resistance to British rule in America. If you take the traditional approach from Monument Street, you'll be following the route the British took; an inscription on the mass grave of some British regulars just before the bridge reads, "They came 3000 miles and died to keep the past upon its throne." The bridge itself, however, looks a bit too well-preserved to provoke much sentiment – no surprise as it's actually a 1954 replica of what was already a replica.

A stone's throw from North Bridge is the gray clap-board **Old Manse**, 269 Monument St (April–Oct Mon–Sat 10am–4.30pm, Sun 1–4.30pm; $5), built for the Ralph Waldo Emerson's grandfather, the Reverend William Emerson, in 1770. The younger Emerson lived here on and off, though this was where, in 1834, he penned *Nature*, the book that signaled the beginning of the Transcendentalist movement. Of the numerous rooms in the house, all with period furnishings intact, the most interesting is the small upstairs study, where Nathaniel Hawthorne, a resident of the house in the early 1840s, wrote *Mosses from an Old Manse*, a rather obscure book that endowed the place with its name. Hawthorne passed three happy years here shortly after getting married to his wife Sophia, who with her wed-ding ring etched the words "Man's accidents are God's purposes" into a window pane in the study. Other con-templative etchings can be found on windows down-stairs. On the first floor, look for the framed swath of original English-made wallpaper, with the British "paper" stamp tax mark on the back.

> **Right in the middle of town is the *Cheese Shop*, at 29 Walden St, a great place to stop for sandwiches.**

Also worth a visit is **The Wayside**, east of the town center at 455 Lexington Rd (April–Oct Tues–Sun 10am–5.30pm; $2), a three-hundred-year-old yellow wooden house that's also a literary landmark, home to both the Alcotts and Hawthornes, though at different times. Louisa May Alcott's girlhood experiences here formed the basis for *Little Women*. Among the antique furnishings, the most unusual is the slanted writing desk at which Hawthorne toiled standing up, in the fourth floor "tower" he added on for that purpose. If you don't feel like taking a guided tour, you can stop in at the small but very well-presented museum at the admissions area for a brief overview. Alcott actually penned her most famous novel, *Little Women*, next door at the **Orchard House**, where the family lived from 1858 to 1867 and her father, Bronson, founded his School of Philosophy.

Just down the road at no. 200, the excellent **Concord Museum** (Mon–Sat 10am–5pm, Sun 1–5pm; $6), on the site of Emerson's apple orchard, has more than a dozen galleries that display period furnishings from eighteenth- and nineteenth-century Concord, including a sizeable collection of Thoreau's personal effects, such as the bed from his Walden Pond hut. More interesting, however, are the Revolutionary War artifacts that are displayed throughout, such as one of the signal lanterns hung from the Old North Church in Boston.

WALDEN POND

Though the tranquility which Thoreau sought and savored at **Walden Pond**, just south of Concord proper off Route

126 ($2), is for the most part gone – thanks mainly to the masses of tourists who pour in to retrace his footsteps – the place itself has remained much the same since the author's famed exercise in independence from 1845 to 1847. Thoreau described his experiment in solitude and self-sufficiency in his 1854 book *Walden*. "I did not feel crowded or confined in the least," he wrote of his life in the simple log cabin. A reconstructed single-room hut, replete with a journal open on its rustic desk, is situated near the parking lot (you'll have to be content with peering through the windows), while the site of the original cabin, closer to the shores of the pond, is marked out with stones. The pond itself is quite popular with long-distance swimmers. Spared from development by a band of celebrities led by ex-Eagle Don Henley, the water looks best at dawn, when the pond still "throws off its nightly clothing of mist"; late-risers should plan an off-season visit to maximize their transcendental experience of it all.

SALEM

Salem, an unpretentious city just sixteen miles north of Boston, is the most intriguing destination on the shore, standing out from the other rustic towns that line the coast if only because of its peculiar history. This is where Puritan self-righteousness reached its apogee in the horrific **witch trials** of 1692, since when it has been trying to shake the stigma. Less known were the many years it spent as a flourishing seaport; the remnants from those years only add to the unsettling aura: abandoned wharves, rows of stately sea captains' homes and the astounding display of their riches at the Peabody Essex Museum – perhaps the finest such collection in the world. Ironically, Salem's darkest days have proven to be its salvation, because were it not for the spruced-up touristy core, all of the once-proud port might look as industrial and unsightly as its immediate environs.

Salem has its own red-lined history trail, the **Salem Heritage Trail**, that links the Peabody Essex Museum, Salem Witch Museum, and The House of the Seven Gables. Also of interest are the Witch Dungeon Museum and sea captains' homes around it, the Witch Trials Memorial and Old Burying Point Cemetery, and the Salem Maritime National Historic Site.

There's no shortage of witches in Salem, as a sizeable and highly visible contingent of latter-day sorceresses known as Wiccans have staked Salem out as their turf. Despite their New Age spirituality, they are more than willing to read your palm or otherwise prognosticate your future for a modest fee. Keep in mind they're as much a part of the tourist industry as everything else in Salem.

The Salem Witch sights

The hokey **Salem Witch Museum**, 19 $^1/_2$ Washington Square (daily: July–Aug 10am–7pm; Sept–June 10am–5pm; $4.50), provides some entertaining orientation on the witch hysteria. It's really just a sound-and-light show that makes ample use of wax figures to depict the events of 1692, housed in a suitably spooky Romanesque one-time church. Right in front of it is the imposing statue of a caped **Roger Conant**, founder of Salem's first Puritan settlement. More evocative is the **Witch Dungeon Museum**, at 16 Lynde St, (daily 10am–5pm, $4.50), on the west side of town near the McIntire architectural district (see below), on the site of the prison where the accused witches were locked up. Inside you're again treated to reenactments of key events, this time by real people: upstairs, it's the farcical trial of Sarah Good, a pipe-smoking beggar woman falsely accused of witchcraft, based on actual transcripts; the actors then escort you to a recreated "dungeon" where you see that some of the prison cells were no bigger than a telephone booth. Dank and supremely eerie, it's not hard to believe claims that the place is haunted.

The **Witch Memorial**, at Charter and Liberty streets, is a simple series of stone blocks etched with the names of the hanged, wedged into a corner of the **Old Burying Point Cemetery**, where one of the witch judges, John Hathorne, is buried.

The Peabody Essex Museum

Mon–Thurs & Sat 10am–5pm, Fri 10am–8pm, Sun noon–5pm; $7.50.

Right up Liberty Street from the Memorial is the **Peabody Essex Museum**, at East India Square on the Essex Street Mall, whose more than thirty galleries hold a mishmash of art and artifacts from around the world. Founded by ship captains in 1799 to exhibit their exotic items obtained while overseas, the museum also boasts the biggest collection of nautical paintings in the world. Other galleries hold Chinese and Japanese export art, Asian, Oceanic and African ethnological artifacts, American decorative arts and, in a preserved house that the museum administers, court documents from the Salem Witch Trials.

The first floor is home to the core museum displays, with creatively curated whaling exhibits that feature not only the requisite scrimshaw but Ambrose Garneray's famous 1835 painting, *Attacking the Right Whale*, and the gaping lower jaw of a sperm whale. Upstairs highlights include a cavernous central gallery with the fanciful figureheads from now demolished Salem ships hung from the walls and the reconstructed salon from America's first yacht, *Cleopatra's*

Barge, which took to the seas in 1816. There's also a decent café in case you're hungry.

Salem Maritime National Historic Site

Daily 9am–5pm; ranger-led tours $3.

Little of Salem's original waterfront remains, although the 2000-ft long **Derby Wharf** is still standing, fronted by the imposing Federalist-style **Custom** at its head. They help comprise the **Salem Maritime National Historic Site**, whose headquarters are at 193 Derby St. Nathaniel Hawthorne had a three-year stint working at the Custom House that he later described as "slavery." You can take tours of the office-like interior at irregular hours, but the warehouse in the rear, with displays of tea chests and such, is usually open for casual inspection. Park rangers also give free tours of the adjacent **Derby House** (daily 9am–5pm), whose millionaire owner had it built here, overlooking the harbor, to monitor the shipping empire over which he presided. Next door, the **West India Goods Store** sells the kinds of spices and nautical knickknacks common to Salem's nineteenth century shops.

House of the Seven Gables

Tours daily July–Aug 10am–7pm, Sept–Oct 9am–6pm; $7.

The most famous sight in this area is undoubtedly the **House of the Seven Gables**, at 54 Turner St, a rambling old mansion by the sea that served as inspiration for Hawthorne's eponymous novel. Still the "rusty wooden house with seven acutely peaked gables" that Hawthorne described, the 1688 three-story house does have some other notable features, such as the bricked-off "Secret Stairway" that leads to a small room. The house was inhabited by

SALEM MARITIME NATIONAL HISTORIC SITE

Susan Ingersoll, a cousin of Hawthorne whom he often visited. The author's birthplace, a small undistinguished house built before 1750, has been moved to the grounds; the lovely gardens feature a wishing well.

Eating and drinking

Café Bagel Company, 122 Washington St ✆978/740-3180. This is a fairly upbeat spot for a bagel and a coffee.
Nathaniel's, 18 Washington Square ✆978/744-4080. Upscale comfort food, like roasted scrod and grilled pork tenderloin.
Salem Beer Works, 278 Derby St ✆978/745-2337. You can try microbrews or nouveau pub food at this glossy brewery.

MARBLEHEAD

Marblehead is a town of winding streets lined with small but well-preserved private sea captain's homes that lead down to its harbor, which makes for a decent respite if (or when) you tire of Salem's witch-related material. Once the domain of Revolutionary War heroes – it was Marblehead boatmen who rowed Washington's assault force across the Delaware River to attack Trenton – it's now mainly home to Boston commuters. One thing that hasn't changed over the years is the town's dramatic setting on series of rocky ledges overlooking the wide natural harbor, which makes it one of the East Coast's biggest yachting centers. The annual Race Week takes place the last week of July.

Settled in 1629, Marblehead has escaped the onslaughts of commercialism thanks to its occupants' affluence and, oddly, a severe shortage of parking. The latter shouldn't deter you from visiting, however, as this is one of the most picturesque ports in New England. You can get a good look at it from **Fort Sewall**, jutting into the harbor at the end of Front Street, the remnants of fortifications the British built in 1742 to protect the harbor from French cruisers (and that later protected the *USS Constitution* in the War of 1812). Closer to the center of town is **Old Burial Hill**, which holds the graves of more than six hundred Revolutionary War soldiers and has similarly sweeping views. **Abbot Hall**, on Washington Street (hours vary greatly, approximately 8am–5pm), an attractive 1876 town hall which can be seen from far out at sea, houses Archibald Willard's famous patriotic painting *The Spirit of '76*.

If you're looking for a **snack**, try *Flynnie's at the Beach*, on Devereaux Beach (summers only), for inexpensive fish and chips. *The Landing*, 81 Front St, serves fresh seafood in a room overlooking the harbor.

GLOUCESTER AND ROCKPORT

Low-key **Cape Ann**, forty miles north of Boston up Route 1 to Route 127, draws visitors for its salty air and seafood restaurants, the latter mostly found in the towns of **Gloucester**, a gritty place high on history but lacking in contemporary goings-on, and **Rockport**, more scenically situated, with decent shops and a lively, if touristy, atmosphere.

Gloucester

Founded in 1623, **Gloucester** is the oldest fishing port in Massachusetts, though years of overfishing the once cod-rich waters have robbed the town of any aura of affluence it may have had in the past. You'd do well to avoid the town's so-called **Rocky Neck Art Colony**, located on a spit of land that juts into the harbor. Though T.S. Eliot was once known to vacation up this way, it's not much of an artists' colony anymore, even if a number of local artists do still live here; most of the galleries are fairly undistinguished, some even a bit tacky. Gloucester's only really compelling attraction is a short drive south along the rocky coast of Route 127: the imposing **Hammond Castle Museum**, at 80 Hesperus Ave (June–Sept daily 10am–5pm, Nov–May weekends 10am–4pm; $6), whose builder, the eccentric financier and amateur inventor John Hays Hammond, Jr, wanted to bring medieval European relics back to the US. The austere fortress, which overlooks the ocean and site of the spot that inspired Longfellow's poem *The Wreck of the Hesperus*, brims with them, from armor and tapestries to the elaborately carved wooden façade of a fifteenth-century French bakery. One of the more interesting artifacts is the partially crushed skull of one of Columbus' shipmates. There's also a murky 30,000-gallon pool which at the switch of a lever can change from fresh to sea water.

Rockport

Rockport, about five miles north of Gloucester, is a coastal hamlet that's more self-consciously quaint, though only oppressively so on summer weekends. Its main drag is a thin peninsula called **Bearskin Neck**, lined with old salt-box fishermen's cottages transformed into art galleries and restaurants. The neck rises as it reaches the sea, and there's a nice view of the rocky harbor from the end of it. Otherwise, aside from some decent antique shopping and strolling around **Dock Square**, at the city's center, there isn't much doing here. Inside the aptly named **Paper House**, a few miles north of here in the small residential neighborhood of Pigeon Cove, everything is made of paper, from chairs and a piano (keys excepted) to a desk made from copies of the *Christian Science Monitor*. It's the end result of a twenty-year project undertaken in 1922 by a local mechanical engineer who "always resented the daily waste of newspaper." He hasn't really helped the cause.

PLYMOUTH

Though the **South Shore** makes a clean sweep of the coast from suburban Quincy to the former whaling port of New Bedford, the only place really of interest is tiny **Plymouth**, America's so-called "hometown," that's forty miles south of Boston. It's mostly given over to commemorating, in various degrees of taste and tack, the landing of the 102 Pilgrims here in December 1620.

See p.9 for information on buses
from Boston to Plymouth.

The proceedings start off with a solemn pseudo-Greek temple by the sea that encloses the otherwise nondescript **Plymouth Rock**, where the Pilgrims are said to have touched land; as is typical with most sites of this ilk, it is of symbolic importance only – they had already spent several weeks on Cape Cod. On the hill behind the rock, **The Plymouth National Wax Museum**, at 16 Carver St (daily: March–May & Nov 9am–5pm; June, Sept & Oct 9am–7pm; July–Aug 9am–9pm; $5), charges admission to its inadvertently kitschy sound-and-light tableaux of the early days of settlement; the various elements could use more than a sprucing up. Down the street is the **Pilgrim Hall Museum**, at 75 Court St (Feb–Dec daily

9.30am–4.30pm; $5.50), where you enter a room filled with furniture that may or may not have come over on the *Mayflower* and numerous pairs of shoes, which the Pilgrims may or may not have worn.

You're better off spending your time at the replica of the Mayflower, called the **Mayflower II** (daily: April–June & Sept–Nov 9am–5pm; July–Aug 9am–7pm; $6), on the State Pier in Plymouth Harbor, which makes no claim to authenticity but tries to meticulously reproduce the experience of the Pilgrims' – staffed by costumed "interpreters," each of whom acts out the part of a specific Pilgrim, Indian or seaman. The charade visitors are expected to perform – pretending to have stepped back into the seventeenth century – can be a little tiresome, but ultimately the sheer depth of detail makes it quite fascinating.

....

**A combined ticket to the Mayflower and
Plimouth Plantation costs $18.50.**

....

Similar in approach and authenticity is the **Plimouth Plantation**, three miles south of town off Route 3, April–June & Sept–Nov daily 9am–5pm, July–Aug daily 9am–7pm). Everything you see in the plantation, such as the Pilgrim Village of 1627 and the Wampanoag Indian Settlement, has been created using traditional techniques; even the farm animals were "backbred" to resemble their seventeeth century counterparts. Again, actors dressed in period garb try to bring you back in time; depending on your resistance, it can be quite enjoyable.

A reasonably interesting way to pass time for free is at **Cranberry World**, at 225 Water St, just past the visitors center on the north side of town (May–Nov daily

9.30am–5pm), a slick little museum sponsored by juice giant Ocean Spray. Exhibits show how the tart crimson berries are harvested from local bogs and then processed; the frequent tours end with free samples of juice.

For **food**, the *John Carver Inn*, 25 Summer St (℃1-800/274-1620), has a tavern and a restaurant, the *Hearth 'n Kettle*, that are excellent settings for a very American meal or a drink; the *Lobster Hut*, on the waterfront (℃508/746-2270), has good, reasonably priced seafood.

PROVINCETOWN

The brash fishing burgh of **PROVINCETOWN** ("P-Town"), at the very tip of Cape Cod, is a popular summer destination for bohemians, artists and general fun-seekers, lured by the excellent beaches, art galleries and welcoming atmosphere. It may be best known for its number of **gay** visitors – and the year-round population of five thousand boasts a high percentage of gays and lesbians – but P-town should not be missed by anyone, especially as its just a few hours' ferry ride from Boston (see box below).

Provincetown by Ferry

During the busy summer season, it's possible to take a **Bay State Cruise** ferry from Boston to Provincetown. Ferries depart from **Commonwealth Pier** at the World Trade Center at 9am and arrive at Provincetown's **Macmillan Wharf** at noon, heading back at 3.30pm for a 6.30pm arrival in Boston. From Memorial Day through June 14, the ferries run on weekends only; from June 20 to Sept 13, they run daily; and weekends thereafter until the end of September. The fare is $30 round-trip, $18 one way. Call ℃457-1428 if you need more information.

PROVINCETOWN

The town and around

Provincetown's town center is essentially composed of two three-mile long streets connected by nearly forty tiny lanes of no more than two short blocks each. The first of these two main strips, the aptly named **Commercial Street**, is where the action is, loaded with restaurants, cafés, art galleries and trendy shops. Jutting right into the middle of Provincetown Harbor, just off Commercial Street, **Macmillan Wharf** is busy with whale watching boats, yachts and colorful old Portuguese fishing vessels. It also houses the new **Whydah Museum**, at no. 16 (July–Oct daily 9am–7pm; $5), which displays some of the bounty from a famous pirate shipwreck off the coast of Wellfleet in 1717. Two blocks north of the wharf, on Town Hill, is the 252-foot granite tower of the **Pilgrim Monument**, named for the Puritans who actually landed near here first before moving on to Plymouth. From the observation deck of the Florentine-style bell tower, accessible by stairs and ramps, the whole Cape (and sometimes Boston) can be seen (July–Aug daily 9am–7pm, May–June & Sept–Oct daily 9am–5pm; $5). At the bottom of the hill on **Bradford Street**, the second of the two strips, is a bas-relief monument to the Pilgrims' **Mayflower Compact**.

In the quiet **West End** of P-Town, many of the weathered clapboard houses are decorated with colored blinds, white picket fences, and wildflowers spilling out of every possible crevice. A modest bronze **plaque** on a boulder at the western end of Commercial Street commemorates the Pilgrim's actual landing place. West of town, **Herring Cove Beach** is easily reached by bike and is justly famous for its sunsets. At the Cape's northern tip, off Route 6, **Race Point Beach** has a wide strip of white sand and is backed by tall dunes – the archetypal Cape Cod beach. It abuts the ethereal **Province Lands**, where vast sweeping moors and bushy dunes are buffeted by a deadly sea, site of some 3000 known shipwrecks.

One of the best things to do around Provincetown is to take an organized, but unusual, tour: choose to either ramble about the dunes in a four-wheel drive vehicle with **Art's Dune Tours**, at Commercial and Standish (April–Oct 10am–dusk; $9; ℂ508/487-1950); or fly over them in a replica 1938 biplane ($60 for one person, $80 for two; ℂ1-888/BIPLANE or 508/428-8732). Twenty-minute flights take off from the Cape Cod Airport, near the intersection of Race Lane and Route 149.

Eating and drinking

Crown and Anchor, 274 Commercial St ℂ508/487-1430. Noisy pub with nightly drag cabaret.

Fat Jack's Café, 335 Commercial St ℂ508/487-4822. Low-priced, no-nonsense breakfasts; and lunch and dinner specials.

Lobster Pot, 321 Commercial St ℂ508/487-0842. Let the neon sign lead you to fresh and affordable crustaceans.

Portuguese Bakery, 299 Commercial St ℂ508/487-1803. An excellent stop for baked goods, particularly the fried *rabanada*, similar to french toast.

PROVINCETOWN: EATING AND DRINKING

LISTINGS

ACCOMMODATION

F or such a popular travel destination, Boston has a surprisingly limited range of well-priced **accommodation**. Though there are still bargains to be found, prices at many formerly moderate **hotels** have inched into the expense-account range. Your best bet is to come off-season, around November through April, when many hotels not only have more vacancies but offer special discounts too. At any other time of year, be sure to make reservations well in advance. September (start of the school year) and June (graduation) are particularly busy months, due to the large student population here.

Increasingly popular are **bed-and-breakfasts**, of which there are a surprising number tucked into renovated brownstones in Beacon Hill, Back Bay and the South End. Short-term **furnished apartments**, spread throughout the city, are another option; most have two-week minimums. There are also a handful of decent **hostels** if you're looking for real budget accommodation.

HOTELS

If Boston's **hotels** are not suited to every traveler's budget, they do cater to most tastes, and range from the usual

Accommodation Prices

Accommodation prices vary throughout the year, with the highest rates from June to September, and around Christmas and other holidays. Our listings for **hotels** and **B&Bs** feature a code (eg 3) for the least expensive double room available for most of the year:

① under $65		⑤ $175–225	
② $65–100		⑥ $225–275	
③ $100–135		⑦ $275–325	
④ $135–175		⑧ $325+	

The prices do not include **tax**, which is 9.7 percent; there are rumours that it may soon be increased to 12 percent. Bed and breakfasts are exempt from tax.

assortment of **chains** to some excellent independently-run hotels, the best of which, not to mention the highest concentration, are in **Back Bay**. Most of the business hotels are located in or around the **Financial District**, and are not bad if you don't mind being away from the nightlife.

DOWNTOWN

Boston Harbor Hotel

Map 3, L4. 70 Rowes Wharf ⓒ439-7000 or 1-800/752-7077, fax 345-6799. Aquarium ⓣ.

This hotel provides opulent accommodation in an atmosphere of studied corporate elegance. There's a health club, pool, kowtowing concierge staff, and rooms with harbor and city views, the former substantially more pricey. ⑧

Boston Marriott Long Wharf

Map 3, L2. 296 State St ⓒ227-0800, fax 227-2867. Aquarium ⓣ

All the rooms here boast harbor views, but this *Marriott* stands out more for its awesome vaulted lobby. ⑥

Harborside Inn

Map 3, J2. 185 State St ⓒ723-7500, fax 670-2010. State Ⓣ.
This small new hotel with a Victorian accent is housed in a renovated mercantile warehouse across from Quincy Market, and it has fairly reasonably priced rooms. ③–④

Le Meridien

Map 3, I5. 250 Franklin St ⓒ451-1900 or 1-800/543-4300, fax 423-2844. State Ⓣ.
Located in the heart of the Financial District, this stern granite building is, appropriately enough, the former Federal Reserve Bank of Boston. The rooms are modern, and the overall atmosphere is a bit stiff. ⑥

Milner Hotel

Map 3, E9. 78 Charles St South ⓒ426-6220, 1-800/453-1731. Boylston Ⓣ.
Recently renovated, this uninspiring but affordable hotel is convenient to the Theater District, Bay Village and the Public Garden. All room rates include a continental breakfast, served in a European-style nook in the lobby. ②

Omni Parker House

Map 3, G4. 60 School St ⓒ227-8600, 1-800/843-6664, fax 742-5729. Park Ⓣ.
No one can compete with the *Parker House* in the history department: it's the oldest continuously operating hotel in the US. Though the present building only dates from 1927, the lobby has been restored to its nineteenth-century splendor of

HOTELS: DOWNTOWN

dark oak and carved gilt moldings. The rooms are small, however, and a bit dowdy. ④–⑤

Regal Bostonian Hotel

Map 3, H2. Faneuil Hall Marketplace ✆1-800/343-0922, fax 523-2454. State Ⓣ.

Splendid quarters in the heart of downtown. The rooms and lobby are festooned with portraits of famous Colonials. ⑥

Swissôtel

Map 3, G6. 1 Avenue de Lafayette ✆451-2600 or 1-800/621-9200, fax 451-2198. Downtown Crossing Ⓣ.

Boston's *Swissôtel* is a plush if peculiarly located option – on the fringes of ragged Downtown Crossing, not the best place to be at night. There's no pedestrian access to the sleek 16-story tower; entry is via the parking garage. ⑤

Tremont House

Map 3, E9. 275 Tremont St ✆426-1400 or 1-800/331-9998, fax 338-7881. Boylston Ⓣ.

The opulent lobby of this 1925 hotel, the former national headquarters of the Elks Lodge, somewhat compensates for its rather small rooms, but if you want to be in the thick of the Theater District you can't do better. ⑤

BEACON HILL AND THE WEST END

Holiday Inn Select – Government Center

Map 3, C2. 5 Blossom St ✆742-7630 or 1-800/HOLIDAY, fax 742-4192. Bowdoin Ⓣ.

Somewhat misleadingly named, as it's located in the West End, and is more convenient to Beacon Hill than Government

Center, this has modern accoutrements, plus a weight room and pool. ④

The John Jeffries House

Map 3, A3. 14 Embankment Rd ⓒ367-1866, fax 742-0313. Charles Ⓣ.

Mid-scale hotel at the foot of Beacon Hill. There's a cozy lounge for hotel guests, and all rooms include kitchenettes. Though wedged in between a busy highway and the T, multi-paned windows keep out most of the sound out. ②

The Shawmut Inn

280 Friend St ⓒ720-5544 or 1-800/350-7784. North Station Ⓣ.

Located in the old West End near the FleetCenter, this place has 66 rooms, all of which come equipped with kitchenettes. ③

BACK BAY AND KENMORE SQUARE

Back Bay Hilton

Map 6, G5. 40 Dalton St ⓒ236-1100 or 1-800/874-0663, fax 867-6139. Hynes Ⓣ.

Though this chain hotel is fairly charmless, it does have good weekend packages and a guaranteed good American-style breakfast at the hotel's informal restaurant, *Boodle's*. It's actually a bit out of Back Bay, closer to the bohemian area of the Berklee College of Music than the shops of Newbury Street – though this is a plus in some folks' eyes. ⑤

Boston Park Plaza Hotel & Towers

Map 3, C9. 64 Arlington St ⓒ426-2000 or 1-800/225-2008, fax 426-5545. Arlington Ⓣ.

The Park Plaza is practically its own neighborhood, housing the original *Legal Seafoods* restaurant alongside three other eateries, plus offices for American, United and Delta airlines. Its old-school elegance and hospitality, and its central location, however, make it stand out; the high-ceilinged rooms, too, are quite comfortable. ⑤

Boston Sheraton Hotel & Towers

Map 6, G5. 39 Dalton St ©236-2000 or 1-800/325-3535, fax 236-1702. Hynes Ⓣ.
Accommodations here are a bit nicer than the nondescript exterior might imply, and they mostly play host to convention-goers, who can walk to the nearby Hynes Convention Center and Prudential Center mall without going outside. ④–⑤

The Buckminster Hotel

Map 6, C2. 645 Beacon St ©236-7050 or 1-800/727-2825, fax 523-2454. Kenmore Ⓣ.
Though recently renovated, the *Buckminster* still has the feel of an old Boston hotel; its Kenmore Square location also puts it within easy walking distance of Fenway Park and Boston University. ③

The Colonnade

Map 6, H5. 120 Huntington Ave ©424-7000 or 1-800/962-3030, fax 424-1717. Prudential Ⓣ.
With its beige poured-concrete shell, the *Colonnade* is barely distinguishable from the buildings of the Church of Christ, Scientist, World Headquarters directly across the street. Still, there are spacious rooms and, in summer, a rooftop pool, the only one in Boston. ⑤

Copley Square Hotel

Map 6, I5. 47 Huntington Ave ℂ536-9000 or 1-800/225-7062, fax 267-3547. Copley Ⓣ.

Situated on the eastern fringe of Copley Square, this is one of the best bargains in the city; it's also home to the *Café Budapest* (see p.201), one of Boston's most romantic restaurants. Low-key, with a European crowd, and room prices as low as $165 a night. ④-⑤

Eliot Hotel

Map 6, F3. 370 Commonwealth Ave ℂ267-1607 or 1-800/442-5468, fax 536-9114. Hynes Ⓣ.

West Back Bay's answer to the *Ritz*, this calm, plush nine-floor suite hotel has rooms with kitchenettes and luxurious Italian marble baths; they also serve a nice breakfast downstairs. ⑥

Fairmont Copley Plaza

Map 6, K4. 138 St. James Ave ℂ267-5300, 1-800/795-3906, fax 375-9648. Copley Ⓣ.

Built in 1912 and it shows, from the somewhat severe façade facing Copley Square to the old-fashioned rooms. The hotel has long boasted Boston's most elegant lobby, with its glittering chandeliers, mirrored walls and trompe-l'œil sky. Even if you don't stay here, have a martini in the fabulous *Oak Bar* (p.221), with its high coffered ceilings and mahogany chairs. ⑧

Four Seasons

Map 6, D8. 200 Boylston St ℂ338-4400 or 1-800/332-3442, fax 426-7199. Arlington Ⓣ.

The tops in city accommodation, with 288 rooms that offer quiet, contemporary comfort. The penthouse level health spa has an indoor pool that seems to float over the Public Garden,

HOTELS: BACK BAY AND KENMORE SQUARE

and the superlative *Aujourd'hui* restaurant is housed here, too.
⑧

The Lenox

Map 6, I4. 710 Boylston St ℂ536-5300 or 1-800/225-7676, fax
266-7905. Copley Ⓣ.
Billed as Boston's version of the *Waldorf-Astoria* when its doors
first opened in 1900, the *Lenox* is a far cry from that now,
though it's still one of the most comfortably upscale and
affordable hotels in the city. Many of the rooms have working
fireplaces. ⑥

Marriott Hotel at Copley Place

Map 6, J5. Copley Place ℂ236-5800 or 1-800/228-9290, fax
236-5885. Copley Ⓣ.
There's not a whole lot of character here, but it's modern,
clean and well-located, with an indoor pool. Ask about lower
weekend rates that include full breakfast. ④–⑥

Ritz-Carlton

Map 6, L3. 15 Arlington St ℂ536-5700 or 1-800/241-3333, fax
536-1335. Arlington Ⓣ.
This is the *Ritz-Carlton* flag ship, and even if the rooms can
seem a bit cramped, the hotel retains a certain air of
refinement. The one thing no one can complain about is the
view of the Public Garden, available from the second-floor
dining room or street-level *Ritz Bar*. ⑧

Westin

Map 6, J5. Copley Place ℂ262-9600 or 1-800/228-3000, fax
424-7483. Copley Ⓣ.
Rooms are modern and spacious at this well-located hotel,

always hopping with convention-goers, and a lively place to hole up in winter. Request a room facing the Charles River.
⑥–⑦

Cambridge Marriott

Map 7, L3. 2 Cambridge Center ℂ494-6600 or 1-800/228-9290. Kendall Ⓣ.
Stately, well-appointed rooms with a minimum of pretension. Many overlook the Charles, while the rest have views of industrial Kendall Square. Some weekend packages include sumptuous free brunch. ④

Charles Hotel

Map 7, D5. 1 Bennett St ℂ864-1200 or 1-800/882-1818. Harvard Ⓣ.
Clean, bright rooms – some overlooking the Charles – have a good array of amenities: radios, cable TV, three phones, mini-bar, Shaker furniture, and access to the adjacent WellBridge Health Spa. There's also an excellent jazz club, *Regattabar* (p.234), and restaurant, *Henrietta's Table* (p.210) on the premises.
⑥

Harvard Square Hotel

Map 7, D5. 110 Mt Auburn St ℂ864-5200 or 1-800/458-5886. Harvard Ⓣ.
The rooms here are only adequate, but it has a great location in the midst of Harvard Square, and is fairly affordable too. ④

Hyatt Regency Cambridge

Map 7, G7. 575 Memorial Dr ℂ492-1234, fax 491-6906. Kendall Ⓣ.
Brick ziggurat-like riverside monolith, with luxurious rooms,

HOTELS: CAMBRIDGE

pool, health club, and a patio with gazebo. Picturesque location on the Charles, but it's a hike from major points of interest. ⑤

Inn at Harvard

Map 7, E5. 1201 Massachusetts Ave ℂ491-2222 or 1-800/222-8733, fax 491-6520. Harvard Ⓣ.
This recently built hotel is carefully designed to give the impression of old-school grandeur, and it is so close to Harvard you can smell the ivy. Pleasant but rather small rooms. ⑥

Royal Sonesta

Cambridge Parkway ℂ491-3600 or 1-800/SONESTA, fax 661-5956. Kendall Ⓣ.
Luxury quarters with views of the downtown Boston skyline. The fancy rooms have big, sparkling bathrooms; the vast lobby is festooned with strikingly bad art. ④–⑤

Sheraton Commander

Map 7, C4. 16 Garden St ℂ547-4800, fax 868-8322. Harvard Ⓣ.
The hotel's name refers to George Washington, who, legend has it, took command of the Continental Army on nearby Cambridge Common (see p.123). Rooms tend to be rather dark and small, though with some cute frills (eg terrycloth robes). ③

Susse Chalet Cambridge

211 Concord Turnpike ℂ661-7800, fax 458-8153.
Modest rooms in a plain motor lodge located right off a highway (a mixed blessing) and next-door to a vintage bowling alley (a definite blessing). Free continental breakfast. ②

BED AND BREAKFASTS

The **bed–and–breakfast** industry in Boston is thriving, largely because it is so difficult to find accommodation here for under $100 a night – and many B&B's offer just that. Some of the best are outside the city, in either **Cambridge** or **Brookline**, though there are nice in-town options as well. You can make reservations directly with the places we've listed; there are also numerous B&B **agencies** that can do the booking for you.

B&B agencies and short-term accommodation

Beacon Inns & Guest Houses (©262-1771 or 266-7142, fax 266-7276). Books guest rooms with private baths and kitch-enettes throughout Back Bay.

Bed & Breakfast Agency of Boston (47 Commercial Wharf, Boston MA 02110; ©720-3540 or 1-800/248-9262, fax 523-5761). Can book you a room in a brownstone, a waterfront loft or even on a yacht.

Bed & Breakfast Associates Bay Colony Ltd (PO Box 57166 Babson Park Branch, Boston MA 02157; ©449-5302 or 1-800/347-5088, fax 449-5958). Has some real finds in Back Bay and the South End.

Bed & Breakfast - Cambridge & Greater Boston (©720-1492 or 1-800/888-0178, fax 227-0021). Has listings of B&Bs, both hosted and unhosted, and furnished apartments throughout central Cambridge and Boston.

Boston Short Term Rental (©262-3100). Furnished apartments throughout the city from $500 per week and up, with a two-week minimum stay.

Beacon Hill Bed & Breakfast

Map 3, A5. 27 Brimmer St ℂ523-7376. Charles Ⓣ.
Only three rooms are available in this well-situated brick townhouse. There are sumptuous full breakfasts; two-night minimum, three on holiday weekends. ③-④

BACK BAY AND THE SOUTH END

463 Beacon Street Guest House

Map 6, G4. 463 Beacon St ℂ536-1302. Hynes Ⓣ.
The good-sized rooms in this renovated brownstone, in the heart of Back Bay, come equipped with kitchenettes and other hotel-style amenities. Ask for the top floor room. ②

82 Chandler Street

Map 6, J5. 82 Chandler St ℂ482-0408. Back Bay Ⓣ.
One of Boston's best in-town B&Bs, this restored 1863 brownstone sits on one of the most up-and-coming streets of the South End. Good breakfasts served on the sun-splashed top floor – where you'll also find the best room in the house. ②

Copley House

Map 6, J4. 239 West Newton St ℂ236-8300 or 1-800/331-1318; fax 424-1815. Copley Ⓣ.
Furnished apartments on an attractive edge of Back Bay, across from the Copley Plaza shopping center. There's a three-night minimum; ask about the lower weekly rates. ②

Newbury Guest House

Map 6, H3. 261 Newbury St ℂ437-7666, fax 262-4243. Copley Ⓣ.

Big 32-room Victorian brownstone that still fills up whenever there's a big convention in town, so call in advance. Continental breakfast included. ➌

Oasis Guest House

Map 6, F6. 22 Edgerly Rd ©267-2262, fax 267-1920. Symphony Ⓣ. Sixteen comfortable, very affordable rooms, some with shared baths, in a renovated brownstone near Symphony Hall. ➊

BROOKLINE

Beacon Inn

1087 and 1750 Beacon St ©566-0088. Dean Ⓣ. Fireplaced lobbies and original woodwork contribute to the relaxed atmosphere in these two nineteenth-century brownstones, part of the same guest house. ➋

Brookline Manor Guest House

32 Centre St ©232-0003 or 1-800/524-1237, fax 734-5815. Dean Ⓣ.
This small guesthouse, on a pleasant stetch off Beacon Street, is just a short subway ride from Kenmore Square. The same management also run the *Beacon Street Guest House*, at 1047 Beacon St (©1-800/575-1009). ➋

CAMBRIDGE

A Cambridge House

2218 Massachusetts Ave ©491-6300 or 1-800/232-998, fax 868-2079. Porter Ⓣ.
A classy B&B, with gorgeous rooms decked out with canopy beds and period pieces. There are full breakfasts plus an evening wine-and-cheese in the parlor. It's a bit far out from any points of interest, but worth the trek. ➌

BED AND BREAKFASTS: BROOKLINE AND CAMBRIDGE

A Friendly Inn

Map 7, E3. 1673 Cambridge St ⓒ547-7851. **Harvard** Ⓣ.
This is a great deal, located just a few minutes' walk from
Harvard Square. The rooms are nothing special, but they do
have private bath and cable TV. Laundry service available. ①-②

Irving House

Map 7, E3. 24 Irving St ⓒ547-4600. **Harvard** Ⓣ.
A small but quaint option near Harvard Square, with laundry
and kitchen facilities. They have both shared and private baths.
①-②

Mary Prentiss Inn

Map 7, C2. 6 Prentiss St ⓒ661-2929, **fax** 661-5989. **Harvard** Ⓣ.
Eighteen clean, comfortable rooms in an impressively
refurbished mid-nineteenth-century Greek Revival building.
Full breakfast and snacks are served in the living room, or,
weather permitting, on a pleasant outdoor deck. Room prices
can, however, be as high as $225. ③

The Missing Bell

Map 7, C2. 16 Sacramento St ⓒ876-0987. **Harvard** Ⓣ.
This Queen Anne-style house, located in a quiet residential
neighborhood, takes its name from a decorative piece that dates
to the original construction of the house in 1883 and has since
disappeared. Rich woodwork, antique furnishings, deck and
gardens, and very friendly proprietors. ②

Prospect Place

Map 7, H4. 112 Prospect St ⓒ864-7500 **or** 1-800/769-5303.
Harvard Ⓣ.
This Italianate edifice boasts a restored parlor with nineteenth-

century period antiques, including two grand pianos, plus newly redecorated rooms. ②

HOSTELS

There are fairly limited **hostel** accommodations in Boston, and if you want to get in on them, you should definitely book ahead, especially in the summertime.

Greater Boston YMCA

Map 6, F6. 316 Huntington Ave ⊘536-7800, fax 267-4653. Symphony Ⓣ.
Good budget rooms, and access to the Y's health facilities (pool, weight room, etc). Singles are $38–56, but you can get a four-person room for $80. Open during summer and early fall only.

HI – Boston

Map 6, G4. 12 Hemenway St ⊘536-1027, fax 424-6558. Hynes Ⓣ.
Around the Back Bay-Fenway border, standard dorm accommodation with 3–4 beds per room. Members $17, nonmembers $20.

HI – Back Bay Summer Hostel

Map 6, C2. 519 Beacon St ⊘353-3294; reservation requests to 1020 Commonwealth Ave, Boston 02215 (⊘739-3017). Kenmore Ⓣ.
This converted BU dorm has 63 beds, but is only open June 16–Aug 26. Members $15, nonmembers $17.

Irish Embassy Youth Hostel

232 Friend St ⊘973-4841, fax 720-3998. North Station Ⓣ.

Boston's only independent youth hostel is above the *Irish Embassy* pub, in the West End and not far from Faneuil Hall. Prices include free admission to pub gigs on most nights, and free barbecues on Tues and Sun. Dorm beds are $15.

YWCA

Map 7, H5. 7 Temple St ☉491-6005. Central Ⓣ.

Spartan quarters in Cambridge for women only (men aren't allowed on the premises, even for a visit), but space is very limited, so call in advance. Members $30 per night, $90 per week, non-members $35/$106.

EATING

There is no shortage of places to **eat** in Boston. The city is loaded with bars and pubs that double as restaurants, cafés that serve full and affordable meals, and plenty of higher-end dinner-only options. There's a new level of dining adventurousness these days, partly in response to the traditional New England-type fare that is still the area's hallmark: hearty standbys like broiled scrod, clam chowder and Yankee pot roast, all of which owe a debt to the cold winter mentality of Boston. Most of this has shown up in the explosion of restaurants, mostly in Back Bay and the South End, serving modern, eclectic food that doesn't always quite hit the mark.

At **lunchtime** many places offer meals for about half the cost of dinner, a plus if you want to sample some of the food at the city's pricier and more exclusive restaurants. Pubs and taverns are also a good bet, serving sandwiches and old-fashioned grub that won't let you go hungry. There are also plenty of gourmet shops (p.264), if you're looking to picnic. **Dinner**, usually from 5pm on, is a much more exciting deal, with a wide array of **restaurants** that range from Boston's own local cuisine to ethnic foods of every stripe. You'll probably want to book ahead if you're planning to show up after 6pm; places are generally open until

10 or 11pm, though in Chinatown, there are numerous **late-night** spots. Also, many restaurants close on Sundays and/or Mondays, when you should call ahead to make sure your choice is open.

As far as Boston's culinary landscape goes, there are ever-popular **Italian** restaurants, both traditional Southern and more trendy Northern, that cluster in the **North End**, mainly on Hanover and Salem streets. The city's tiny **Chinatown** packs in not only a fair number of **Chinese** spots, but **Japanese**, **Vietnamese** and **Malaysian** too. *Dim sum*, where you choose selections from carts wheeled past your table, is especially big here, and you can find it anytime, though mostly at lunch – the best places are always packed on weekends, with lines down the streets. Boston's trendiest restaurants, mostly serving vogueish **New American** cuisine, tend to cluster in **Back Bay** and the **South End**.

Cambridge eating life centers around Harvard and Inman squares, and is perhaps best distinguished for its proliferation of **Indian** restaurants, forever competing against each other to offer lower prices, and resulting in some of the best food values in the city.

BREAKFASTS, SNACKS AND QUICK MEALS

In most places, save certain areas of downtown, you won't have a problem finding somewhere to grab a quick bite, whether it's a diner, deli or some other kind of snack joint. The establishments we list are all good for light meals, late-night snack or desserts; see also the bars and cafés listed on p.215, many of which offer food all day.

DOWNTOWN

Brigham's

Map 3, H3. 50 Congress Street ℂ523-9372. State Ⓣ.

The closest thing downtown has to a coffee shop, with an excellent soda fountain. Stick to basic ice cream flavors – chocolate chip, vanilla – and you'll be happiest.

Finagle-a-Bagel

Map 3, H5. 70 Franklin St ⑦261-1900. Downtown Crossing Ⓣ.
Map 6, I4. 535 Boylston St ⑦266-2500. Copley Ⓣ.
A small Boston chain with more than fifteen varieties of bagels, from Pumpkin Raisin to Triple Chocolate Chip, that are always served fresh.

Kam Lung Bakery and Restaurant

Map 3, G8. 77 Harrison St ⑦542-2229. Chinatown Ⓣ.
Tiny take-out joint that vends dim sum as well as bakery treats (sweet rolls, sugary moon pies) and more exotic delicacies (pork buns, meat pies).

Milk Street Café

Map 3, I4. 50 Milk St ⑦542-3663. State Ⓣ.
Map 3, I5. Post Office Square Park ⑦350-7273. Downtown Crossing Ⓣ.
Kosher and quick are the keys at these two downtown eateries, popular with suits for the large designer sandwiches and salads.

Sultan's Kitchen

Map 3, J4. 72 Broad Street ⑦728-2828. Aquarium Ⓣ.
The best Turkish food in Boston, this lunch spot is favored by businessmen who queue up for the agreeably spicy Ottoman classics. Take a table in the casual upstairs toom and you'll feel a million miles away from nearby tourist-laden Quincy Market.

DOWNTOWN

Verdura

Map 3, I4. 82 Water Street Ⓒ357-9013. State Ⓣ.
You can get fresh Mediterranean-style salads and sandwiches at this airy downtown lunch spot; on a warm day order a box lunch and enjoy it in the mini-park of Post Office Square next door.

NORTH END

Ernesto's

Map 4, B6. 69 Salem St Ⓒ523-1373. Haymarket Ⓣ.
The cheap, oversized slices of thin-crust pizza served here can't be beat for a quick lunch.

Galleria Umberto

Map 4, C6. 289 Hanover St Ⓒ227-5709. Haymarket Ⓣ.
When a place is open only from 11am to 2pm daily and there is a line out the door, you know something good is cooking. Here, it's pizza, cut in squares, that's cheap, greasy and delicious.

Rabia's

Map 4, C5. 73 Salem St Ⓒ227-6637. Haymarket Ⓣ.
The best thing about this small restaurant is the "Express Lunch" special. A heaped plate of pasta, chicken parmigiana and similar dishes are yours to savor for a mere $4 from noon until 2pm, daily.

CHARLESTOWN

Sorelle Bakery and Café

Map 5, E2. 1 Monument Ave Ⓒ242-2125.
Phenomenal muffins and cookies, plus pasta salads and other lunch fare which you can enjoy on a delightful hidden patio.

Buzzy's Fabulous Roast Beef

Map 3, B3. 327 Cambridge St ✆242-7722. Charles Ⓣ.
The lunch and after-hours crowds gather here for – what else?
– roast beef sandwiches, which really do live up to the hype.
Open 24 hours.

Paramount

Map 3, B4. 44 Charles St ✆720-1152. Charles Ⓣ.
The Hill's neighborhood diner serves Belgian waffles and
frittatas to the brunch crowd regulars by day, decent American
standards like hamburgers and meatloaf by night.

Ruby's Diner

Map 3, C2. 280 Cambridge St ✆367-3224. Charles Ⓣ.
Very basic breakfast chow, eggs and such, done cheaply and
well. Open all night Thurs–Sat.

Café de Paris

Map 6, L5. 19 Arlington St ✆247-7121. Arlington Ⓣ.
The Parisian pretensions of this spot, where you order your
sandwich off a wall menu or select a pre-prepared salad from
the counter, are sort of a joke, though people still line up. If
you want a pastry, ask for the freshest to avoid
disappointment.

Café Jaffa

Map 6, G4. 48 Gloucester St ✆536-0230. Hynes Ⓣ.
Boston's best falafel and other Middle Eastern staples are served
in this cool, inviting space with polished wood floors.

Emack & Bolio's

Map 6, H4. 290 Newbury St ⓒ247-8772. **Copley** Ⓣ.
Pint-sized ice cream parlor named for a long-defunct rock
band. Try a scoop each of Chocolate Moose and Vanilla Bean
Speck in a chocolate-dipped waffle cone to get hooked.

Fuel

Map 6, I2. 636 Beacon St ⓒ266-0011. **Copley** Ⓣ.
Basically a juice and coffee bar, but you can also get fresh baked
goods and made-to-order sandwiches.

Mike's City Diner

1714 Washington St ⓒ267-9393. **Back Bay** Ⓣ.
Classic diner breakfasts and lunches (greasy but good) in an
out-of-the-way setting in the South End.

Stephanie's on Newbury

Map 6, J3. 190 Newbury St ⓒ236-0990. **Copley** Ⓣ.
A prime people-watching spot that used to be the beloved
Harvard Bookstore Café, and now serving relatively disappointing
salads and the like, though that doesn't stop folks from coming.

The Ultimate Bagel Company

Map 6, G4. 335 Newbury St ⓒ247-1010. **Hynes** Ⓣ.
Whoever says New York has the best bagels may have
overlooked this upper Newbury spot, where the cinnamon
glazed is a dream and the onion bagel uncommonly good.

KENMORE SQUARE

Deli-Haus

Map 6, C2. 476 Commonwealth Ave ⓒ247-9712. **Kenmore** Ⓣ.

This Kenmore Square student haunt is open 24 hours; try any of the breakfast fare, served all day, or the club sandwich.

C'est Bon

Map 7, D5. 1432 Massachusetts Ave St ©661-0610. Harvard Ⓣ.
Map 7, D5. 110 Mt Auburn St ©492-6465. Harvard Ⓣ.
Small, centrally located shop, in two branches, both of which serve up excellent coffee and the best falafel in the area at inexpensive prices. Open late.

Darwin's Ltd

Map 7, C5. 148 Mt Auburn St ©354-5233. Harvard Ⓣ.
The squalid exterior conceals a delightful deli serving the best sandwiches in the Square – wonderfully inventive combinations, such as roast beef, sprouts, and apple slices, served on freshly baked bread. There's also a selection of pastries, deli foodstuffs, alcohol, and frozen treats.

Herrell's Ice Cream

Map 7, D5. 15 Dunster St ©497-2179. Harvard Ⓣ.
The best ice cream in Cambridge, if not anywhere. If you don't believe it, just ask one of the patrons in the always-long lines, or check out the profusion of "Best of Boston" awards adorning the walls. Better yet, try the stuff yourself. The chocolate pudding ice cream is a particular delight, especially combined with "smoosh-ins," such as Junior Mints or crushed Oreo cookies. Open until midnight.

Lee's Sandwich Shop

Map 7, D5. 61 Church St ©876-4090. Harvard Ⓣ.
An old-fashioned lunch counter, simple and unpretentious.

The burgers are great – if you love beef, ask for the DBCB (double bacon cheeseburger).

Porter Square Café and Diner

Map 7, A1. 1933 Massachusetts Ave ℂ354-3898. Porter Ⓣ.
This place manages to pull off the unlikely combination of coffeehouse and diner culture. It's best for good, cheap American breakfast fare: specials are served all day, and there's a make-your-own omelette option, too.

Scoops and Beans

Map 7, D5. 56 JFK St ℂ576-3532. Harvard Ⓣ.
A rising star in the competitive pantheon of Harvard Square ice cream spots, *Scoops* earned its stars by offering an especially intriguing range of flavors, including burnt sugar and green tea.

RESTAURANTS

Boston's restaurants are fairly well spread out, though Back Bay, the South End and Harvard Square probably have the highest concentrations of worthwhile spots. You should make reservations ahead of time, especially at the more expensive places.

DOWNTOWN/**AMERICAN AND NEW AMERICAN**

Abigail's Restaurant

Map 3, F5. 100 Tremont St ℂ423-9898. Park Ⓣ. Inexpensive.
The menu promises "robust" American food, and that's what the kitchen delivers at this homespun spot near the Park Street Church, with sizeable and inexpensive portions of staples like meatloaf, turkey with gravy, and Boston scrod.

Restaurant prices

The restaurant listings are price-coded into five categories: **cheap** (under $10), **inexpensive** ($10–15), **moderate** ($15–25), **expensive** ($25–40) and **very expensive** (over $40). This assumes a three-course meal for one person, not including drinks, tax or tip. Much depends of course on what you order, with meat and seafood, as you might expect, on the pricier side of things. Restaurant tax in Massachusetts is five percent. Most places accept all major credit cards, but eateries in the North End are renowned for accepting only cash.

Bakey's

Map 3, J3.
Easily recognized by its decorative sign of a man slumped over an ironing board, *Bakey's* was one of the first after-hours Irish pubs to surface in the Financial District. Though it tends toward the pricey side ($9 for a turkey sandwich), it's a safe bet if you're caught hungry wandering around this part of town.

Bay Tower Room

Map 3, H3. 60 State St ©723-1666. State Ⓣ. Very expensive.
Located on the 33rd floor of a downtown high-rise, the Bay Tower is notable mostly for its spectacular views of Boston Harbor. The food is less remarkable, though good enough – standard fancy American cuisine, filet mignons and the like.

The Blue Diner

Map 3, I9. 150 Kneeland St ©695-0087. South Station Ⓣ.
Inexpensive–moderate.

Campy bar and restaurant with a rare feature among retro diners – good food. A popular spot for a late-night nosh – it's open until 4am on weekends

Country Life

Map 3, K4. 200 High St ©951-2534. Aquarium Ⓣ. Inexpensive.
An all-vegetarian buffet near the Waterfront, whose cheap and quick meal options vary daily; call the menu hotline (©951-2462) to find out what's cooking.

Dakota's

Map 3, G5. 34 Summer Street in the 101 Arch Street Building ©737-1777. Downtown Crossing or Park Ⓣ. Expensive.
Frequented mainly by office workers for lunch and pre-commute dinners, the clubby feel of this expansive American grill restaurant and great food make it the perfect place to dine after visiting nearby *Filene's Basement*. There are also very good salads, pasta dishes and Key Lime Pie. Closed weekends.

David's

Map 3, D9. 123 Stuart St ©367-8405. Boylston Ⓣ. Expensive.
This striking Theater District eatery serves the most delectable New American food in Boston. Chef Stephen Lancaster used to cook at the British Embassy in Washington, but this stuff – from date ravioli with curried goat cheese and sliced apples to banana chocolate strudel with butterscotch sauce and homemade white chocolate ice cream – is as far from stodgy as you can get.

Durgin-Park

Map 3, I2. 340 Faneuil Hall Marketplace ©227-2038.
Government Center Ⓣ. Expensive.

A Boston landmark in operation since 1827, *Durgin-Park* has a no-frills Yankee atmosphere and a somewhat surly waitstaff. That doesn't stop folks from coming for the pricey if sizeable pot roast and roast beef dinners in the upstairs dining room. The downstairs raw bar is considerably livelier.

Locke-Ober Café

Map 3, F5. 3 Winter Place Ⓒ**542-1340. Park** Ⓣ**. Very expensive.**
Don't be fooled by the name: *Locke-Ober* is very much a restaurant, and one of the most bluebloded in Boston. The fare consists of things like steak tartare and oysters on the half shell, while the setting is dark, ornate and stuffy. There's an archaic dress code, too – jacket and tie for men.

Mercury Bar

Map 3, E8. 116 Boylston St Ⓒ**482-7799. Arlington** Ⓣ**. Expensive.**
Known more for its faux-hip scene than its Mediterranean-American entrées and reasonably-priced tapas, *Mercury Bar* also has a small dance club in the rear (see p.236).

Mr. Dooley's Boston Tavern

Map 3, J3. 77 Broad St Ⓒ**338-5656. State** Ⓣ**. Inexpensive.**
Another downtown Irish pub, though with a quieter and more atmospheric interior than the rest. Also known for its live music acts and Traditional Irish Breakfast Sundays – nice, since finding *anything* open around here on Sunday is a challenge.

Seasons

Map 3, H2. North and Blackstone sts, in the *Regal Bostonian Hotel* Ⓒ**523-4119. Government Center or State** Ⓣ**. Very expensive.**
Inventive, truly excellent Modern American fare, such as stone crab with smoked corn minestrone, atop a luxurious hotel.

RESTAURANTS: DOWNTOWN

Silvertone

Map 3, G5. 69 Bromfield St ☏338-7887. Downtown Crossing ⓣ.
Inexpensive.

Though cocktails are the big draw at this Downtown Crossing
basement bar and eatery, its Caesar salads and roasted salmon
with homemade potato chips are surprisingly inexpensive.

DOWNTOWN/CHINESE, VIETNAMESE AND MALAYSIAN

Buddha's Delight

Map 3, G8. 5 Beach St ☏451-2395. Chinatown ⓣ. Inexpensive.
Menu items are inside quotation marks, basically because the
"beef" and "chicken" are actually made from tofu. In fact,
everything served here is Vietnamese vegetarian fare, and while
the ersatz meats don't exactly taste like the real thing, they're
still good.

Chau Chow

Map 3, H8. 52 Beach St ☏426-6266. Chinatown ⓣ. Moderate.
One of the first Chinatown restaurants to specialize in seafood,
and still one of the best. The setting is stripped-down so there's
nothing to distract you from delicious salt-and-pepper shrimp
or, if you're in a more adventurous mood, sea cucumber. The
Grand Chau Chow, just across Beach Street, serves basically the
same food at somewhat higher prices and with fancier
accoutrements such as tablecloths and linen napkins.

East Ocean City

Map 3, H8. 25-29 Beach St ☏542-2504. Chinatown ⓣ. Moderate.
Another seafood specialist, full of aquariums where you can
greet your dinner before it appears on your plate. They have
especially good soft-shell crabs.

> **Many of Chinatown's restaurants stay open past 2am, when a fairly lively after-hours scene starts.**

King Fung Garden

Map 3, F9. 74 Kneeland St ©357-5262. **Chinatown** Ⓣ. **Inexpensive.**
The interior won't impress with its size or style, but the authentic Shangdong province food they serve here will. Inexpensive and delicious, the *King* is best on classics, like pot stickers, scallion pancakes, and (if you let them know in time) Peking duck.

Penang

Map 3, F8. 685 Washington St ©451-6373. **Chinatown** Ⓣ.
Moderate.
A newcomer to Chinatown scene, this Malaysian restaurant has a painfully overdone interior but consistently good food to counter it.

Pho Pasteur

Map 3, F8 & 9. 682 Washington St and 8 Kneeland St ©482-7467. **Chinatown** Ⓣ. **Budget.**
Two restaurants, both offering a multitude of variations on "pho," a Vietnamese noodle dish. The Kneeland location serves only pho, while the one on Washington has other Vietnamese specialties as well – and it's all incredibly cheap.

DOWNTOWN/FRENCH

Ben's Café

Map 3, G4. 45 School Street ©227-3370. **Government Center or Park** Ⓣ. **Expensive.**
This relaxed French eatery is situated in a French Second Empire building that for a hundred years served as Boston's City Hall. Ask for a table in "The Vault" and go with the prix

RESTAURANTS: DOWNTOWN

fixe menu; otherwise head for its airy, hideaway bar, where the price of a drink includes free hors d'oeuvres. Upstairs is the more formal *La Maison Robert*. Closed on weekends.

Les Zygomates

Map 3, I8. 129 South St Ⓒ542-5108. South Station Ⓣ. Expensive.
The name comes from the French term for the facial muscles that make you smile. An eclectic crowd ranging from bankers to black-clad artistes gather for the inventive Modern French cuisine served here. The wine selection is among Boston's best – more than a hundred varieties from around the world are available, all bottled or by the glass, to encourage exploration.

DOWNTOWN/**GERMAN**

Jacob Wirth

Map 3, E9. 31 Stuart St Ⓒ338-8586. Arlington Ⓣ. Moderate.
A German-themed Boston landmark, around since 1868; even if you don't like bratwurst washed down with a hearty lager, something is sure to please. This is a Boston must.

DOWNTOWN/**ITALIAN**

Café Marliave

Map 3, F5. 10 Bosworth Street Ⓒ423-6340. Park Ⓣ. Moderate.
This Italian-American hideaway is one of Boston's oldest restaurants. Go for the first-rate ravioli and unmistakably Bostonian ambience, as it's located behind the *Omni Parker House Hotel* and next to the Province House Steps – the remains of the seventeenth-century British Government House.

DOWNTOWN/**JAPANESE**

Ginza

Map 3, H8. 16 Hudson St Ⓒ338-2261. Chinatown Ⓣ. Moderate.

Open until 4am on weekends, *Ginza* is a popular after-hours spot serving perhaps the best sushi in the city. Any of the vast number of options goes well with a pitcher of warm house sake.

Jae's Café

Map 3, D9. 212 Stuart St ℂ451-7788. Arlington Ⓣ. Moderate.
The first floor of the popular Theater District place is a sushi bar and jazz room, while the third is a Korean barbecue where chefs slice and dice at your table. In between is the main café, with an emphasis on Korean seafood, though you can also create your own noodle dish. There's another location in Cambridge, at 1281 Cambridge St ℂ497-8380; #69 bus.

DOWNTOWN/MEXICAN

Zuma's Tex-Mex Café

Map 3, I2. 7 North Market St ℂ367-9114. State Ⓣ. Inexpensive.
Tex-Mex is a long way from home in Boston, but *Zuma's* comes up with a close approximation, complemented by a garish interior and sassy waitstaff. Especially good are the fajitas, which come to your table billowing smoke, and the salty, tangy margaritas.

DOWNTOWN/SEAFOOD

The Chart House

Map 3, L2. 60 Long Wharf ℂ227-1576. Aquarium Ⓣ. Expensive.
Rich food for the rich, though worth the prices if you can afford them; the lobster and swordfish are particularly good. For a less highbrow experience, try the downstairs café.

The Daily Catch

Map 2, I4. 261 Northern Ave ℂ338-3093. South Station Ⓣ. Moderate.

RESTAURANTS: DOWNTOWN

Seafood with a Modern Italian flair that provides a solid
alternative to the standard Yankee scrod-and-chips thing.

Jimbo's Fish Shanty

Map 2, I4. 245 Northern Ave ℂ542-5600. South Station Ⓣ. Moderate.
Operated by the proprietor's of *Jimmy's Harborside*, (below),
serving basically the same food at lower prices and in a more
casual atmosphere, without the picturesque views.

Jimmy's Harborside

Map 2, I4. 242 Northern Ave ℂ423-5000. South Station Ⓣ.
Expensive.
Jimmy's aesthetic is totally tacky, but the harbor views and
seafood are beyond reproach. House specialties include the
sizeable King Lobsters and the Shore Dinners, a panoply of
shellfish harvested along the New England seashore.

Salty Dog

Map 3, I2. Faneuil Hall Marketplace ℂ742-2094. Government
Center Ⓣ. Expensive.
It's worth braving the long waits here for the fresh seafood,
such as particularly good raw oysters and clams, and a generous
lobster dinner, all best enjoyed in the outdoor dining area.

Union Oyster House

Map 3, H2. 41 Union St ℂ227-2750. Government Center or
State Ⓣ. Expensive.
The oldest continuously operating restaurant in America has
two big claims to fame: French King Louis-Phillipe lived over
the tavern during his youth, and, perhaps apocryphally, the
toothpick was first used here. The food is good too: fresh and
well-prepared seafood, plus some of Boston's best raw bars.

Assaggio

Map 4, D5. 29 Prince St ℰ227-7380. Haymarket Ⓣ. Moderate.
An extensive wine list allows *Assaggio* to stand on its own as a
wine bar, but it's reliable for classic Italian fare with
contemporary touches, too. The main dining room, with its
ceiling mural of the Zodiac and steady stream of opera music, is
calm and relaxing.

Dolce Vita

Map 4, E5. 237 Hanover St ℰ720-0422. Haymarket Ⓣ. Inexpensive.
Sit in the quiet upstairs dining room in this long-standing
North End spot to savor their famous Ravioli Rose, in a tomato
cream sauce. Don't come here if you're in a hurry, though.

Giacomo's

Map 4, F3. 355 Hanover St ℰ523-9026. Haymarket Ⓣ. Moderate.
Among the handful of truly great restaurants in Boston, this
small eatery, with its menu written on a chalkboard attached to
a brick wall, serves fresh and flavorful seafood and pasta
specialties; try the pumpkin tortellini in sage butter sauce.

Il Panino

Map 4, C5. 11 Parmenter St ℰ720-1336. Haymarket Ⓣ.
Inexpensive.
A *bona fide* Boston best, with incredible pasta specials at lunch;
a bit more formal by night.

Mama Maria

Map 4, E6. 3 North Square ℰ523-0077. Haymarket Ⓣ. Expensive.
A favorite special-occasion restaurant, and considered by some
to be the best the district has to offer; in any case its location,

on historic North Square, is as good a reason as any to come. The Northern Italian fare is of consistently impeccable quality. Dinner only.

Marcuccio's

Map 4, D3. 125 Salem St ℂ723-1807. Haymarket Ⓣ. Expensive. Contemporary Italian food in a nice setting, with pop art updates of Renaissance masterpieces on the walls. The chef has a light, piquant touch that works particularly well with seafood dishes, risottos and salads. No cards; dinner only.

Monica's

Map 4, C4. 67 Prince St ℂ720-5472. Haymarket Ⓣ. Inexpensive. Some of the most intensely flavored Italian fare around, prepared and served by Monica's three sons, one of whom drew the cartoons plastered over the walls. They do a brisk take-out (sandwiches and such) at lunch, though the best dishes are reserved for dinner. Monica herself has a gourmet shop around the corner at 130 Salem St (see p.264).

Pizzeria Regina

Map 4, B3. 11½ Thacher St ℂ227-0765. Haymarket Ⓣ. Inexpensive. Tasty pizza, served in a neighborhood feed station where the wooden booths haven't budged since the 1940s. Vintage North End.

NORTH END/SEAFOOD

The Daily Catch

Map 4, F4. 323 Hanover St ℂ523-8567. Haymarket Ⓣ. Moderate. Ocean-fresh seafood, notably calamari and shellfish, draws big lines to this tiny storefront resto. The cooking is Sicilian-style with megadoses of garlic.

Figs

Map 5, D4. 67 Main St ℰ242-2229. Moderate.

This noisy, popular offshoot of *Olives* (see below) has excellent thin-crusted pizzas, topped with such savory items as figs and prosciutto or caramelized onions and arrugula. They have another location in Beacon Hill at 42 Charles St (ℰ742-3447).

Olives

Map 5, D5. 10 City Square ℰ242-1999. Very expensive.

Olives is consistently rated Boston's best restaurant, and justifiably so. Chef Todd English turns out New Mediterranean food of unforgettable flavor and sizeable portions, the cause of long lines if you show up after 6pm —there are no reservations save for parties of six or more. Closed Sun and Mon.

Gabriele's

Map 5, H3. 1 First Ave (Charlestown Navy Yard) ℰ242-1722. Moderate.

This upscale Italian eatery between the USS Constitution Museum and the arrival area for the Long Wharf ferry features the usual suspects – bruschetta, spinach ravioli, chicken parmigiana – but with unusually good execution. Dine on the terrace to catch the breeze on a hot summer's day.

Grand Canal

Map 3, G1. 57 Canal St ℰ523-1112. North Station Ⓣ. Moderate.

Atmospheric West End Irish pub and restaurant with nineteenth-century accoutrements, such as the linen tablecloths

RESTAURANTS: CHARLESTOWN

and a great mahogany bar with a mirror behind. Cheap, relatively inexpensive lobster dinners as well as American comfort food.

The Hungry I

Map 3, B4. 71 Charles St ⊘227-2524. Charles T. Very expensive. A pricey menu and hyped-up romantic surroundings, but the food is delectable – classic American fare with creative twists that change nightly.

Rebecca's

Map 3, B4. 21 Charles St ⊘742-9747. Charles T. Expensive. This place brought New American to Beacon Hill when it was still new. The nouvelle cuisine is still good, if a little more tame these days.

Road Trip

Map 3, G1. 54 Canal St ⊘720-2889. North Station T. Expensive. An almost too-hip West End spot, with retro decor and a theme menu, based on "indigenous" American cuisines. You can start with an appetizer from California (brie salad) or New England (Maine crab cakes), and move on to an entree from the Heartland (rib eye steak) or the Southwest (mole chicken). It's gimmicky, but the food is good.

BEACON HILL AND THE WEST END/ITALIAN

Ristorante Toscano

Map 3, B4. 47 Charles St ⊘723-4040. Charles T. Moderate. In the midst of the New Italian craze, this place stayed traditional, and survived. It serves particularly good southern Italian food, made with classic flair and fresh ingredients.

Lala Rokh

Map 3, C5. 97 Mt Vernon St ⓒ720-5511. Park T. Moderate.
Have the waitstaff help you with the inscrutable menu at this exotically plush Persian restaurant.

The King & I

Map 3, B3. 145 Charles St ⓒ227-3320. Charles ⓣ.
Inexpensive–moderate.
Excellent, inventive Thai with bold, but not overbearing flavors. The "Shrimp in Love" is worth trying for its name alone.

575

Map 6, F4. 94 Massachusetts Ave ⓒ247-9922. Hynes ⓣ. Moderate.
This cavernous restaurant/bar has an Asian-influenced grazing menu and dark paneling designed to attract Boston's beautiful people – which to a certain extent it does.

Anago

Map 6, I3. 65 Exeter St (in the Lenox Hotel) ⓒ266-6222. Copley ⓣ. Expensive.
Comfort food like spit-roasted pork and rotisserie chicken prepared with a thoughtful and not overblown New American accent; desserts include the likes of coconut crème brûlée and ginger poached pear dipped in chocolate.

Back Bay Brewing Company

Map 6, I4. 755 Boylston St ⓒ424-8300. Copley ⓣ. Moderate.

Of all the brewpubs in Boston, this feels the least like a glorified bar: the breakfast fare is every bit as good as the inventive lunch and dinner offerings. If you just want a brew, though, settle into the comfortable second-floor lounge and take your pick.

Biba

Map 6, L4. 272 Boylston St ©426-5684. Arlington Ⓣ. Very expensive.

Chef Lydia Shire takes culinary eclecticism to absurd heights at this pricey spot, which would be more at home in trendy LA. The food is description-resistant, and there's a category on the menu called "Offal" – draw your own conclusions. *Biba*'s bar is a safe, if overcrowded and pretentious, alternative (see p.220).

Cottonwood Restaurant & Café

Map 6, L4. 222 Berkeley St ©247-2225. Arlington Ⓣ. Moderate–expensive.

Creative and tasty Southwestern fare served in a bright setting on the ground floor of the 22-story Houghton Mifflin Building. Locally (and justly) famous for its margaritas, this is one of Back Bay's best bets for lunch or Sunday brunch with a twist.

Dixie Kitchen

Map 6, F5. 182 Massachusetts Ave ©536-3068. Hynes Ⓣ. Moderate.

Safe bets at this easygoing New Orleans-style eatery include jambalaya, fried crawfish and chicken gumbo. Great pies.

Top of the Hub

Map 6, H5. 800 Boylston St ©536-1775. Prudential Ⓣ. Expensive.

There are several benefits of dining atop the 50th floor of the Prudential Tower, not the least of which is enjoying the

excellent city views. There's also surprisingly inventive New
England fare and a big, bright space in which to enjoy it.

BACK BAY/FRENCH

Ambrosia

Map 6, I5. 116 Huntington Ave ⓒ247-2400. Prudential or Copley
ⓣ. Expensive–very expensive.
When you get the craving for a Peruvian Purple Potato
Springroll or Grilled Pulled Pig Sandwich with Indonesian
BBQ Sauce Oil, this is your place. The French Provençal-
meets-Asia fusion cuisine is inventively prepared in a high-tech
but accessible environment of dazzling floral arrangements,
hand-blown crystal and intricate metalwork, though the flavors
don't always measure up to the elaborate presentation. At lunch
most salads, gourmet sandwiches and other entrées are priced
under $12.

Café Budapest

Map 6, I5. 90 Exeter St (in the *Copley Square Hotel*) ⓒ266-1079.
Copley ⓣ. Expensive.
Some call it the most romantic restaurant in Boston, but really
elegance and inadvertent camp (live piano-and-violin
renditions of *Hello, Dolly*, for example) are what this gaily-hued
basement-level fixture do best. That and iced tart cherry soup
followed by chicken paprika.

Du Barry Restaurant Français

Map 6, H3. 159 Newbury St ⓒ262-2445. Copley ⓣ. Expensive.
A bastion of tradition on otherwise trendy Newbury Street, *Du
Barry* is one of few classic French restaurants in Boston.
Nothing too inventive, just good, hearty staples like boeuf
bourguignon, and a hidden terrace on which to enjoy them in

warmer weather. The quiet bar is popular with the area's writers.

L'Espalier

Map 6, G3. 30 Gloucester Street ℂ262-3023. Hynes Ⓣ. Very expensive.

A ravishing French restaurant in a Back Bay brownstone. The food is first rate, but the minimalist portions suggest that the ambience is also factored into your bill.

Sonsie

Map 6, F4. 327 Newbury St ℂ351-2500. Hynes Ⓣ. Expensive.

The pretension factor is high at this *kaffeeklatsch*, where the ultra-trendy meet over strange marriages of French and Asian food (miso clam soup with spring morels and tofu, grilled salmon with edible blossoms). Worth a try, though.

Zinc

Map 6, J5. 35 Stanhope St ℂ262-2323. Back Bay Ⓣ. Expensive.

French bistro fare, and a raw bar, in a hideaway but increasingly hip location straddling the South End.

BACK BAY/**INDIAN**

Bombay Café

Map 6, F4. f 175 Massachusetts Ave ℂ247-0555. Hynes Ⓣ. Inexpensive.

The chicken tikka and stuffed nan are solid bets, as is anything with seafood, at this casual Indian restaurant.

Kashmir

Map 6, G4. 279 Newbury St ℂ536-1695. Hynes Ⓣ. Moderate.

The food and decor are equally inviting at Newbury Street's only Indian restaurant. Sound bets include shrimp samosas, tandoori rack of lamb and vegetarian curries, all of which go well with the excellent nan bread

Papa Razzi

Map 6, J4. 271 Dartmouth St ©536-9200. Copley ⓣ. Moderate.
Though this urbane, basement-level eatery doesn't look like a chain restaurant, it is – a fact reflected in the menu of standard-issue bruschetta, salads and pastas. It's all good, but for more authentic takes head to the North End.

Spasso

Map 6, L3. 160 Commonwealth Ave ©536-8656. Arlington ⓣ. Moderate.
A Back Bay trattoria, with all that implies (good location, hip ambience, so-so in the sustenance department). Salads and pastas are generally OK, but the big draw is the sunken al fresco terrace that fronts the Commonwealth Avenue Mall.

Gyuhama

Map 6, G4. 827 Boylston St ©437-0188. Hynes ⓣ. Expensive.
A very noisy basement-level sushi bar, favored by many college students for late-night Japanese snacks.

Kaya

Map 6, I4. 581 Boylston St ©236-5858. Copley ⓣ. Expensive.
This is the place to go when the craving for Japanese-Korean food kicks in; try the teriyaki salmon or steaming shabu shabu.

Miyako

Map 6, G3. 279 Newbury St ©236-0222. Copley Ⓣ. Expensive.
Authenticity comes at a price at this Japanese standby, which has a
popular terrace on Newbury Street, a sleek sushi bar inside and a
minimalist decor of muted greys and bright floral arrangements.

BACK BAY/**MEXICAN AND LATIN AMERICAN**

Cactus Club

Map 6, F4. 939 Boylston St ©236-0200. Hynes Ⓣ. Inexpensive.
Cavernous Tex-Mex restaurant with funky decor and
surprisingly tasty nibbles (including great quesadillas), but
equally sought out for its popular bar.

Mucho Gusto Café

Map 6, E4. 1124 Boylston St ©236-1020. Symphony Ⓣ. Inexpensive.
Good-sized portions of Cuban cuisine – a welcome alternative to
the ubiquitous Tex-Mex – and a room brimming with
grandmotherly bric-a-brac that will either attract or repel you
from this bohemian eatery and Berklee College of Music hangout.

BACK BAY/**MIDDLE EASTERN**

Steve's Greek-American Cuisine

Map 6, F4. 316 Newbury St ©267-1817. Hynes Ⓣ. Inexpensive.
Excellent Greek food makes this one of Boston's classic cheap
eats. Steve's Greek Salad is a favorite among the Newbury
Street lunch crowd, and the Grilled Chicken Sandwich could
convert a vegetarian.

BACK BAY/**SEAFOOD**

Legal C Bar

Map 3, C9. Park Plaza Hotel ©426-5566. Arlington Ⓣ. Expensive.

A small outpost of *Legal Seafoods* (below) less than a stone's throw from the original, with delights from the sea prepared in a variety of Cajun and Caribbean styles. Go for the acra (codfish cakes), Bermuda fish chowder, and the solid range of rum drinks.

Legal Seafoods

Map 3, C9. 35 Columbus Ave in the *Park Plaza Hotel* ①426-4444. Arlington ⓣ.
Map 6, J4. 100 Huntington Ave, Level Two Copley Place ①266-7775. Copley ⓣ.
Map 6, H5. 800 Boylston St, Prudential Center ①266-6800. Prudential ⓣ.
Map 7, L3. 5 Cambridge Center ①864-3400. Kendall ⓣ. Expensive.
This local chain is probably the best-known seafood restaurant in America, and for many the best as well. Its trademark is freshness: the clam chowder, Boston scrod and lobster are all top quality. There are some new Asian offerings on the menu, too. Go early to avoid long lines, no matter the location or day of the week.

Skipjack's

Map 6, K4. 199 Clarendon St ①536-3500. Arlington ⓣ. Expensive.
A cool, South Beach-style decor and bold menu distinguish this seafood spot from its rival, the always-busy *Legal Seafoods* – you're as likely to find fresh mahimahi dipped in lemon and soy as fried scrod with tartar sauce. The Sunday jazz brunch is quite popular.

Turner Fisheries

Map 6, I5. 10 Huntington Ave ①424-7425. Prudential ⓣ. Expensive.
The traditional New England seafood at this cheerful spot –

scrod, Boston clam chowder, lobster bisque – is as good as any in the city. Most nights feature live jazz, too.

Thai Basil

Map 6, J3. 132 Newbury St ✆424-8424. Copley Ⓣ. Moderate.
With its excellent seafood and vegetarian dishes, great pad Thai and a cool, soothing decor in which to enjoy it all, this is the best Thai restaurant in Boston.

SOUTH END/**AMERICAN AND NEW AMERICAN**

Claremont Café

Map 6, I7. 535 Columbus Ave ✆247-9001. Back Bay Ⓣ. Expensive.
Diverse appetizers, imaginatively garnished entrees and particularly flavorful desserts, including a stellar banana creme pie. Closed Mondays.

Franklin Café

Map 6, L8. 278 Shawmut Ave ✆350-0010. Back Bay Ⓣ.
Moderate–expensive.
One of the hottest new spots in Boston, this upscale diner has earned local fame for its tasty renditions of Yankee comfort food.

Geoffrey's

Map 6, K7. 578 Tremont St ✆266-1122. Back Bay Ⓣ. Inexpensive.
This cheerful eatery serves a nice range of salads and sandwiches from a menu that also includes treats like seven-vegetable couscous, asparagus mousse ravioli and huge portions of cake.

Moka

Map 6, J6. 130 Dartmouth St ✆424-7768. Back Bay Ⓣ. Inexpensive.

One of the first California-style cafés to appear on the Boston dining landscape, *Moka* has lots of salads, grilled pizzas and the like, though the service is a bit lacking. There's also cheap breakfasts, fresh baked goods and fruit smoothies.

Hamersly's Bistro

Map 6, K7. 553 Tremont St ☏423-2700. Back Bay Ⓣ Ⓣ. Expensive.
Hamersly's is widely regarded as one of the best restaurants in Boston, and with good cause. Every night star chef-owner Gordon Hamersley dons a baseball cap and takes to the open kitchen, where he dishes out unusual – and unforgettable – French-American fare that changes seasonally.

Mistral

Map 6, K5. 221 Columbus Ave ☏867-9300. Back Bay Ⓣ. Expensive.
Boston's restaurant of the moment serves pricey modern Provençal food in a bright, airy space above the Turnpike. How long its star will keep rising is anyone's guess, as the food is mediocre considering the cost. Dinner only.

On the Park

Map 6, K8. One Union Park ☏426-0862. Back Bay Ⓣ. Moderate.
The French Country fare here is as much of a draw at this neighborhood restaurant as its secluded setting on the quiet south side of Union Park. The vegetarian cassoulet is a winner.

Bertucci's Brick Oven Pizzeria

Map 6, K5. 43 Stanhope St ☏247-6161. Back Bay Ⓣ. Inexpensive.

Though it may not be the best pizza in Boston, *Bertucci's* more than does the trick; there's also great free garlic bread in this funky South End location.

Giacomo's

Map 6, I6. 431 Columbus Ave ℭ536-5723. Back Bay Ⓣ. Moderate.
South End sister of the original in the North End; see p.195. Dinner only, closed Mondays.

KENMORE SQUARE, THE FENWAY AND BROOKLINE

Anna's Taqueria

Map 2, D5. 1412 Beacon St ℭ739-7300. Coolidge Corner Ⓣ. Budget.
Exceptional tacos, burritos and quesadillas are the only things on the menu at this bright Mexican eatery, but they're so good a second branch had to be opened around the corner (at 446 Harvard St) to accommodate its legions of devotees.

Audubon Circle

Map 6, C2. 838 Beacon St ℭ421-1910. Kenmore Ⓣ. Moderate.
The seemingly endless bar grabs your attention first, but it's the food that's worth staying for. Any of the appetizers are good bets, as is anything grilled – from burgers with chipotle ketchup to grilled tuna with banana salsa and fufu (fried plantains mashed with coconut milk). There's a limited but homemade dessert selection.

Piccolo Pomodoro

Map 6, E5. 58 Hemenway St ℭ421-0800. Symphony Ⓣ. Moderate.
Upbeat Italian spot behind Symphony Hall with great wood-fired pizza, homemade pastas, and fish dishes.

Amrhein's

Map 2, H5. 80 W Broadway, South Boston ℂ268-6189. Broadway Ⓣ. Moderate.

A Southie landmark and a favorite of local politicians for generations. The good old American comfort food won't dazzle your palate, but it's reasonably priced and you get a lot of it.

Bella Luna

Map 2, E7. 405 Centre St, Jamaica Plain ℂ524-6060. Green St Ⓣ. Moderate.

Nouvelle pizza with a funky array of fresh toppings (you can order from their list of combinations or design your own) is available in this festive space. Jazz brunch on Sunday mornings and live entertainment on most weekends.

Bob the Chef

Map 6, G8. 604 Columbus Ave, Roxbury ℂ536-6204. Mass Ave Ⓣ. Inexpensive–moderate.

The best soul food in New England. Good chitterlings, black-eyed peas and collard greens, and don't miss the "glori-fried chicken," the house specialty. Live jazz on weekends.

Five Seasons

Map 2, E7. 669A Centre St, Jamaica Plain ℂ524-9016. Green St Ⓣ. Moderate.

Though this restaurant has a few chicken and fish entrees, it's their vegetarian options, such as millet-butternut croquettes in a spicy ginger and snow pea sauce, that truly distinguish it.

CAMBRIDGE/**AMERICAN AND NEW AMERICAN**

Cambridge Common

Map 7, C4. 1667 Massachusetts Ave ⊘547-1228. Harvard or Porter Ⓣ. Inexpensive.

Not quite a bar, not quite a restaurant; more a popular after-work place for young professionals, where everyone orders drinks with their dinner. The "Ultimate Nachos" are an appetizer, but could be a meal in themselves. A downstairs music venue, the *Lizard Lounge* (p.232), has decent rock and jazz acts almost nightly.

Charlie's Kitchen

Map 7, D5. 10 Eliot St ⊘452-9646. Harvard Ⓣ. Inexpensive.

Marvelously atmospheric townie hangout in the heart of Harvard Square, with red vinyl booths, sassy waitresses with beehive hairdos, and greasy diner food. The patrons here were smoking cigars before it was hip, and will be doing so long after the craze ends. Try the cheap but filling "Double Cheeseburger Special."

Henrietta's Table

Map 7, D5. 1 Bennett St, in the *Charles Hotel* ⊘661-5005. Harvard Ⓣ. Very expensive.

One of the only restaurants in Cambridge that serves classic New England fare. Rich entrées such as roasted duck or pork chops work well with side dishes of wilted greens or mashed potatoes – although some would say a trip to Henrietta's is wasted if it's not for their famous brunch, served every Sunday from noon to 3pm; it costs $32 per person but allows unlimited access to a cornucopia of the farm-fresh treats from around New England.

House of Blues

Map 7, D5. 96 Winthrop St ⊘491-2583. Harvard Ⓣ. Moderate.

This is the original *House of Blues*, and it has mediocre Southern food, like jambalay and ribs, served by a desultory waitstaff. The décor is carefully manufactured to effect a casual roadhouse look. The real reason to come here is for the big name blues performers at the upstairs venue (see p.233).

Mr & Mrs Bartley's Burger Cottage

Map 7, E5. 1246 Massachusetts Ave ℂ354-6559. Harvard Ⓣ. Inexpensive.

The walls are decorated with political humor and popular culture items; names of the dishes poke fun at celebrities of the hour; and the food is loaded with cholesterol. A burger and "frappe" (milkshake) here is a definite experience.

Nick's American Bar and Grill

Map 7, C3. 1688 Massachusetts Ave ℂ491-9882. Porter Ⓣ. Inexpensive.

From the mirrored walls to tacky lighting fixtures shaped like yule logs, *Nick's* is incredibly garish and hyper-American. It also has cheap drinks and a great double cheeseburger special.

Upstairs at the Pudding

Map 7, D5. 10 Holyoke St ℂ864-1933. Harvard Ⓣ. Very expensive.

The dining room was converted from what was originally the eating area for Harvard's ultra-elite Hasty Pudding Club, and the attitude lingers on. The food is excellent, though, falling somewhere in between New American and Old Colonial, and done with surprising verve – even old standards like a Porterhouse Steak. Advance reservations are essential.

RESTAURANTS: CAMBRIDGE

CAMBRIDGE/CHINESE AND VIETNAMESE
Pho Pasteur

Map 7, D5. 35 Dunster St, in the Garage ℂ864-4100. Harvard Ⓣ.
Budget.
This Harvard Square incarnation of the successful Chinatown
string of Vietnamese joints serves a variety of noodle soup
("pho"), filling and delicious, for prices that range around $5.
The spring rolls are also a treat.

CAMBRIDGE/FRENCH
Chez Henri

Map 7, C3. 1 Shepard St ℂ354-8980. Harvard Ⓣ. Very expensive.
Does paying more at a fancy restaurant actually mean you'll get
a vastly superior meal? At *Chez Henri*, the answer is an emphatic
yes. If you can get a table (no reservations, and the weekend
wait tops one hour even late at night), you'll enjoy what may
well be Cambridge's finest cuisine. Chef Paul O'Connell's
experiment in fusion brings Modern French together with
Cuban influences, best sampled in the light salads and excellent
Cuban crab cakes for starters, and the chicken asado to follow.

CAMBRIDGE/INDIAN
Café of India

Map 7, C5. 52a Brattle St ℂ661-0683. Harvard Ⓣ. Inexpensive.
This Indian spot stands out primarily because of its interior. Its
best dishes are tried-and-true Indian standards – chicken tikka,
saag paneer, and particularly light and delectable nan bread.

Tandoor House

Map 7, H5. 569 Massachusetts Ave ℂ661-9001. Central Ⓣ.
Inexpensive.
Consistently at the top of the list of Cambridge's many fine

Indian restaurants, *Tandoor* has excellent chicken saag and a
great mushroom bhaji. Definitely the best Indian outside
Harvard Square, perhaps in the whole city.

Trattoria Pulcinella

Map 7, A3. 147 Huron Ave ℂ491-6336. Porter Ⓣ. Expensive.
They manage to do a lot with the not-so-original Modern
Italian genre. Creative menu blends fresh ingredients and
prepares them with Continental flair. Unusually attentive
waitstaff manage to keep your water glass full without making
their presence intrusive.

CAMBRIDGE/MEXICAN AND LATIN AMERICAN
Boca Grande

Map 7, B2. 1728 Massachusetts Ave ℂ354-7400. Porter Ⓣ.
Budget.
Somewhere in between a restaurant and a taco stand, crowded
Boca vends delectable, if not quite authentic, Mexican fare at
low, low prices – no entrée costs more than $5. The
overstuffed burritos are excellent meals in themselves.

Border Cafe

Map 7, D5. 32 Church St ℂ864-6100. Harvard Ⓣ. Moderate.
Cambridge's most popular (and nearly only) Tex-Mex place.
It's pretty good, though not nearly so much as to justify the
massive crowds that form to wait for seats on weekend nights.
The margaritas are salty and strong, and the food so pungent
that you'll carry its aroma with you for hours afterward.

Iruna

Map 7, D5. 56 JFK St ℂ868-5633. Harvard Ⓣ. Inexpensive.

RESTAURANTS: CAMBRIDGE

213

Located in a diminutive, unassuming spot in an alley off JFK Street, *Iruna* is a fairly uncrowded with authentic Spanish fare. Lunch specials are incredibly cheap, including paella and a rich *arroz con pollo*; dinner is more expensive but equally good.

CAMBRIDGE/**THAI**

Siam Garden

Map 7, E5. 45½ Mt Auburn St ⓒ354-1718. Harvard Ⓣ. Inexpensive.

Tasty Thai fare in an atmosphere strenuously attempting to invoke images of the exotic East.

DRINKING

Despite – or perhaps because of – the lingering Puritan ethic that pervades Boston, people here tend to **drink** more than they do in the rest of the country, with the consequence that few other cities offer as many different kinds of places to get ploughed per capita in the whole of the United States.

The most prevalent of these is the Irish pub, of which there are high concentrations in the **West End** and downtown around **Quincy Market**. Among many unextraordinary watering holes, several are the real deal, and draw as many Irish expatriates as they do Irish-American locals. More upscale are the bars and lounges of **Back Bay**, along Newbury and Boylston streets, which offer attitude as much as anything else. The most popular bars in this area are actually often adjuncts of restaurants and hotels rather than stand-alone bars. The rest of the city's neighborhood bars, pick-up joints and yuppie hotspots are differentiated by their crowds: **Beacon Hill** tends to be older and a bit stuffy; **downtown**, mainly around Quincy Market and the Theater District, draws a healthy mix of tourists and locals; **Kenmore Square** and **Cambridge** are fairly student-oriented.

The **café** scene is not quite as diverse, but still offers a decent range of places to hang out. The toniest spots are again those that line the Back Bay's **Newbury Street**, where you pay as much for the fancy environs as for the quality of the coffee. Value is much better in the **North End**, whose Italian caffès have somewhat less expensive but generally excellent beverages and desserts. The most lively cafés, however, are across the river in **Cambridge**, unsurprisingly catering to the large student population.

BARS

Bars stop serving at 2am (at the latest), and most strictly enforce the drinking-age minimum of 21. Be prepared to show at least one form of valid identification, either a driver's license or passport. The one potential for after-hours drinking is **Chinatown**, where some restaurants will bring you a pot of beer if you ask for the "cold tea."

DOWNTOWN

Bell in Hand Tavern

Map 3, H2. 45 Union St ℡227-2098. State or Government Center Ⓣ.

The oldest continuously operating tavern in Boston draws a fairly exuberant mix of tourists and young professionals.

The Black Rose (Roisin Dubh)

Map 3, I3. 160 State St ℡742-2286. State T.

Down-home Irish pub specializing in imported beers from the Emerald Isle: Harp, Bass Ale, Murphy's, and especially Guinness all flow freely, and things get pretty boisterous on weekends.

Emily's

Map 3, F5. 48 Winter St ℡423-3649. Park Ⓣ.

Red velvet curtains and floor-to-ceiling mirrors give this
downtown spot as much style as any place in Back Bay –
without the accompanying attitude. It's mellow on weeknights;
on weekends, a DJ spins top-40 mixes to over-enthusiastic
dancers.

The Good Life

Map 3, G6. 28 Kingston St ©451-2622. Downtown Crossing Ⓣ.
This trendy bar (and restaurant) near Downtown Crossing has
generated quite a buzz since its recent opening, due as much to
its potent martinis as its 1970s decor.

Governor's Alley

Map 3, G4. 42 Province St ©426-3333. Park Ⓣ.
Although this casual weekday lunch and dinner spot is just off
the the Freedom Trail, it is happily far from the Trail's crowds.
Secure a wooden booth and enjoy big portions of Yankee pub
grub, from deli sandwiches to baked stuffed scrod and crab
cakes, or repair upstairs to the *Gargoyle Bar* – about as close to a
real *Cheers* as you'll find in Boston.

Green Dragon Tavern

Map 3, H2. 11 Marshall St ©367-0055. Government Center Ⓣ.
Another tavern that dates to the Colonial era, this was a
popular meeting place for Patriots during the Revolution. A
standard selection of tap beers, and a raw bar and full menu rife
with twee historical humor ("One if by land, two if by
seafood").

The Littlest Bar in Boston

Map 3, G4. 47 Province St ©523-9766. Downtown Crossing Ⓣ.
The tiny size of this place is part of the charm, as are the

BARS: DOWNTOWN

quality pints of Guinness and free music by bands crammed into an alcove – perhaps also the littlest performance space in Boston.

The Purple Shamrock

Map 3, H2. 1 Union St ✆227-2060. State or Government Center Ⓣ.
A lively watering hole that draws a broad cross-section of folks, the *Shamrock* has one of Boston's better straight singles scenes, which isn't saying much. It gets very crowded on weekends.

The Rack

Map 3, I2. 20 Clinton St ✆725-1051. Government Center Ⓣ.
Well-dressed twenty- and thirty-somethings convene at this pool hall to dine, smoke cigars, drink a bewildering variety of cocktails, and, of course, shoot a rack or two. While there are 35 pool tables and a fair share of wanna-be hustlers, about half the crowd shows up just to see-and-be-seen.

CHARLESTOWN

Warren Tavern

Map 5, C2. 2 Pleasant St at Main St ✆241-8142.
An atmospheric place to enjoy a drink, and the oldest standing structure in Charlestown. They also have a generous menu of good tavern food.

BEACON HILL AND THE WEST END

21st Amendment

Map 3, F4. 150 Bowdoin St ✆227-7100. Bowdoin Ⓣ.
This dimly lit, down-home watering hole is a favorite haunt of legislators from the adjacent State House and students from nearby Suffolk University.

The Bull & Finch Pub

Map 3, B6. 84 Beacon St ℗227-9605. Arlington Ⓣ.
If you don't already know, and if the conspicuous banners
outside don't tip you off, this is the bar that served as the
inspiration for the TV show *Cheers*. If you've gotta go, be
warned – it's packed with camera-toting tourists; the inside
bears little resemblance to the NBC set; the food, though
cutely named (eNORMous burgers), is pricey and
mediocre; and it's almost certain that nobody will know
your name.

Fours

166 Canal St ℗720-4455. North Station Ⓣ.
The classiest of the West End's sports bars, with an army of
TVs to broadcast games from around the globe, and
paraphernalia from the Celtics, Bruins, and other local teams.
Coach Rick Pitino has been spotted here after Celtic
victories.

Hill Tavern

Map 3. D2. 228 Cambridge St ℗742-6192. Bowdoin Ⓣ.
A classic yuppie bar, with suit-wearing folk consuming a lot of
pricey imported beers; there's often a long line to get in on
weekend nights.

Irish Embassy

234 Friend St ℗742-6618. North Station Ⓣ.
Up in the West End, this is one of the city's most authentic
Irish (rather than Irish-American) pubs, with the crowd to
match. Live Irish entertainment most nights, plus broadcasts of
Irish soccer games.

McGann's

197 Portland St ℅227-4059. North Station Ⓣ.
Similar to the nearby *Irish Embassy*, but with a more
upmarket, restauranty feel. There are British eats like
shepherd's pie and pan-seared calf's liver if you're in the
mood.

Sevens Ale House

Map 3, B3. 77 Charles St ℅523-9074. Charles Ⓣ.
While the tourists pack into the *Bull and Finch*, you can drop
by this cozy joint to get a taste of what a real Boston
neighborhood bar is like. Wide selection of draught beers plus
daily specials, solid food, darts, and a relaxed feel.

BACK BAY AND THE SOUTH END

Back Bay Brewing Company

Map 6, I4. 755 Boylston St ℅424-8300. Copley Ⓣ.
This is actually more a restaurant than bar – despite the name –
but the second-floor lounge is one of the city's most inviting
spaces to drink a tasty draught. See also p.199.

Biba

Map 6, L4. 272 Boylston St ℅426-5684. Arlington Ⓣ.
The first floor is a chic bar packed with Back Bay
executives; upstairs is home to *Biba's* trendy restaurant (see
p.200).

Bristol Lounge

Map 3, C8. 200 Boylston St ℅351-2053. Arlington ⓉⓉ.
A posh lobby-side lounge in the *Four Seasons Hotel* where the
desserts are as popular as the drinks.

The Claddagh

Map 6, J6. 113 Dartmouth St ℂ262-9874. Back Bay Ⓣ.
Big, two-room Irish-flavored bar and restaurant on the
northern cusp of the South End.

Dad's

Map 6, G4. 911 Boylston St ℂ296-3237. Hynes Ⓣ.
Dim lights and scantily clad barmaids make this a fairly un-
Back Bay drinking hole. Down that $6 martini and prepare to
cruise.

Daisy Buchanan's

Map 6, H4. 240A Newbury St ℂ247-8516. Copley Ⓣ.
A real-life beer commercial: young guys wearing baseball
caps, professional sports on TV, and a pervasive smell of
booze.

Division Sixteen

Map 6, F4. 955 Boylston St ℂ353-0870. Hynes Ⓣ.
The diminutive entrance hides a huge bar-restaurant in a
converted police livery. They have fine martinis – try the white
chocolate – a wide array of cigars, and huge portions of
delicious, if standard, American fare, like burgers and hand-cut
french fries.

Oak Bar

**Map 6, J4. 138 St. James Ave (in the *Fairmont Copley Plaza
Hotel*) ℂ267-5300. Copley Ⓣ.**
Rich wood paneling, high ceilings, swirling cigar smoke and
excellent martinis make this one of the more genteel Back Bay
spots to drink.

KENMORE SQUARE AND THE FENWAY

Bill's Bar

Map 6, C3. 7 Lansdowne St Ⓒ421-9678. Kenmore Ⓣ.

A fairly relaxed and homey Landsowne Street spot, with lots of beer, lots of TV, and occasional live music – in which case expect a cover charge of $5.

Boston Beer Works

Map 6, B3. 61 Brookline Ave Ⓒ536-2337. Kenmore Ⓣ.

A brewery located right by Fenway Park – and as such a popular place for the Red Sox faithful to drink before games and drown their sorrows after. Their signature ale is "Boston Red," but the seasonal brews are also worth a taste. Decent food too.

Copperfield's/Down Under

Map 6, A4. 98 Brookline Ave Ⓒ247-8605. Kenmore Ⓣ.

Two adjoining bars, with two names, though the difference is minimal. Both offer cheap drafts and pool, and are frequented by a raucous collegiate crowd. Cover of $5 on weekends to see loud bands.

CAMBRIDGE

The Cellar

Map 7, F5. 991 Massachusetts Ave Ⓒ876-2580. Harvard Ⓣ.

If *Cheers* were set in Cambridge, this would be it. Two floors, each with a bar, are pleasantly filled with a regular crowd of older students, faculty, and locals who imbibe finer beers and killer Long Island iced teas.

The Druid

Map 7, G2. 1357 Cambridge St Ⓒ497-0965. #69 bus.

Twee Inman Square bar featuring an old Celtic motif, with murals of druid priests and ever-present pints of Guinness. It's blessedly free of the college scene, too.

Finnegan's Wake

Map 7, A1. 2067 Massachusetts Ave ©576-2240. Porter Ⓣ.
Yet another Irish pub, this one with two floors: upstairs is rather sedate, where you can get food as well as beer; downstairs – "the Snug" – is loud, with darts, pool, occasional live music, and a rough-and-tumble crowd.

Grafton Street

Map 7, E5. 1280 Massachusetts Ave ©497-0400. Harvard Ⓣ.
A recent addition to the Harvard bar scene with authentic Irish atmosphere and a relaxing coziness. Higher prices draw an older, classier set to enjoy smooth drafts and equally good food.

Grendel's Den

Map 7, D5. 89 Winthrop St ©491-1160. Harvard Ⓣ.
A favorite spot of locals and grad students who drink ale in these dark, conspiratorial environs. The *Den* was recently saved by Harvard Law professor Larry Tribe, who lobbied against Puritan blue laws when a nearby church tried to get the place closed. Fantastic happy-hour special offers big plates of appetizers (fried calimari, nachos) for just $1.50 each.

Miracle of Science

Map 7, I5. 321 Massachusetts Ave ©868-2866. Central Ⓣ or #1 bus.
Suprisingly hip despite its status as an MIT hangout. There's a *noir* decor and a trendy crowd of well-dressed professionals; quite crowded on weekend nights.

BARS: CAMBRIDGE

Rialto

Map 7, D5. 1 Bennett St ✆661-5050. Harvard Ⓣ.

The bar adjunct to the chi-chi restaurant of the same name caters to a wealthy crowd that matches the plush atmosphere. Dress semi-formally and be prepared to pay big-time for the drinks and cocktails, which are excellent.

Shay's

Map 7, D5. 58 JFK St ✆354-9038. Harvard Ⓣ.

Very relaxed bar stands in contrast to the crowded, sweaty student-oriented sports bars of Harvard Square. It's all about wine and quality beer here, and you can relax amid a sedate, grad-student-oriented crowd.

CAFÉS

At many **cafés** in Boston and Cambridge, you can just as easily get an excellent full meal as you can a cup of coffee. Below are the best choices for casual hanging out, day or night; there are also plenty of cafés more suited for meals listed throughout the "Eating" chapter (p.179).

NORTH END

A Different Drummer Café

Map 4, C5. 135 Salem St ✆523-6263. Haymarket Ⓣ.

Have a grilled cheese sandwich with your coffee at this small, decidedly un-Italian café in the middle of the Italian North End.

Café Pompeii

Map 4, E5. 280 Hanover St ✆227-1562. Haymarket Ⓣ.

Though you may not enjoy the garish murals, mediocre pizza or marginal homemade ice cream, this is the only real late night joint in the North End, open till 4am.

Caffé Vittoria

Map 4, E5. 294 Hanover St ℗227-7606. Haymarket Ⓣ.
A Boston institution, the *Vittoria*'s atmospheric original section, with its dark wood paneling, pressed tin ceiling, murals of the Old Country, and Sinatra-blaring Wurlitzer, is vintage North End. There's also a cavernous downstairs grotto, and a no-smoking-allowed street-level addition, both equally fine for sipping one of their excellent cappucinos.

Caffé dello Sport

Map 4, F4. 308 Hanover St ℗523-5063. Haymarket Ⓣ.
A continuous stream of *Rai Uno* soccer matches broadcast from the ceiling-mounted TV sets, and make for an agreeable din and a very local crowd. Opens very early.

Caffé Paradiso

Map 4, E5. 255 Hanover St ℗742-1768. Haymarket Ⓣ.
Not much on atmosphere, but the pastries are hands-down the best in the North End.

BEACON HILL

Curious Liquids

Map 3, F4. 22B Beacon St ℗720-2836. Park Ⓣ.
What makes this one of Boston's premier cafés is not the specialty coffees (though the "midnight silk mocha" is outstanding), but the stylish setting, with two floors of comfy overstuffed chairs, as well as books and games for your amusement.

CAFÉS: BEACON HILL

Panificio

Map 3, B3. 144 Charles St ℡227-4340. Charles Ⓣ.
Damn fine cups o' Joe, fresh tasty pastries (*biscotti* is the standout), and some of the best home-baked bread in the city.

BACK BAY AND THE SOUTH END

29 Newbury

Map 6, L3. 29 Newbury St ℡536-0290. Arlington Ⓣ.
A small upscale café/bar and eatery with good, if pricey, salads and the like. In warmer weather, the self-consciously hip crowd migrates to the sidewalk terrace. Wear black, dangle sunglasses, enjoy the crème brûlée. Open until 1.30am.

Caffé Romano

Map 6, L3. 33 Newbury St ℡266-0770. Arlington Ⓣ.
Affordable pastries, sandwiches and coffee drinks on the first and toniest block of Newbury Street. Those who require a dose of aesthetics will be gratified by the rotating installations of contemporary paintings.

The Delux Café & Lounge

Map 6, K6. 100 Chandler St ℡338-5258. Back Bay Ⓣ.
The South End's cool spot of the moment is this retro hideaway *boîte*; the menu is loosely American fusion, but you basically go for the buzz.

Francesca's Espresso Bar

Map 6, K7. 565 Tremont St ℡482-9026. Back Bay Ⓣ.
This very contemporary café, situated next to Union Park, is a popular meeting spot and also a comfortable place to imbibe on one's own. There's a good selection of fresh baked goods.

The Other Side Cosmic Café

Map 6, F4. 407 Newbury St ⓒ536-9477. Hynes Ⓣ.

This ultra casual spot on "the other side" of Massachusetts Avenue, cut off from the trendy part of Newbury Street, offers gourmet sandwiches, "creative green salads," and fresh juices. Local band videos and short art films are shown Monday nights; there's a jazz/ambient brunch on weekends.

Trident Booksellers & Café

Map 6, G4. 338 Newbury St ⓒ267-8688. Copley Ⓣ.

A window seat at this bookstore café (see p.256), perennially popular with the cool student set, is the ideal vantage point from which to observe the flood of young passersby outside.

Twelve Church

Map 6, L6. 12 Church St ⓒ348-0012. Arlington Ⓣ.

Tiny neighborhood coffeehouse in Bay Village with a solid range of fresh baked goods.

SOUTHERN DISTRICTS

Black Crow Caffe

Map 2, E7. 2 Perkins St, Jamaica Plain. Green St Ⓣ.

Great coffee and lunch fare in a stylish space adorned with the work of local artists. A focal point of the offbeat JP scene.

CAMBRIDGE

1369 Coffeehouse

Map 7, G2. 757 Massachusetts Ave ⓒ576-4600. Central Ⓣ; 1369 Cambridge St ⓒ576-1369. #69 bus.

The *1369* mixes earnest thirty-something leftists with youthful hipsters in a relaxed environment; your best bets are the standard array of caffeinated beverages and particularly exquisite desserts.

Algiers

Map 7, D5. 40 Brattle St Ⓒ492-1557. Harvard Ⓣ.
A fashionably cramped North African café popular with the artsy set; while the food is so-so and the service slow, there are few more atmospheric spots in which to sip first-rate coffee.

Bookcellar Café

Map 7, A1. 1971 Massachusetts Ave Ⓒ864-9625. Porter Ⓣ.
Cozy and very relaxed basement coffeehouse. Furnishings consist primarily of a few folding chairs and old sofas on the concrete floor, but the coffee is good – and cheap – and you can peruse the wide range of magazines and used books while you imbibe.

Café Gato Rojo

Map 7, D5. Basement of Lehman Hall (Dudley House), Harvard Yard Ⓒ496-4658. Harvard Ⓣ.
One of the least-known of the Harvard Square coffeehouses, this place is hip without being overbearing, run by and for grad students, though the general public is welcome too.

Café Liberty

Map 7, H5. 497b Massachusetts Ave Ⓒ492-9900. Central Ⓣ.
Vogueish basement café frequented by Central Square locals and indie rock fans going to the nearby *Middle East* (see p.232). Unusually spacious and comfortable for a Cambridge coffeehouse, there's a supply of books to read and even computers with internet connections.

Café Pamplona

Map 7, E5. 12 Bow St. No phone. Harvard Ⓣ.

Eurochic trendiness hits its pretentious peak in this tiny basement café. The coffee is surprisingly average, the waitstaff a bit snooty. The patio seating on balmy evenings provides refuge from thick blue clouds of clove cigarette smoke.

Caffé Paradiso

Map 7, D5. 1 Eliot St ✆868-3240. Harvard Ⓣ.

This glossy Italian café strikes a bright, comfortable contrast to the atmospheric dimness of most Harvard Square coffeehouses. The coffee's good (and reasonably priced), the service is swift, and the setting free of pretension.

Loulou's Tealuxe

Map 7, D5. 0 Brattle St ✆441-0077. Harvard Ⓣ.

In a cool twist on the standard coffeehouse thing, what was once a curiosity shop called *Loulou's Lost and Found* has reincarnated itself as the only teahouse in Harvard Square. They stock over 100 varieties of tea, loose and by the cup. The place itself is smaller than a teacup, festooned with art deco pieces to create a stylish space where you can "skip the java in flavor of tea."

CAFÉS: CAMBRIDGE

NIGHTLIFE

n recent years Boston's **nightlife** has received something of a wake-up call, with stylish new **clubs** springing up in places, such as Downtown Crossing, that were previously ghost towns at night. Though Boston is by no means a 24-hour city, these spots have breathed fresh air into a scene that lived in the shadow of the city's so-called highbrow culture. Most of the clubs, however, tend to be geared toward – or at least chiefly attract – either monied students, suburbanites or the office, which doesn't make the after-hours scene inauthentic but can make it more than a trifle dull.

For listings of the city's best gay clubs, see p.249.

The **live music** scene plays perhaps a bigger part in the city's nightlife: many of the bars and clubs, especially around Kenmore Square and Harvard Square, are just as likely, if not more, to have a scruffy garage band playing for only a nominal cover as they are to have a slick DJ spinning house tunes. And Boston has spawned its share of enormous **rock** acts, from the ever-enduring Aerosmith – who are part-owners of *Mama Kin*, one of the city's better music clubs – to the Cars, pop ska-sters Mighty Mighty

Bosstones, hip-hop teen heartthrobs Marky Mark and the New Kids on the Block, and, more recently, a deluge of post-punk and indie groups such as the Pixies, Sebadoh and Folk Implosion. There is a bit less in the way of **jazz** and **blues**, but you can usually pretty much find something cheap and to your liking almost any day of the week.

For listings of classical music venues, see p.240.

For **club and music listings**, check Thursday's *Boston Globe* "Calendar" or the *Boston Phoenix*; alternately, the two best Web sites for Boston's entertainment scene – each with daily listings and search engines – are *http://www.boston.com* and *http://boston.sidewalk.com*.

LIVE MUSIC

The strength of Boston's **live music** is its diversity, and the city serves both as a stop on the world tours of superstar performers and a hotbed of small, experimental acts. Two of the biggest venues are a ways out of town: the *Great Woods Auditorium*, south of the city in Mansfield (✆508/339-2333), and the *Worcester Centrum*, an hour or so west in Worcester (✆508/798-8888). There are still, however, plenty of adequate places to see either name bands or obscure experimental acts; if all else fails, there's always street music at "The Pit" in Harvard Square (p.121), where you're bound to hear some free amateur acts whether you like it or not.

ROCK

FleetCenter

50 Causeway St ✆624-1750. North Station Ⓣ.
This arena, up in the West End, attracts a decent number of the

LIVE MUSIC: ROCK

big-name acts that pass through New England, usually at a hefty price.

Harborlights Pavilion

Map 2, J4. Fan Pier, Northern Ave ℭ374-9000. South Station Ⓣ.
During the summer, concerts by well-known performers from Mel Tormé to the Gipsy Kings are held here under a huge white tent at Boston Harbor's edge.

Lizard Lounge

Map 7, C4. 1667 Massachusetts Ave ℭ547-1228. Harvard or Porter Ⓣ.
The downstairs portion of the restaurant *Cambridge Common* (p.209), this place has rock and jazz acts pretty much nightly, for a fairly nominal cover charge.

Mama Kin

Map 6, C3. 36 Lansdowne St ℭ536-2100. Kenmore Ⓣ.
One of the cooler places on Lansdowne Street, due in no small part to the fact that Aerosmith is the co-owner (it's named after one of their songs). The bands here are usually local and rock-oriented. A small theater upstairs is sometimes used for club events, at other times for bona fide theatrical productions.

Middle East

Map 7, H5. 472 Massachusetts Ave ℭ864-3278, Central Ⓣ.
Local and regional progressive rock acts regularly stop in at this Cambridge institution. Downstairs hosts bigger acts, smaller acts ply their stuff in a tiny upstairs space. A third venue, the "Corner" has free acts every night, with belly dancing every Wednesday. The attached restaurant has decent – you guessed it – Middle Eastern food.

Orpheum Theater

Map 3, F5. Hamilton Place ⓒ482-0630. **Park** or **Downtown Crossing** Ⓣ.

Once an old-school movie house, this is now a venue for big-name music acts. The small space means you're closer to the action, but it sells out quickly and the cramped seating discourages dancing.

Paradise Rock Club

Map 6, C3. 967 Commonwealth Ave ⓒ562-8800. **Kenmore** Ⓣ.

Usually a dance club (see *M-LXXX*, p.237), but occasionally hosting mid-level music shows. Crazy decor and pricey drinks, but it rarely sells out and the acoustics are quite good.

T.T. the Bear's

Map 7, I5. 10 Brookline St ⓒ492-2327. **Central** Ⓣ.

A downmarket version of the *Middle East:*, with lower quality acts, but in a space that has a grittiness and intimacy its neighbor lacks. All kinds of bands appear, mostly punk, rock and electronica.

JAZZ, BLUES AND FOLK

The House of Blues

Map 7, D5. 96 Winthrop St, Cambridge ⓒ491-2583. **Harvard** Ⓣ.

The first in the corporate monolith spawned by the same evil geniuses who started the Hard Rock Cafe conglomerate. The faux-roadhouse decor and stiff, middle-class patrons are painfully inauthentic, but the house still features top blues acts.

Johnny D's Uptown

17 Holland St, Somerville ⓒ776-2004. **Davis** Ⓣ.

This is a totally mixed bag: acts include garage bands,

LIVE MUSIC: JAZZ, BLUES AND FOLK

progressive jazz sextets, traditional blues artists, and some uncategorizables.

Passim

Map 7, D5. 47 Palmer St, Harvard Square ℘492-7679. Harvard Ⓣ. Folkie hangout where Joan Baez and Suzanne Vega got their starts. There's also world music and spoken word performances.

Regattabar

Map 7, D5. 1 Bennett St ℘354-8238. Harvard Ⓣ. This place draws top jazz acts, though as its location in the swish *Charles Hotel* suggests, the atmosphere – and clientele – is decidedly sedate. Dress nicely and prepare to pay at least $10 cover.

Wally's Cafe

Map 3, G8. 427 Massachusetts Ave, Roxbury ℘424-1408. Massachusetts Ⓣ. This refreshingly unhewn bar hosts lively jazz and blues shows that draw a vibrant crowd. It gets pretty packed on weekends, but that's part of the experience. No cover.

Western Front

Map 7, G6. 343 Western Ave, Cambridge ℘492-7772. Central Ⓣ. The *Front* puts on rollicking jazz, blues, and reggae shows for a dance-crazy audience. Drinks are cheap, and the Jamaican food served on weekends is delectably authentic.

NIGHTCLUBS

Boston's **nightclubs** are mostly clustered in downtown's Theater District and around Kenmore Square, with a few prominent ones in Back Bay and the South End. Many of the Back Bay and South End venues are **gay clubs**, and are often the most happening in town. For a complete listing of these, see "Gay Boston," p.249; otherwise, a number of the clubs listed below have special gay nights. The music also changes almost nightly; to keep apprised of what's on, check the "Calendar" section in Thursday's *Boston Globe* or the listings in the weekly *Boston Phoenix*. **Cover charges** are generally in the $5–10 range, though sometimes there's no cover at all.

DOWNTOWN

Alley Cat Lounge

Map 3, E8. 1 Boylston Place ℂ351-2510. Boylston Ⓣ.
Dance to the sounds of the 1970s, 1980s and 1990s at this decidedly non-techno club, a perennial favorite with the collegiate set.

Avenue C

Map 3, E8. 25 Boylston Place ℂ423-3832. Boylston Ⓣ.
The musical menu at this small, casual (but no baseball caps or sneakers, please) club ranges from classic alternative to Top 40 and techno, depending on which DJ happens to be on duty.

Club Europa/Buzz

Map 3, E9. 67 Stuart St ℂ267-8969. Boylston Ⓣ.
On the edge of the Theater District, this is one of Boston's better dance clubs. Most of the action is on the third floor; the second tends to be louder and more crowded. On Saturday night the club becomes "Buzz," the most plugged-in gay disco in Boston.

NIGHTCLUBS: DOWNTOWN

The International

Map 3, J5. 184 High St ⓒ542-4747. State Ⓣ.

Snazzy club addition to an American bistro-style restaurant, in the quiet (by night) Financial District. Wednesdays are fairly reliable for "Smoke," which features live jazz.

Joy

Map 3, G6. 533 Washington St ⓒ424-7747. Downtown Crossing Ⓣ.

Located on the fringe of Downtown Crossing near a cluster of abandoned grand old theaters, this bi-level club packs in the international poseur crowd for its mix of techno music. Friday night is gay night.

The Roxy

Map 3, F7. 279 Tremont St ⓒ338-7699. Boylston Ⓣ.

Located in the former grand ballroom of the *Tremont House Hotel*, this Theater District club is a magnet for Eurotrash, who brave the most byzantine admission process – lots of doors and a mandatory inkstamp on the hand – and long queues even in winter to gyrate to the loud techno music.

BACK BAY AND THE SOUTH END

The Big Easy

Map 3, E8. One Boylston Place ⓒ351-7000. Boylston Ⓣ.

New bar and jazz club with a New Orleans theme; for the best people-watching go on a weeknight.

Mercury Bar

Map 3, E8. 116 Boylston St ⓒ482-7799. Boylston Ⓣ.

You'll hear everything from Eurohouse and classic dance hits to traditional Greek music at the small dance club tucked into the rear of this popular restaurant/bar (p.189).

KENMORE SQUARE AND THE FENWAY

Avalon

Map 6, C3. 15 Lansdowne St ☏262-2424. Kenmore Ⓣ.
Its 1500-person capacity makes it the biggest dance club in Boston, and any weekend night the place is positively jamming. The cavernous central floor is flanked on either side by bars. Sunday is gay night.

Axis

Map 6, C3. 13 Lansdowne St ☏262-2437. Kenmore Ⓣ.
Adjacent to *Avalon* (and at times physically connected to it) but with more techno and trance leanings.

Karma Club

Map 6, C3. 9 Lansdowne St ☏421-9595. Kenmore Ⓣ.
This multi-roomed, faux-hip dance *boîte* aspires with limited success to a futuristic Hindu temple decor. Jazz acts perform Tuesday; Thursday is gay night.

M-LXXX (M-80)

Map 6, A1. 967 Commonwealth Ave ☏562-8800. Boston University Ⓣ.
Boston's substantial pack of international students sweats here to redubbed mainstream hits and foreign disco beats. Everyone's dressed to the nines and able to afford the exorbitant prices for drinks; there's also a $10 cover. Open Wed, Fri and Sat.

Q

Map 6, C2. 575 Commonwealth Ave ☏267-7707. Kenmore Ⓣ.
New dance club in the heart of Kenmore Square, with International Night Fridays and Asian Night on Saturdays.

NIGHTCLUBS: KENMORE SQUARE AND THE FENWAY

The Spot

Map 6, D3. 1270 Boylston St ⒸV424-7747. Kenmore Ⓣ.

This club on the northern perimeter of the Fenway alternates deep house, gothic, funk, Top 40 and "club classics," among others. Two floors, a lounge, and a roof deck with a great view of downtown ensure plenty of space to groove and cruise. Friday is gay night.

THE PERFORMING ARTS AND FILM

Boston's **cultural scene** is famously vibrant, and many of the city's artistic institutions are second to none in the US. Foremost among these is the **Boston Symphony Orchestra**, which gave its first concert on October 22, 1881; indeed Boston is arguably at its best in the **classical music** department, and there are many smaller but internationally known chamber and choral music groups, from the Boston Symphony Chamber Players to the Handel & Hayden Society, to shore up its reputation. The **Boston Ballet** is also considered world-class, though it's probably best known in Boston itself for its annual holiday production of *The Nutcracker*.

The **theater** here is quite active too, even if it is a shadow of its 1920s heyday, when more than forty playhouses were crammed into the **Theater District**, south of Boston Common. Boston remains a try-out city for Broadway productions, however, and smaller companies have an increasingly high visibility, and it's a real treat to see a play or musical at one of the opulent old theaters such as the *Colonial* or *Emerson Majestic*. For current productions, check the listings in the *Boston Globe*'s Thursday "Calendar" section or the *Boston Phoenix*.

The **film** scene is dominated by the Sony conglomerate, which runs several theater multiplexes featuring major first-run movies. For foreign, independent, classic or cult cinema, you'll have to look mainly to other municipalities – Cambridge is best in this respect, though Brookline and Somerville have their own art-movie and re-run houses.

CLASSICAL MUSIC

Boston prides itself on being a sophisticated city of high culture, and nowhere does that show up more than in its proliferation of **orchestras and choral groups** – and the venues to house them. This is helped in no small part by the presence of three of the foremost music academies in the nation: the Peabody Conservatory, New England Conservatory and Berklee College of Music.

Berklee Performance Center

Map 6, F6. 136 Massachusetts Ave ℂ266-1400. Symphony Ⓣ.
Berklee College of Music's main performance center, known for its contemporary repertoire.

Isabella Stewart Gardner Museum

Map 6, A7. 280 The Fenway ℂ734-1369. Museum Ⓣ.
Chamber and classical concerts, including many debuts, are regularly held on weekends at 1.30pm in the museum's Tapestry Room. The $15 ticket price includes admission to the museum.

Chamber Music Ensembles

Boston has a formidable range of **chamber music** groups, many affiliated with the local universities. Except where otherwise noted, the companies perform at various venues; check the usual local listings sources for up-to-date concert information, or call the groups direct.

Alea III (©353-3340). A high-caliber chamber group affiliated with Boston University; they give concerts at the school's Tsai Performance Center.

Boston Baroque (©641-1310). One of the country's oldest baroque orchestras.

Boston Camerata (©262-2092). Regular performances of choral and chamber concerts, from medieval to early American, at various locations.

Boston Cecilia's (©232-4540). Choral group that performs at the New England Conservatory's Jordan Hall.

Boston Chamber Music Society (©422-0086). This society has members who are soloists of international renown; they perform at Jordan Hall and the Sanders Theater in Harvard.

Boston Musica Viva (©353-0556). This group gives five concerts per season, a double bill of a contemporary work with a classic, at BU's Tsai Performance Center.

Boston Symphony Chamber Players (©266-1492). The only permanent chamber group sponsored by a major symphony orchestra and made up of its members; they perform at Jordan Hall.

The Cantata Singers & Ensemble (©267-6502). Boston's premier choral group; they performs oratorios and the like at Jordan Hall.

Handel & Hayden Society (☎266-3605). Chamber and choral performances since 1815; they take place at Symphony Hall.

Pro Arte Chamber Orchestra (☎661-7067). Sunday afternoon concerts at Sanders Theater in Harvard.

Jordan Hall

Map 6, E6. 30 Gainsborough St ☎536-2412. Symphony Ⓣ.
The impressive concert hall of the New England Conservatory, just one block west from Symphony Hall, is the venue for many chamber music performances as well as those by the Boston Philharmonic (☎868-6696).

Museum of Fine Arts

Map 6, B7–C7. 465 Huntington Ave ☎369-3306 ext 4. Museum Ⓣ.
During the summer, the MFA's "Concerts in the Courtyard" take place each Wednesday at 7.30pm; a variety of indoor performances are also scheduled for the rest of the year.

Symphony Hall

Map 6, F6. 301 Massachusetts Ave ☎266-1492 or 1-800/274-8499. Symphony Ⓣ.
This is the regal, acoustically perfect venue for the Boston Symphony Orchestra; the famous Boston Pops concerts happen in May and June; in July and August the BSO retreats to Tanglewood, in the Berkshires.

Tsai Performance Center

Map 6, A1. 685 Commonwealth Ave ☎353-8724. Boston University Ⓣ.
Improbably tucked into Boston University's School of Management, this mid-sized hall is a frequent venue for

CLASSICAL MUSIC

chamber music performances, prominent lecturers, and plays, often affiliated with BU and either free or very inexpensive.

DANCE

The longest-running **dance** company in the city is **Boston Ballet** (℡695-6950), which has an unparalleled reputation in America, and beyond. The troupe performs at the Wang Center (p.245). For a more modern take, **Dance Umbrella** (℡492-7578) represents and promotes a number of contemporary acts, and most often performs at the Emerson Majestic (p.244).

THEATER

It's quite possible to pay dearly for a night at the theater. Tickets to the bigger shows range from $25–75 depending on the seat, and there is, of course, the potential of a pre- or post-theater meal (see p.186 for restaurants in the Theater District). Your best option is to pay a visit to **Bostix** (℡482-BTIX), a half-price, day-of-show ticket outlet and Ticketmaster center with three locations: Faneuil Hall (Tues–Sat 10am–6pm, Sun 11am–4pm), Copley Square (Mon–Sat 10am–6pm, Sun 11am–4pm), and the Holyoke Center in Harvard Square (same hours as Copley Square). The half-price tickets here go on sale at 11am, and only cash is accepted. You can also call **Ticketmaster** direct (℡931-2000), or call the individual theater direct or visit its box office in advance of the performance. The **smaller venues** tend to showcase more offbeat and affordable productions; shows can be under $10 – though you shouldn't bank on that.

DANCE, THEATER

American Repertory Theater at the Loeb Drama Center

Map 7, C5. 64 Brattle St ✆547-8300. Harvard Ⓣ.
Excellent theater near Harvard Square known for its stagings of plays by such postmodern heavyweights as Ionesco and Stoppard, as well as the works of Shaw, Wilde and other big names.

Charles Playhouse

Map 3, D8. 74 Warrenton St ✆426-6912. Boylston Ⓣ.
The *Charles* has two stages, one of which is more or less the permanent home of *Shear Madness*, a participatory, comic murder mystery that's now the longest-running non-musical in American theater. The other stage hosts somewhat edgier material.

Colonial Theatre

Map 3, E8. 106 Boylston St ✆426-9366. Boylston Ⓣ.
Built in 1900 and since refurbished, this is the glittering *grande dame* of Boston theaters, known primarily for its Broadway-scale productions.

Emerson Majestic Theatre

Map 3, E8. 219 Tremont St ✆578-8727. Boylston Ⓣ.
Emerson College, a communications and arts school, took stewardship of this 1903 Beaux-Arts beauty in 1983. A lavish venue, with its soaring Rococo ceiling and Neoclassical friezes, it hosts productions of the Emerson Stage company, the Boston Lyric Opera and Dance Umbrella.

Huntington Theatre Company

Map 6, F6. 264 Huntington Ave ✆266-0800. Symphony Ⓣ.
Productions here range from the classic to the contemporary,

but they are consistently well-staged at this small playhouse, the official theater of Boston University.

Shubert Theatre

Map 3, E9. 265 Tremont St *(*426-4520. Boylston ⓣ.
Stars from Sir Laurence Olivier to Kathleen Turner have played the Shubert at some point in their careers; today the 1680-seat theater accommodates mostly big Broadway-style productions.

Wang Center for the Performing Arts

Map 3, E9. 270 Tremont St *(*482-9393. Boylston ⓣ.
The biggest performance center in Boston opened in 1925 as the Metropolitan Theater, a movie house of palatial proportions – and its 3800 seats, Italian marble and gold leaf ornamentation, and crystal chandeliers all remain. The Boston Ballet (*(*695-6950) is headquartered here; when their season ends, Broadway musicals often take center stage.

Wilbur Theatre

Map 3, E8. 246 Tremont St *(*423-7440. Boylston ⓣ.
A Streetcar Named Desire, starring Marlon Brando and Jessica Tandy, debuted in this small Colonial Revival theater before going to Broadway, and the *Wilbur* is still working on getting back to that level. In winter, avoid the seats toward the back, where the loud, old heating system may leave you straining to hear.

SMALL VENUES

Boston Center for the Arts

Map 6, K7. 539 Tremont St *(*496-8400. Back Bay ⓣ.
Several theater troupes, many experimental, stage productions at the *BCA*, which incorporates a series of small venues on a single South End property. One of these is the Cyclorama

THEATER: MAJOR VENUES, SMALL VENUES

245

Building, originally built to house a monumental painting called *The Battle of Gettysburg*.

Institute of Contemporary Art Theatre

Map 6, G4. 955 Boylston St ⊘927-6620. Hynes Ⓣ.
Count on the unconventional at the theater of the ICA, Boston's leading venue for all things postmodern and cutting-edge.

Hasty Pudding Theatre

Map 7, D5. 12 Holyoke St ⊘496-8400. Harvard Ⓣ.
Harvard University's Hasty Pudding Theatricals troupe, one of the country's oldest, mounts one show per year (usually a musical comedy; Feb–March) at this theater, then hits the road, after which the Cambridge Theatre Company takes over.

Lyric Stage

Map 6, K4. 140 Clarendon St ⊘437-7172. Copley Ⓣ.
Both premieres and modern adapatations of classic and lesser-known American plays take place at this small theater in the big YWCA building.

Paramount Penthouse

Map 6, L5. 58 Berkeley St ⊘728-1388. Arlington Ⓣ.
Open City, one of Boston's newest theater companies, stages experimental productions at this small playhouse.

Terrace Room

Map 3, C9. *Park Plaza Hotel*, 64 Arlington St ⊘666-8888. Arlington Ⓣ.
An intimate space for appropriately small, but often very worthwhile productions, from the spoof *Forbidden Broadway* to Spanish *Café Teatro*, a Flamenco dance show.

FILM

In Boston, as in any other large American city, it's easy enough to catch general release films – and the usual listings sources carry all the details you need. If you're looking for out-of-the-ordinary film fare, however, you'll have to venture out a bit from the centre. Whatever you're going to see, admission will cost you about $7.50, though matinees before 6pm can be considerably cheaper. You can call ©333-FILM for automated film listings.

Brattle Theater

Map 7, D5. 40 Brattle St ©876-6837. Harvard Ⓣ.
A historic cinema that pleasantly looks its age. They have thematic presentations like "Film Noir," and the movies of Alfred Hitchcock, plus occasional author appearances and readings.

Coolidge Corner Moviehouse

Map 2, D5. 290 Harvard St, Brookline ©734-2500. Coolidge Corner Ⓣ.
Film buffs flock to this classic theater for foreign and independent movies. The interior has balconies and is adorned with Art Deco murals.

Harvard Film Archive

Map 7, D5. Carpenter Center, 24 Quincy St ©495-4700. Harvard Ⓣ.
They show a mixed bag of artsy, foreign and experimental films.

Kendall Square Cinema

Map 7, J3. One Kendall Square, Cambridge, ©494-9800. Kendall Ⓣ.
All the neon decoration, cramped seating, and small screens of

FILM

your average multiplex, but this also has the area's widest selection of first-rate foreign and independent films.

Museum of Fine Arts Theater

Map 6, B7–C7. 465 Huntington Ave Ⓒ**267-9300. Museum** Ⓣ. Offbeat art films and documentaries, mostly by locals, and often accompanied by lectures from the filmmaker.

Somerville Theatre

55 Davis Square, Somerville Ⓒ**625-5700. Davis** Ⓣ. Wacky home for camp and cult films, as well as a mixed bag of independent and foreign flicks and the occasional old classic. It's way out in more ways than one, too – past Cambridge – but it's always cheap; tickets are a mere $2.50.

Sony Nickelodeon

Map 6, A1. 606 Commonwealth Ave Ⓒ**424-1500. Kenmore** Ⓣ. Originally an art-flick place, now taken over by the Sony group, but it features the better of the first-run flicks.

GAY BOSTON

Boston is a fairly gay-friendly city and has a decent number of establishments that cater to a gay crowd. The center of the **gay scene** is the South End, a largely residential neighborhood whose gay businesses, mostly restaurants and cafés, are concentrated on a short stretch of Tremont Street above Union Park. Adjacent to the South End, on the other side of Arlington Street, is tiny **Bay Village**, which has most of the gay bars and clubs in the city. The **lesbian scene** is pretty well mixed-in with the gay scene, and there are very few exclusively lesbian bars or clubs.

Many of Boston's more popular clubs designate a few nights a week as gay nights. Of these, Sunday nights at *Avalon* is usually the most happening. See p.237 for that and other listings.

The best sources of club **information** are the weeklies *Boston Phoenix* and *Bay Windows*. The latter, along with *in newsweekly*, are Boston's two area **gay newspapers**; both are free, and can be found in certain bookstores, notably *Glad Day Bookstore*, 673 Boylston Street, and *We Think the World of You*, 540 Tremont Street. In *Glad Day*'s vestibule is a gay community bulletin board, with postings for apartment rentals, club happenings and so forth. Other **resources** for the gay community include the *Gay and Lesbian Helpline* (℃267-9001), a general information source; the *AIDS Action Hotline* (℃1-800/235-2331 or 536-7733); and *Fenway Community Health Center*, 7 Haviland St (℃267-0159), which offers HIV testing during weekdays.

In the summer, the Charles River Esplanade between Dartmouth and Fairfield streets, at the northern perimeter of Back Bay, is a popular spot for **cruising**. Footbridges lead from the end of both streets over Storrow Drive to a narrow urban beach alongside the river. You can't swim in the Charles, but it's more than acceptable to wear a bathing suit anyway. The area, however, can get a bit dodgy at night, as can the rest of the Esplanade.

GAY BARS AND CLUBS

Campus/ManRay

Map 7, I5. 21 Brookline St ℃864-0400. **Central** Ⓣ.
One massive space – with five bars and two dance floors – with two very different theme nights. Campus, on Thursday and Sunday nights, hosts a gay night that's relatively wholesome, with many J. Crew types and plenty of straights as well. The other five nights, the club becomes ManRay, a fetish-and-bondage fest, replete with leather and dominatrices galore.

Chaps

Map 6, L4. 100 Warrenton St ℃695-9500. **Arlington** Ⓣ.
The biggest and flashiest gay disco in town features a bar and lounge area (open from 1pm daily) and a cavernous dance room, with two additional bars. The sounds range from house

and techno to oldies and Latin; call ahead to make sure it's to your liking. Dancing starts at 10pm nightly, and the cover varies.

Club Café

Map 6, J6. 209 Columbus Ave ©536-0966. Back Bay Ⓣ.
A rather understated combination restaurant, video bar (Moonshine) and club, the latter of which attracts jazz acts, that caters to a gay South End crowd.

Jacque's

Map 3, E8. 79 Broadway ©338-7472. Boylston Ⓣ.
Priscilla, Queen of the Desert invades New England at this drag queen's dream where the action gets so hot they have to close at 2am. The scene: past-it divas lip-synching *I Love the Nightlife*, younger folks exploring their friskier sides and she-male prostitutes trying very hard to indulge them. Bring the family!

Jox/Luxor

Map 6, L4. 69 Church St ©423-6969. Arlington Ⓣ.
Jox is a plain gay sports bar that usually seems empty, whereas the affiliated *Luxor*, upstairs, is a popular gay video bar with a more modern look. A small lounge area to the right of the main barroom offers a respite from the cruising and boozing.

Napoleon Club

Map 6, L4. 52 Piedmont St ©338-7547. Arlington Ⓣ.
A dark, historic gay piano bar – one of the country's first – that's very much a neighborhood kind of place, where anti-show tune comments will not be much appreciated. The weekend disco upstairs attracts a younger crowd.

Ramrod

Map 6, E4. 1254 Boylston St ⓒ266-2986. Kenmore Ⓣ.
Not quite as hardcore as the name suggests, this Fenway meat market gets a pretty hungry leather-and-Levi's crowd. The last Saturday of each month is Fetish Night, and each Sunday is Mandance, a sweaty techno dancefest, with a $2 cover.

Wet Bar

Map 3, G5. 137 Pearl St ⓒ473-3827. Downtown Crossing Ⓣ.
One of the city's few lesbian-dominated spots, this Financial District lounge and dance club features Sunday tea dances.

SHOPPING

Though Boston has its share of chain stores and typical mall fare, there are plenty of unusual and funky places to **shop** here. You can find pretty much anything at any price, though the city is perhaps best known for its bookstores and designer boutiques. Best of all, Boston is an extremely pleasant place to shop, with high quality, unique stores clustered on atmospheric streets like **Charles Street**, in Beacon Hill, and **Newbury Street**, in Back Bay. The former is best known for its antique shops, while the latter is an eight-block stretch that starts off quite trendy and upmarket, then begins to cater to more of a student population as it moves west past Exeter Street. Record stores and novelty shops take over and continue the theme out to **Kenmore Square**. This span also has its fair share of big bookstores, but the best are clustered in and around **Harvard Square**, across the Charles River in Cambridge.

Otherwise, most of the action takes place in various downtown quarters, first and foremost at the **Faneuil Hall Marketplace**. This area has become more commercialized over the years, but there's still enough homespun boutiques, plus the many food stalls of **Quincy Market**, to make a trip here worthwhile. Otherwise, there's the somewhat downmarket **Downtown Crossing**, at Washington and

Summer streets, centered on **Filene's Basement**, a bargain-hunter's delight.

- -

**Stores are generally open 9.30am or 10am to 6pm
or 7pm Mon through Sat (sometimes later on
Tues/Wed) and Sun noon to 6pm.**

- -

Shopping Categories

ANTIQUES

The Firm of Scrooge and Marley

Map 3, B4. 65 Chestnut St. No phone. Charles Ⓣ.
This store claims "A collection of the unusual past and present," and it doesn't disappoint, with lots of old ceramic animals and chess sets with scary gargoyle pieces.

Judith Dowling Asian Art

Map 3, B3. 133 Charles St ℗523-5211. Charles Ⓣ.
A first-rate selection of Asian pieces from all periods, though at prices that encourage browsing rather than buying.

Marcoz Antiques

Map 6, I3. 177 Newbury St ℂ262-0780. Arlington ⓣ.

An atmospheric antiques boutique with French, English and American furniture and accessories.

S.W. Alan

Map 3, B3. 131 Charles St ℂ720-7808. Charles ⓣ.

Tucked away on the first floor of a recessed building, it's easy to miss, but inside is a varied array of Continental antiques – eighteenth- and nineteenth-century Italian and French – and nineteenth-century Chinese formal pieces.

Twentieth Century Limited

Map 3, B4. 73 Charles St ℂ742-1031. Charles ⓣ.

Antique pieces from the early part of the century, with a focus on American Art Deco and works from the Roaring Twenties.

BOOKSTORES

Boston has a history as a literary city, enhanced by its numerous universities and the authors and publishing houses that once called it home. This is well-reflected in the quality and diversity of **bookstores** to be found both in Boston and neighboring Cambridge.

NEW

Barnes & Noble

Map 3, H4. Downtown Crossing ℂ426-5502. Downtown Crossing ⓣ. **Map 6, C2.** 660 Beacon St ℂ267-8484. Kenmore ⓣ.

Two large outposts of the national bookstore chain, with a decent newsstand and a good selection of bargain books and calendars. The one on Beacon Street is topped off by the neon Citgo sign (p.94).

Harvard Book Store

Map 7, E5. 1120 Massachusetts Ave ⊘661-1515. Harvard ⊤.
Three huge rooms of new books upstairs, a basement for used volumes and remainders down. Academic and critical work in the humanities and social sciences dominate, with a healthy dose of fiction thrown in.

Trident Booksellers & Café

Map 6, G4. 338 Newbury St ⊘267-8688. Copley ⊤.
This somewhat New-Agey hangout is a preferred lair of Back Bay Gen-Xers. If the aroma of one too many essential oils doesn't deter you, buy an obscure magazine and pretend to read it over coffee in the café (see p.227).

Waterstone's

Map 6, I3. 26 Exeter St ⊘859-7300. Copley ⊤.
Quartered in the substantial 1884 brownstone temple of the "Working Union of Progressive Spiritualists," this may be the finest bookstore in the city. Check out the extensive travel section and café on the first floor (one flight up from the entrance); the third floor is a frequent venue for readings by prominent authors.

USED

Avenue Victor Hugo Bookshop

Map 6, G4. 339 Newbury St ⊘266-7746. Hynes ⊤.
One of Boston's best used bookstores, this upper Newbury fixture is the place to find recent editions at unbeatable prices. Vintage postcards and back issues of *Life* and other American magazines, dating from 1854 to the present, also fill the stacks.

Brattle Book Shop

Map 3, H4. 9 West St ⓒ542-0210. **Downtown Crossing** Ⓣ.
In these fairly dingy digs is one of the oldest antiquarian
bookstores in the country. Three levels, with a good selection
of yellowing travel guides on the second.

Bryn Mawr Books

Map 7, A3. 373 Huron Ave ⓒ661-1770. **Porter** Ⓣ.
This neighborhood bookstore vends used titles in a friendly,
relaxed Cambridge setting. Weather permitting, there are
sidewalk displays for pedestrian browsers.

House of Sarah

Map 7, G2. 1309 Cambridge St ⓒ547-3447. **Central** Ⓣ.
An Inman Square spot to browse used fiction and scholarly
work in eccentrically stylish environs. You may find a 25¢ copy
of Danielle Steele or some remaindered Foucault, and there are
often coffee and snacks, compliments of the proprietors.

Starr Bookshop

Map 7, E5. 29 Plympton St ⓒ547-6864. **Harvard** Ⓣ.
A bit like a library hit by a tornado, with books lying about or
spilling over desks and tables, but if you're patient – or ask for
help – you can find great discounts on literature and art
criticism.

TRAVEL

Boston Globe Store

Map 3, H4. 1 School St ⓒ367-4000. **Park** Ⓣ.
Small shop in the historic Old Corner Bookstore building with
New England travel guidebooks, Internet access and lots of
stuff emblazoned with the *Boston Globe* logo.

BOOKSTORES: USED, TRAVEL

Globe Corner Bookstore

Map 6, C2. 500 Boylston St ⊘859-8008. Kenmore Ⓣ.
Map 7, D5. 28 Church St ⊘497-6277. Harvard Ⓣ.

These travel specialists are well-stocked with maps, travel literature and guidebooks, with an especially strong New England section.

Willowbee & Kent

Map 6, D2. 519 Boylston St ⊘437-6700. Kenmore Ⓣ.

The first floor of this roomy store has a good range of travel guidebooks and gear; the second is given over to a travel agency.

GAY AND LESBIAN

Glad Day Bookshop

Map 6, C2. 673 Boylston St ⊘267-3010. Kenmore Ⓣ.

This second-floor gay bookstore is easily recognized from the sidewalk by the big rainbow flag draped from the inside window. A good selection of reasonably-priced books, cards and pornography and a vast community bulletin board at the entrance.

We Think the World of You

Map 6, K7. 540 Tremont St ⊘423-1965. Back Bay Ⓣ.

With its cool music and good selection of international magazines, this bright, upscale South End gay bookstore invites lingering.

SPECIALTY

Grolier Poetry Bookstore

Map 7, E5. 6 Plympton St ⊘547-4648. Harvard Ⓣ.

Diminutive store specializing in in-print poetry. With 14,000 volumes of verse, it has gained an international following among poets and their fans, and it hosts frequent readings.

Lucy Parsons Center

Map 7, H5. 3 Central Square ©497-9934. Central Ⓣ.

The radical left lives on in this shrine to socialism, with a particular bent toward women's issues, labor issues and radical economics. They also have plenty of free pamphlets on local demonstrations, and occasional readings and lectures.

New Words

Map 7, H5. 186 Hampshire St ©876-5310. Central Ⓣ.

Well-organized feminist bookstore with tons of books on history criticism, lesbian studies, and the like. It also serves as a community center for women's issues and feminist events.

Nini's Corner/Out of Town News

Map 7, D5. Harvard Square. Harvard Ⓣ.

These two good, old-fashioned newsstands lie directly across from each other in the heart of Harvard Square. Few published magazines cannot be found at one of these two spots.

CLOTHES

DESIGNER STORES

Alan Bilzerian

Map 6, K3. 34 Newbury St ©536-1001. Arlington Ⓣ.

International *haute couture* from Jean-Paul Gaultier and Comme des Garçons alongside the owner's own label. Menswear and accessories occupy the first floor and womenswear the second; clubwear roosts in a small basement section.

Allston Beat

Map 6, F4. 348 Newbury St ℂ421-9555. Copley Ⓣ.
This small but dense fashion den may exceed the vinyl per
square foot limit – cutting-edge designer wear, ogled by
teenagers too young to afford it and others too old to wear it.

Culture Shock

Map 6, G4. 286 Newbury St, ℂ859-7508. Copley Ⓣ.
Even if you're not in the market for local designer Patrick
Petty's trendy creations, nip into his suave shop to browse
around and pick up flyers on club happenings.

Gypsy Moon

Map 7, B2. 1780 Massachusetts Ave ℂ876-7095. Porter Ⓣ.
For the well-dressed Wiccan, eccentric women's wear sold by a
staff that can advise on a dress for your next coven meeting.

Jet Screamer

Map 7, B2. 1735 Massachusetts Ave ℂ661-8826. Porter Ⓣ.
Aggressively hip shoe boutique aimed mostly at women, with
everything from formal leather shoes to glittery silver platforms.

J. Press

Map 7, D5. 82 Mt Auburn St ℂ547-9886. Harvard Ⓣ.
Old Harvard lives on in J. Press' sober collection of men's suits;
rates are mid-level (from $400–1000 per suit) for their high
quality and the store's genteel clientele.

Louis, Boston

Map 6, H4. 234 Berkeley St ℂ956-6100. Arlington Ⓣ.
Occupying a stately, freestanding building from 1863 that once

housed Boston's Museum of Natural History (which became the Museum of Science), this is Boston's classiest and most expensive clothes emporium. Though mostly geared toward men, the top floor is reserved for designer womenswear.

Riccardi

Map 6, I3. 116 Newbury St ℂ266-3158. Arlington Ⓣ
The hippest designer *schmatta* shop in Boston could hold its own in Paris or New York. A few of the labels on parade are Dolce & Gabbana, Romeo Gigli and Jean-Paul Gaultier.

Suzanne

Map 6, J3. 81 Newbury St ℂ266-4146. Arlington Ⓣ.
Women's special occasion apparel by leading international designers such as Montana and Thierry Mugler.

CHAIN STORES

Burberrys

Map 6, L3. 2 Newbury St ℂ236-1000. Arlington Ⓣ.
The famously conservative British clothier seems right at home in its four-story Newbury Street digs, across from the *Ritz-Carlton Hotel.*

Patagonia

Map 6, G4. 346 Newbury St ℂ424-1776. Copley Ⓣ.
Patagonia invented the soft, synthetic fleece called "Synchilla," and there's still no better way to fend off a Boston winter than in a jacket or vest lined with the colorful stuff.

USED AND THRIFT

The Closet Upstairs

Map 6, H3. 223 Newbury St ℂ267-5757. Copley Ⓣ.

CLOTHES: CHAIN STORES

The most atmospheric of Newbury Street's numerous retro clothes stores, this oversized second-floor closet is stuffed with everything from silly hats to designer shoes.

Dollar-a-Pound

Map 7, J3. 200 Broadway ©876-1122. Kendall ⓣ.
Warehouse full of bins crammed full of used togs. If you have the time to sift through the leftovers of twentieth-century fashion, you'll happen upon some great bargains – all at the universal rate of a buck for every pound of clothing.

Mass Army & Navy Store

Map 6, C2. 895 Boylston St ©267-1559. Boston University ⓣ.
You can stock up on camouflage duds and combat boots at this military surplus store, and there is also a good and inexpensive range of (mostly men's) pants, shirts and shoes worth inspecting.

CRAFTS

Artsmart

Map 3, K6. 272 Congress St ©695-0151. South Station ⓣ.
Everyday objects made beautiful. You can buy a pink neon toothbrush holder or a chair in the shape of a shoe so even dental hygiene and at-home loafing have an artistic flair.

Beadworks

Map 6, G4. 349 Newbury St ©247-7227. Hynes ⓣ.
With so many kinds of beads, it's a good thing sales staff can assist you in creating a "distinctly personal adornment." Buttons too.

Rugg Road Paper Co

Map 3, B3. 105 Charles St ⌀742-0002. Charles Ⓣ.

They've got fancy paper products of all kinds, including lovely cards, stationery and wrapping paper.

Simon Pearce

Map 6, J3. 115 Newbury St ⌀450-8388. Arlington Ⓣ.

Hand-blown glassware from Irish-born, Vermont-based craftsman.

FOOD AND DRINK

BAKERIES

Bova's Bakery

Map 4, D4. 76 Prince St ⌀523-5601. Haymarket Ⓣ.

The North End's all-night bakery, with plain and chocolate cannollis, oven-fresh cakes and whoopie pies is also famously cheap, with most items around $5.

LMNOP Bakery

Map 3, C9. 79 Park Plaza ⌀338-7500. Arlington Ⓣ.

Purveyor of bread to the adjacent restaurant, this hideaway is the best gourmet bakery in Boston. Besides those breads, pastries and cookies, they also have great sandwiches and pasta specials at lunchtime.

Mike's Pastry

Map 4, E5. 300 Hanover St ⌀742-3050. Haymarket Ⓣ.

The famed North End bakery is one part Italian, two parts American, meaning in addition to cannolli and tiramisu, you'll find counters-full of brownies and cookies. The gelato, only served in summer, is not to be missed.

FOOD AND DRINK: BAKERIES

Panini

Map 7, E2. 406 Washington St ℂ666-2770. #86 bus.

Baguettes and bruschetta, desserts and danishes – *Panini* offers a diverse array of baked goods, all created on the premises. It's hard to find a place to sit on weekends.

Rosie's Bakery

Map 7, G2. 243 Cambridge St ℂ491-4988. #69 bus.

This pastel-link bakery features the richest, most decadent desserts in Cambridge. Their specialty is a fudge brownie called the "chocolate orgasm," though the less raunchily named lemon squares are just as good.

GOURMET FOOD AND WINE SHOPS

Baci's

Map 6, F4. 61 Massachusetts Ave ℂ266-2200. Hynes Ⓣ.

Gourmet food shop with prepared pastas, salads, pizzas by the slice and desserts, plus a nice selection of wines.

Barsamian's

Map 7, F5. 1030 Massachusetts Ave ℂ661-9300. Harvard or Central Ⓣ.

Fresh, gourmet meats, cheeses, coffee and bread plus a great range of desserts, including the best tart in Cambridge.

Monica's Salumeria

Map 4, C5. 130 Salem St ℂ742-4101. Haymarket Ⓣ.

Lots of imported Italian cheeses, cooked meats, cookies and pastas.

Polcari's Coffee

Map 4, B6. 105 Salem St ℂ227-0786. Haymarket Ⓣ.

Old and fusty, but brimming with coffees and every spice you could think of. Worth going inside just for the aroma.

Savenor's

Map 3, B3. 160 Charles St ©723-6328. Charles Ⓣ.
Known for its meats, this small gourmet food shop in Beacon Hill also has a better-than-average produce selection, in addition to prepared foods – ideal for taking to the nearby Charles River Esplanade for an impromptu picnic.

See Sun Co

Map 3, G7. 19 Harrison St ©426-0954. Chinatown Ⓣ.
The most accessible of Chinatown's markets, they've got all the basics, like huge bags of rice and a dizzying range of soy sauces; you can also get more exotic delicacies like duck's feet.

V. Cirace & Sons

Map 4, D6. 173 North St ©227-3193. North Station Ⓣ.
A great liquor store, with the expected range of Italian wines –it's in the North End, after all – and much more.

HEALTH FOOD

Bread & Circus

Map 6, F6. 15 Westland Ave ©375-1010. Symphony Ⓣ.
The Boston branch of this New England wholefoods chain, near Symphony Hall, has all the alternative foodstuffs you'd expect, plus one of the best salad bars in town.

Nature Food Centers

Map 6, I4. 545 Boylston St ©536-1226. Copley Ⓣ.
If you're looking for vitamin-enriched fruit juices, organic

FOOD AND DRINK: HEALTH SHOPS

produce, and other healthful items, this small store in Copley Square is bound to have it.

GALLERIES

Many of Boston's **art galleries** are on Newbury Street, and there are dozens of them. You may not be in the market for fine art, but the galleries are generally browser-friendly. South Street, in downtown's so-called Leather District, has more contemporary art galleries.

Alianza

Map 6, K3. 154 Newbury St Ⓒ262-2385. Arlington Ⓣ.
An artsy American crafts gallery where the strong suits are creative ceramics, glass work and jewelry, with funky sculptural clocks and picture frames as well.

American Animated Classics

Map 6, K3. 154 Newbury St Ⓒ262-2385. Arlington Ⓣ.
An animation art gallery specializing in original production and limited edition reels from biggies like Disney and Warner Bros.

Arden Gallery

Map 6, K3. 129 Newbury St Ⓒ247-0610. Arlington Ⓣ.
The focus is on abstractionist contemporary paintings, vivid examples of which are displayed in the oversized second-story bowfront window.

Galerie Europeenne

Map 6, K3. 123 Newbury St Ⓒ859-7062. Arlington Ⓣ.

Always-interesting works often include classic European landscapes interpreted with evocative, contemporary touches.

Gallery NAGA

Map 6, L3. 67 Newbury St ℂ267-9060. Arlington Ⓣ.

Contemporary painting, sculpture, studio furniture and photography from Boston and New England artists, located in the Gothic Revival Church of the Covenant.

International Poster Gallery

Map 6, J3. 205 Newbury St ℂ375-0076. Copley Ⓣ.

This browser-friendly gallery has more than 6000 posters from 1895 through World War II.

Mario Diacono Gallery

Map 3, I8. 207 South St ℂ350-3054. South Station Ⓣ.

Artist-specific shows, of a contemporary nature, on a rotating basis. Call ahead; the gallery has unpredictable hours.

The Society of Arts and Crafts

Map 6, K3. 175 Newbury St ℂ266-1810. Arlington Ⓣ.

The oldest non-profit crafts group in America has two floors here. The first is its commercial outpost, with a wide range of ceramics, glass and jewelry. The second floor is reserved for themed (and free) special exhibitions.

MALLS AND DEPARTMENT STORES

MALLS

CambridgeSide Galleria

Map 7, L1. 100 Cambridgeside Place ℂ621-8666. Kendall Ⓣ.

Not too different from any other American shopping mall, though somewhat larger than most. The haze of neon and packs of hairsprayed teens can be depressing, but there's no similarly dense conglomeration of all kinds of shops in Cambridge.

Copley Place

Map 6, I5. 100 Huntington Ave ©375-4400. Copley Ⓣ.
This ambitious, upscale office-retail-residential complex features more than 100 stores and an 11-screen multiplex. The best of the shops are a *Rizzoli* bookshop, a *Nieman Marcus* department store, the gift shop for the Museum of Fine Arts, and the Artful Hand Gallery, representing solely American artists; the rest is pretty generic.

Faneuil Hall Marketplace

Map 3, I2. Faneuil Hall ©338-2323. Government Center Ⓣ
The city's most famous market, with a hundred or so shops, plus next door's Quincy Market. It's a bit tourist-oriented, but still worth a trip.

The Heritage on the Garden

Map 3, C8. Corner of Arlington and Boylston sts ©423-0002. Arlington Ⓣ.
Not so much a mall as a very upscale mixed-use complex across from the Public Garden that consists of condos, restaurants and boutiques. The latter include Arche Shoes, Escada, Sonia Rykiel and St John boutiques, Villeroy Boch and Hermés.

The Shops at Prudential Center

Map 6, H5. 800 Boylston St ©267-1002. Prudential Ⓣ.
This is a fairly new conglomeration of a hundred or so mid-

MALLS AND DEPARTMENT STORES

market shops, heavily patronized by local residents and conventioneers from the adjacent Hynes Convention Center who seem to genuinely enjoy buying T-shirts and ties from the center-atrium pushcarts.

DEPARTMENT STORES

Filene's

Map 3, G5. 426 Washington St ℂ357-2100. Downtown Crossing Ⓣ.
The merchandise inside downtown Boston's oldest department store is standard issue; the stunning 1912 Beaux Arts façade is not. You'll have better luck downstairs, in *Filene's Basement* (below).

Filene's Basement

Map 3, G5. 426 Washington St ℂ542-2011. Downtown Crossing Ⓣ.
Established in 1908, *Filene's Basement* is now a separate business from *Filene's*, and although it has become a chain, nothing beats the original. The discounted merchandise comes not only from *Filene's*, but other big-name department stores and a few Boston boutiques. The markdown system works like this: after 14 days, merchandise is discounted 25 percent, after 21 days, 50 percent and after 28 days, 75 percent. Anything that lasts more than 35 days goes to charity. Be warned: dressing rooms are communal.

The Harvard Coop

Map 7, D5. 1400 Massachusetts Ave ℂ499-2000. Harvard Ⓣ.
Harvard's local department store, with a wide selection of fairly expensive insignia clothing and the like.

Loehmann's

Map 3, G5. 385 Washington St ℂ338-7177. Downtown Crossing Ⓣ.
Well-known chain that specializes in dramatically discounted designer-label womenswear.

MALLS AND DEPARTMENT STORES

Lord & Taylor

Map 6, I4. 760 Boylston St ℂ262-6000. Copley Ⓣ.
This human-scale department store is an excellent place to stock up on high-end basics, from sweaters and suits to jewelry and cosmetics.

Macy's East

Map 3, G5. 450 Washington St ℂ357-3000. Downtown Crossing Ⓣ.
Much the generic urban department store, with all the basics covered, including a better-than-average cosmetics section and a men's department that outshines that of *Filene's* next door.

Neiman Marcus

Map 6, I5. 5 Copley Place ℂ536-3660. Copley Ⓣ.
Part of a Texan chain, *Neiman's* is the most luxurious of Boston's department stores, with prices to match. Three levels, with an impressive menswear collection on the first.

MUSIC

The best places for new and used **music** in Boston are on Newbury Street in Back Bay, around Massachusetts Avenue near Kenmore Square and up in Harvard Square.

NEW

Boston Beat

Map 6, G3. 297 Newbury St ℂ247-2428. Hynes Ⓣ.
A second-floor store stocking lots of independent dance and techno labels, along with a small selection of club clothes.

Newbury Comics

Map 6, F4. 332 Newbury St ℂ236-4930. Hynes Ⓣ.

Boston's biggest alternative record store carries lots of
independent labels you won't find at the national chains, and a
substantial array of vinyl 12-inches and singles, as well as
posters, 'zines, and kitschy T-shirts. It's also a good place to
pick up flyers on local club happenings.

Nuggets

Map 6, B2. 486 Commonwealth Ave ©536-0679. Kenmore Ⓣ.
American jazz, rock and R&B are the strong suits at this
venerable new and used record store.

Satellite

Map 6, F5. 49 Massachusetts Ave ©536-5482. Hynes Ⓣ.
This storefront hideaway has a great selection of imported
techno and trance, in both CD and vinyl format.

Tower Records

Map 6, F4. 360 Newbury St ©247-5900. Hynes Ⓣ.
Typically vast representative of this music superstore chain,
with a standard selection of popular music, as well as jazz,
classical, world beat, and the like. You can listen to the music
before you buy. The building itself started out as an early
1900s warehouse, but was given an overhaul by architect Frank
Gehry in 1989.

USED/VINTAGE

Cheapo

Map 7, H5. 645 Massachusetts Ave ©354-4455. Central Ⓣ.
Narrow, two-story Cambridge shop stuffed with bargains on
just about every genre of used music. Slogging through the
dense collection will produce considerable discoveries.

MUSIC: USED/VINTAGE

Disc Diggers

401 Highland Ave, Somerville ℂ776-7560. Davis Ⓣ.
The largest selection of used CDs in New England, though
higher in quantity than quality. Forgotten albums by one-hit
wonders abound.

Planet Records

Map 6, B2. 536 Commonwealth Ave ℂ353-0693. Kenmore Ⓣ.
To buy that old Duran Duran or Styx LP missing from your
collection – or to sell one you've listened to a tad too much –
head to this second-floor, secondhand music shop in Kenmore
Square. Buy and sells CDs, too.

Pipeline

Map 7, D5. 1110 Massachusetts Ave ℂ661-6369. Harvard Ⓣ.
This alluringly bizarre store defies categorization. Mainly used
CDs and vinyl, particularly deep on indie and imports. Also
new music, kitsch Americana, and videos of the Russ Meyer
film ilk.

Skippy White's

Map 7, H5. 538 Massachusetts Ave ℂ491-3335. Central Ⓣ.
Excellent collection of jazz, blues, R&B, gospel, funk, P-funk,
funkadelic, and hip-hop. Hum a few bars and the salesfolk will
guide you to your soul's content.

Stereo Jack's

Map 7, B2. 1686 Massachusetts Ave ℂ497-9447. Porter Ⓣ.
Jazz and blues specialists, mostly used, but with some new stuff
too. CDs, tapes, and vinyl.

Twisted Village

Map 7, D5. 12 Eliot St ℂ354-6898. Harvard Ⓣ.

A really weird mix of fringe styles, among them avant-garde, beat, spoken word and psychedelic rock.

SPECIALTY SHOPS

Black Ink

Map 3, B3. 101 Charles St ℂ723-3883. Charles Ⓣ.

Eclectic assortment of things you don't really need but are cool anyway: rubber stamps, a smattering of clothes, campy refrigerator magnets, and a panoply of Tintin paraphernalia.

Justin Tyme Emporium

Map 7, G6. 91 River St ℂ491-1088. Central Ⓣ.

Justin's is all about pop culture artifacts, featuring boffo American detritus like lava lamps, Donny and Marie Osmond pin-ups, and campy T-shirts with iron-ons.

Kakadu

Map 6, J3. 237 Newbury St ℂ266-9707. Arlington Ⓣ.

This uplifting shop offers brightly painted wooden houseware items from Israel and animal-themed ceramics from South Africa.

Koo de Kir

Map 3, B4. 34 Charles St, ℂ723-8111. Charles Ⓣ.

Their motto, "Ars longa, vita brevis," reflects their sales philosophy – to make even the most everyday objects artistic and beautiful. For a pretty penny, you can buy those objects here.

Leavitt and Pierce

Map 7, D5. 1316 Massachusetts Ave Ⓒ547-0576. Harvard Ⓣ.
Old-school tobacconists that have been around almost as long as Harvard. An outstanding selection of cigars, imported cigarettes and smoking paraphernalia (lighters, rolling papers, ashtrays), plus an upstairs smoking loft right out of the carefree past.

The London Harness Company

Map 3, H5. 60 Franklin St Ⓒ543-9234. Downtown Crossing Ⓣ.
Chiefly known for its high quality luggage goods, this atmospheric shop reeks of traditional Boston – indeed, Ben Franklin used to shop here. They also vend a wide array of items like chess sets, clocks, candlesticks and inlaid decorative boxes.

Loulou's Lost & Found

Map 6, I3. 121 Newbury St Ⓒ859-8593. Arlington Ⓣ.
They say Loulou scours the globe in search of such essentials as tableware embossed with French cruise ship logos and silverware from long-gone five-star restaurants. A fine place to indulge your inner Martha Stewart.

Marquis de Sade Emporium

Map 6, L5. 73 Berkeley St Ⓒ426-2120. Back Bay Ⓣ.
Proffering a wide range of leather items and hardcore sexual paraphernalia, this South End shop leaves little to the imagination.

Matsu

Map 6, H3. 237 Newbury St Ⓒ266-9707. Copley Ⓣ.
A hip little shop featuring a medium-sized range of sleek

Japanese knick-knacks (desk clocks, stationery, funky pens) and contemporary home decor items.

Million-Year Picnic

Map 7, D5. 99 Mt Auburn St ℂ492-6763. Harvard Ⓣ.

For the comic obsessive. Japanese anime and Superman, Tank Girl and Dilbert. Stronger on current stuff than old material. The staff has encyclopedic knowledge, and is tolerant of browsers.

Sherman's

Map 3, G5. 11 Bromfield St ℂ482-9610. Downtown Crossing Ⓣ.

Forget those overpriced travel boutiques in the malls; this cavernous Downtown Crossing emporium stocks not only an impressive range of luggage but just about every travel gadget imaginable.

Union Shop

Map 3, D8. 356 Boylston St ℂ536-5651. Arlington Ⓣ.

The retail outpost of this long-established private social services organization features quality handmade household knick-knacks, toys, wrapping paper, stationery and a range of antiques.

SPORTS AND OUT-DOOR ACTIVITIES

Bostonians have an acute love-hate relationship with their professional **sports** teams, obsessing over the four major franchises – baseball's Red Sox, football's Patriots, basketball's Celtics, and hockey's Bruins – with evangelical fervor. After years of watching their teams narrowly miss championship bids, hope is extended cautiously here. Despite this pessimism, Boston's sports fans have an admirable tenacity, following their teams closely through good seasons and bad; indeed, supporters seem to love bemoaning their teams' woes nearly as much as they do celebrating their victories. This lively, vocal fan base makes attending a game a great way to get a feel for the city, as do Boston's fine sports venues. While the Patriots' Foxboro Stadium is located out of town and has little to recommend it, the new FleetCenter, where the Celtics and Bruins play, makes up in convenience what the classic old Boston Garden possessed in history, and for fans of baseball, there is no more essential pilgrimage than to the Red Sox' idiosyncratic Fenway Park.

> If you're a fan of an opposing team going to a
> game to root against Boston, be warned: you're in
> store for censure – and perhaps even violence –
> from the local faithful.

Boston isn't a city where **participatory sports** particularly thrive, due mostly to the area's often dreary weather. There are, however, more than a number of good areas for jogging, biking, rollerblading and the like. The **Metropolitan District Commisson (MDC)**, 20 Somerset St (©727-9650), oversees most facilities.

BASEBALL

The Boston **Red Sox** have tormented fans with an uncanny ability to choke late in the season: they haven't won a World Series since 1918, although they've come extremely close on several occasions (see p.96). In recent years they have been up and down, making the playoffs as recently as 1995, though they've lost some of the faithful·by not resigning their longtime star pitcher **Roger Clemens**. They somewhat overcompensated in winter 1997 by giving Cy Young winner Pedro Martinez, a new acquisition, the largest contract in baseball history – reportedly $75 million over six years.

Even when the team isn't performing well, it's worth going to a game just to see **Fenway Park**, at 24 Yawkey Way, one of America's sports treasures. It's the oldest baseball stadium in the country, and one of bizarre dimensions – best represented by the abnormally tall (37-ft) left-field wall, dubbed the "Green Monster." Though grandstand tickets can cost $20 or so, a bleacher seat only costs around $10 and puts you amid the raucous fans; there are few better ways to spend a Sunday summer afternoon in Boston.

BASEBALL

The stadium is near the Kenmore Ⓣ stop; for ticket information, call Ⓒ267-1700.

FOOTBALL

For years, the New England **Patriots** were saddled with the nickname "Patsies" and generally considered to be a laughing stock. But with changes of ownership, improvements in coaching, and some great draft picks in the early 1990s, the Pats have developed into one of the better teams in professional **football**, reaching the Super Bowl in January 1997. However, going to a game isn't a very reasonable goal unless you have connections or are willing to pay a scalper upwards of $100; games are sold out far in advance and in any case the stadium is located in distant Foxboro, just north of the Massachusetts-Rhode Island border (for ticket information, call Ⓒ508/543-1776). Better to drop by a sports bar on a Sunday afternoon during the fall season; the best ones are located in the West End (see p.218).

BASKETBALL

While Boston's other sports franchises have a reputation for falling just short of championships, basketball's **Celtics** have won 16 NBA championships – more than any other professional sports team except the New York Yankees. But while they enjoyed dynastic success in the 1960s and 1980s, the Celts have recently fallen on hard times; in the 1996-97 season, they had the second-worst record in the NBA. However, star coach Rick Pitino, hired after the 1997 season, has a great track record and should bring the Celts back to glory sooner rather than later. They play in the **FleetCenter**, 150 Causeway St (Ⓒ624-1000), located near the North Station Ⓣ stop in the West End. Most tickets are pricey – good seats run at least $50 – but you can sometimes snag some for as little as $20.

HOCKEY

Until a few years ago, ice hockey's **Boston Bruins** were a consistently successful franchise, at one point running up a streak of 26 straight winning seasons that was the longest in professional sports, including appearances in the Stanley Cup finals on two occasions, 1988 and 1990, both of which they barely lost. A series of retirements, injuries and bad luck turned things around fast, and in the 1996-97 year they posted the worst record in the National Hockey League. The team has bounced back just as quickly, though, and is again exciting to watch. You can catch the Bruins at the **FleetCenter**, 150 Causeway St (North Station Ⓣ; ✆624-1000), where tickets are expensive ($30–75), especially if a good team is in town.

A cheap and exciting alternative to the Bruins is **college hockey**. The biggest event is the "Beanpot," an annual competition that takes place on the first two Mondays in February, in which the four big local teams – **Boston University**, who play at Walter Brown Arena, 285 Babcock St (✆353-3838); **Harvard**, at Bright Hockey Center, N Harvard St, Allston (✆495-2111); **Boston College**, at the Conte Forum, Chestnut Hill (✆552-3000); and **Northeastern**, at Matthews Arena, St Botolph St (✆373-4700) – compete for city bragging rights. BU tends to dominate the Beanpot and are consistently at the top of the national rankings, though BC and Harvard are generally competitive as well. Beanpot tickets are hard to come by, but regular-season seats go for around $5 and the games are quite fun.

HOCKEY

RUNNING, ROLLERBLADING AND BICYCLING

On the rare days that Boston is visited by pleasant weather, residents take full advantage of it, turning up in droves to engage in **outdoor activities**. The most popular of these are **running**, **rollerblading** and **cycling**, and they all pretty much take place along the banks of the Charles River, where the **Esplanade** provides eighteen miles of well-kept, picturesque trails stretching from the Museum of Science all the way down to Watertown and Newton. On the Cambridge side of the Charles is **Memorial Drive**, closed off to traffic between Western Avenue and Eliot Bridge (May–Oct daily 11am–7pm) – a prime place for blading and tanning. Blades are available for rent at *Beacon Hill Skate Shop*, 135 Charles St (✆482-7400) or *Eric Flaim's Motion Sports*, 349 Newbury St (✆247-3284), for about $15 per day.

Call the Metropolitan District Commission (✆727-9650) for local trail information.

Two of the most popular **bike trails** in the area are the Dr Paul Dudley White Bike Path (really just another name for the Esplanade loop) and the Minuteman Bikeway, which runs 10.5 miles from Alewife station on the Red Line in Cambridge through Lexington to Bedford. The MDC has information about area these trails, as does the Massachusetts Bicycle Coalition, 214A Broadway, Cambridge (✆491-7433), which also sells a Boston bike map ($5). The Charles River Wheelmen (✆332-8546) organize frequent, usually free, bike tours. You can rent bikes at *Community Bicycle Supply*, 496 Tremont St (Boylston Ⓣ; ✆542-8623); *Earth Bikes*, 35 Huntington Ave (Copley Ⓣ; ✆267-4733); or at the *Bicycle Workshop*, 259 Massachusetts Ave, Cambridge (Harvard Ⓣ; ✆876-6555), which also does repairs.

ICE SKATING

The MDC operates several **ice skating rinks** in the Boston area, of which the best-kept and most convenient to downtown is the **Steriti Memorial Rink**, at 550 Commercial St (✆523-9327; $3) in the North End. It's open sporadically; to find out dates and times, and indeed to keep tabs on skating availability throughout the city, including at Frog Pond on Boston Common and the lagoon in the Public Garden – both of which when cold enough offer free skating – call the MDC skating hotline (✆727-5283).

POOL

There are plenty of places to shoot **pool** in the Boston area, and not just of the divey variety you'll invariably find in some of the city's more down-and-out bars. One of the best is *Boston Billiard Club*, 126 Brookline Ave (Kenmore ⓣ; ✆536-7665), a classy and serious pool hall that also has a nice bar. *Flat Top Johnny's*, at One Kendall Square in Cambridge (Kendall ⓣ; ✆494-9565), draws a mixed clientele in a smoky environment; and there's also *The Rack* in Faneuil Hall (Government Center ⓣ; ✆725-1051), a slick joint that draws as many well-heeled yuppies as it does ardent pool players.

BOWLING

Boston's variation on tenpin bowling is **candlepin bowling**, in which the ball is smaller, the pins narrower and lighter, and you have three rather than two chances to knock the pins down. It's a popular recreation, as it's difficult to be very bad or very good at candlepins, and Boston's serious bowlers stick to the tenpin variety. The best candlepin spot is the **Ryan Family Amusement Center**, 64 Brookline Ave (Kenmore Ⓣ; Sun, Mon, Wed & Thurs noon–11pm, Tues 9am–11pm, Fri & Sat noon–midnight; Ⓒ267-8495), while **Lanes and Games**, 159 Concord Turnpike out in Somerville (Alewife Ⓣ; daily 9am–midnight; Ⓒ876-5533), is a good spot that has both tenpin and candlepin.

MISCELLANEOUS

Among the other forms of sportslike entertainment in the city, perhaps the oddest (and most fun) is **paintball** – a kind of simulated warfare, where you shoot paintballs rather than bullets (and they do sting), while scampering around an area full of bunkers and obstacles. The proceedings take place in an old North End warehouse at **Boston Paintball**, 131 Beverly St, sixth floor (North Station Ⓣ; reservations Ⓒ742-6612; $39).

KIDS' BOSTON

O ne of the best aspects of traveling with **kids** in Boston is the feeling that you're conducting an ongoing history lesson; while that may grow a bit tiresome for teens, younger children tend to eat up the Colonial-period costumes, cannons and the like. The various points on the **Freedom Trail** are, of course, best for this. The outdoor **parks**, notably Boston Common, the Public Garden – where you can ride the **Swan Boats** in the lagoon – and Franklin Park, make nice settings for an afternoon with the children. The best outdoor option, however, may be **Fenway Park**, the country's oldest baseball stadium; Fenway is easily reachable in the city, and games are very affordable (see p.277). **Harbor cruises** are also fairly popular, and are also a unique way to see Boston – as is ascending to the tops of various city **skyscrapers**. There is also a number of **museums** aimed at kids, most of which are located along one waterfront or another.

MUSEUMS AND SIGHTS

Boston Tea Party Ship & Museum

Map 3, K7. Congress Street Bridge ℂ338-1773. South Station Ⓣ.

March–Nov daily 9am–5pm; $7, kids $6, students $3.50.
This traces the history of the infamous tea party and gives kids the chance to toss some of their own.

Children's Museum

Map 3, L7. 300 Congress St ℰ338-1773. South Station Ⓣ.
Tues–Sun 10am–5pm (Fri until 9pm); $7, kids $6, Fri 5–9pm $1
The hands-on exhibit phenomenon is said to have started here; while this may be difficult to prove, no kid has complained yet.

Computer Museum

Map 3, L7. 300 Congress St ℰ423-6758. South Station Ⓣ.
Tues–Sun 10am–5pm (Fri until 9pm); $7, kids $5, Sun 3–5pm half price.
This museum counts among its thirty-odd hands-on exhibits an oversized PC that kids under fourteen can walk inside.

Franklin Park Zoo

Map 2, F8. 1 Franklin Park Rd 442-2002. Forest Hills Ⓣ.
April–Oct Mon–Fri 10am–5pm, Sat–Sun until 6pm, Nov–March daily 10am–4pm; $6.
The city zoo's many gorillas, monkeys and pygmy hippos are sure to please kids, plus there's a specific Children's Zoo here, which allows kids to pet and feed rhinos and other big animals.

John Hancock Observatory

Map 6, J4. 200 Clarendon St ℰ572-6429. Copley Ⓣ.
Mon–Sat 9am–11pm, Sun 10am–11pm; $4.25.
Kids under five are admitted free to the sixtieth-floor observatory of Boston's tallest skyscraper.

Museum of Science

At the Charles River Dam ✆723-2500. Science Park Ⓣ.
Daily 9am–5pm (Fri until 9pm); $8.

This has all the fun scientific-themed exhibits you'd expect, from an incubator with freshly-hatched chicks to a musical staircase that sounds off when you step on it. There's also the Planetarium and the domed Mugar Omni Theater.

New England Aquarium

Map 3, L2. Central Wharf ✆973-5200. Aquarium Ⓣ.
Mon–Tues & Fri 9am–6pm, Wed–Thurs 9am–8pm, Sat–Sun and holidays 9am–7pm; weekdays $10.50; weekends $12.

The centerpiece of this family attraction is a huge transparent vertical tank of various exotic sea creatures, around which a ramp circles to the top.

SHOPS

The Chocolate Dipper

Map 3, I2. 200 State St (Quincy Market) ✆439-0190.
Government Center Ⓣ. Map 3, H4. 278 Washington St ✆227-0309. Downtown Crossing Ⓣ.

Strawberries, pineapple slices, cookies, brownies and more all get a quick bath in chocolate , either milk or dark, at these two stores – guaranteed to please kids and add to your future dental bills.

Cybersmith

Map 3, I2. 1 Faneuil Hall Marketplace ✆367-1777. Government Center Ⓣ.

Kids' tours

Boston is a great place for kids to see on a **tour**, in part due to the means of transportation: mostly trolleys and ships. Of the latter, the best options are Boston Harbor Cruises (℃227-4321) and Boston Duck Tours (℃723-DUCK). You can also take a ride on the schooner Liberty (℃742-0333), which sails for two hours around Boston's Harbor Islands. The New England Aquarium leads whale watch trips out into the harbor, too (℃973-5277). One tour designed specifically for kids is Boston By Little Feet (℃367-2345), which is a one-hour Freedom Trail walk for ages six to twelve; tours include a free map and Explorer's Guide.

Kids can surf the Net or play virtual reality games to their heart's delight at this popular cybercafé.

F.A.O. Schwarz

Map 6, H4. 440 Boylston St ℃262-5900. Arlington Ⓣ

Whether or not you're turned on by toys, the huge bronze teddy bear plunked on the sidewalk in front of this colorful emporium is worth a look. Inside is a two-level childrens' paradise of huge stuffed animals, a Barbie boutique, the latest home video games and many other useless but fun pieces of molded plastic.

Oilily

Map 6, K3. 31 Newbury St ℃247-9299. Arlington Ⓣ.

Bright and hip kids' clothes from Sweden.

THEATER AND PUPPET SHOWS

If you want to take the kids to the theater, you can try the **Boston Children's Theater**, at 55 Temple St (℃424-

6634), where productions of kids' classics are performed at the C. Walsh Theater, on the Beacon Hill campus of Suffolk University. Otherwise, head out to Brookline for the **Puppet Showplace Theater**, 32 Station St (©731-6400); tickets are $6 a head – big or small.

FESTIVALS

I t's always good to know ahead of time what **festivals** or **annual events** are scheduled to coincide with your trip to Boston, though even if you don't plan it, there's likely to be some sort of parade, public celebration or seasonal shindig going on. Summer is usually best for these, as the warmer weather allows for more outdoor festivals to take place. For written information, call the Boston Convention and Visitors Bureau (©1-888/SEE-BOSTON); the City of Boston Special Events Line (©822-0038) has recorded information on the month's festivals.

JANUARY

Chinese New Year
Dragon parades and firecrackers punctuate these festivities throughout Chinatown. It can occasionally fall in February, depending on the Chinese lunar calendar (©542-2574).

FEBRUARY

The Beanpot
First two Mondays. At the FleetCenter, Boston's four major

college hockey teams (Boston University, Boston College, Northeastern and Harvard) compete (℃624-1000).

MARCH

St Patrick's Day Parade and Festival

March 17. Boston's substantial Irish–American community, along with much of the rest of the city, turns out for this parade through South Boston, which culminates in Irish folk music, dance and food at Faneuil Hall. This also happens to be the anniversary of the day that George Washington drove the British out of Boston during the Revolutionary War (℃536-4100).

New England Spring Flower Show

Winter-weary Bostonians turn out in droves to gawk at hothouse greenery in this week-long horticulture-fest, which takes places down in Dorchester's Bayside Expo Center either the second or third week in March (℃536-9280).

APRIL

Patriot's Day

Third Monday. A celebration and re-creation of Paul Revere's (and William Dawes') famous ride, from the North End to Lexington, that alerted locals that the British army had been deployed against the rebel threat (℃536-4100).

Boston Marathon

Third Monday. One of America's premier athletic events, an enormous spectacle with a world-class field (℃236-1652).

MAY

Blacksmith House Dulcimer Festival

Early May in Cambridge, workshops and performance by experts of both mountain and hammer dulcimers (℡547-6789).

Greater Boston Kite Festival

In mid-May, Franklin Park gets taken over by kite-lovers during this celebration, which also includes kite-makers, flying clinics, and music (℡635-4505).

Lilac Sunday

Third Sunday of May. In the Arnold Arboreturm there are more than three hundred lilac varieties in full bloom (℡524-1717).

JUNE

Bunker Hill Weekend

Sunday nearest June 17. In Charlestown, a parade celebrates the Battle of Bunker Hill, even though it actually took place on Breed's Hill – and the Americans lost (℡242-5641).

Boston Dairy Festival.

First week of June. Cows and other animals are brought back to Boston Common to graze. There's also an event here known as the "Scooper Bowl," which, for a modest donation, allows you unlimited samples of Boston's best ice creams.

Boston Early Music Festival

This only happens every other year, and the next one is scheduled for 1999. It's a huge Renaissance fair with a music theme, and concerts, costumes shows and exhibitions take place throughout town (℡661-1812; Web site *http://www.bemf.org*).

Boston Globe Jazz Festival

The city's leading newspaper sponsors a weeklong series of jazz events at various venues, usually in mid- to late June. Some are free, though shows by big names can be pricey (℃929-2000).

JULY

Harborfest

From late June, culminating in the weekend nearest July 4, Harborfest hosts a series of concerts on the waterfront, mostly jazz, blues, and rock. On the July 4 weekend there's the annual turnaround cruise of the USS Constitution, the highly competitive "Chowderfest," and tons of fireworks (℃227-1528).

Boston Pops Concert and Fireworks

July 4. A wildly popular yearly event at the Hatch Shell, for which people sometimes line up at dawn to get good seats for the evening concert by the scaled-down version of the Boston Symphony Orchestra (℃266-1492).

AUGUST

August Moon Festival

Near the end of the month, Chinatown's merchants and restaurateurs hawk their wares on the street amid dragon parades and firecrackers (℃542-2574).

Italian Festas

The last two weekends in August feature music, dancing, and games throughout the North End. In weekend parades, statues of the Virgin Mary are borne through the streets as locals pin dollar bills to the floats.

SEPTEMBER

Cambridge River Festival

In mid-September, Memorial Drive is closed off from JFK Street to Western Avenue for music shows, dancing, and eclectic food offerings, all along the Charles River (✆349-4380).

Boston Film Festival

Boston theaters screen independent films, with frequent discussions by directors and screenwriters, for approximately two weeks in early to mid-September (✆1-888/SEE-BOSTON).

Art Newbury Street

Typically the weekend after Labor Day, when Newbury Street is blocked off from traffic and thirty galleries open their doors to the public (✆859-8500).

OCTOBER

Columbus Day Parade

Second Monday of October. Kicked off by a ceremony at City Hall at 1pm, the raucous, Italian-flavored parade continues into the heart of the North End.

Head of the Charles Regatta

Hordes of well-to-do prep school alumni descend on the Harvard Square area, ostensibly to watch the crew races that take place on the second to last weekend in October, but really more to pal around with their cronies and get loaded (✆864-8415).

Salem Haunted Happenings/Halloween
The two weeks of witch-related kitsch – seances and the like – end fittingly with the Halloween celebrations. (℃1-800/777-6848).

NOVEMBER
Thanksgiving Celebrations
In Plymouth, they commemorate the first thanksgiving ever held, with tours of old houses and traditional feasts (information ℃1-800/USA-1620, reservations ℃508/746-1622).

DECEMBER
Boston Tea Party Reenactment
Sunday nearest Dec 16. A lusty reenactment of the march from Old South Meeting House to the harbor, and the subsequent tea-dumping that helped spark the American Revolution, hosted by the Boston Tea Party Museum (℃338-1773).

First Night
December 31. A family-friendly festival to ring in the New Year, featuring parades, ice sculptures, art shows, plays, and music throughout Downtown and the Back Bay, culminating in a spectacular fireworks display over Boston Harbor (℃542-1399).

CITY DIRECTORY

AIRLINES American Airlines ☏1-800/433-7300; British Airways ☏1-800/247-9297; United Airlines ☏1-800/241-6522; US Airways ☏1-800/428-4322; Virgin Atlantic ☏1-800/862-8621. American and United have offices in the Park Plaza Hotel (in addition to one at Logan Airport); the British Airways office is across from the Government Center Ⓣ station.

BANKS Bank of Boston and Fleet Bank are the biggest banks, with branches and ATMs throughout the city.

BICYCLES Back Bay Bikes & Boards, 333 Newbury St (☏247-2336); Community Bicycle Supply, 496 Tremont St (☏542-8623); Earth Bikes n' Blades Rentals, 35 Huntington Ave (☏267-4733); Bicycle Workshop, 259 Massachusetts Ave, Cambridge (☏876-6555).

CONSULATES Canada, 3 Copley Place ☏262-3760; France, 31 St. James Ave ☏542-7374; UK, 600 Atlantic Ave ☏248-9555.

DISABILITY Boston is fairly well-equipped for disabled travelers: for general help and information, call the Massachusetts Office on Disability ☏727-7440; for

transportation from the airport, call Airport Handicap Van
℃561–1769.

EMERGENCIES Dial ℃911 for emergency assistance.

EXCHANGE Bureaux de change are not very prevalent. You
can find locations at Logan Airport Terminal E (International);
Thomas Cook, 399 Boylston St; and many Bank of Boston
branches.

FILM Almost any kind of film can be found at pharmacies and
camera specialty shops around town. For one-hour developing
service, try Moto Photo, with locations in the Financial
District, 101 Summer St (℃423-6848); Back Bay, 657 Boylston
St (℃266-6560); and Harvard Square, 19 Dunster St (℃497-
0731).

HEALTH Mass General Physician Referral Service ℃726-
5800.

HOSPITALS Massachusetts General Hospital, 55 Fruit St
(℃726-2000); Beth Israel Deaconess Medical Center, 330
Brookline Ave (℃667-7000); Brigham and Women's Hospital,
75 Francis St (℃732-5500); New England Medical Center, 750
Washington St (℃636-5000); and Children's Hospital, 300
Longwood Ave (℃355-6000).

INTERNET There are two cybercafés in town, both called
Cybersmith: one's in Faneuil Hall Marketplace, the other in
Cambridge at 36 Church St. They charge around $10 per hour
for Internet use.

LAUNDRIES Back Bay Laundry Emporium, 409-A
Marlborough St (daily 7.30am–11pm, last wash at 9pm) is a

good, clean bet; drop-off service is 90¢ per pound of clothing.

LIBRARIES The biggest and best library is the main branch of the Boston Public Library, at Copley Square (Mon–Thurs 9am–9pm, Fri–Sat 9am–5pm, Sun 1–5pm; ✆536-5400).

MAIL The biggest post office downtown is J. W. McCormack Station in Post Office Square, at 90 Devonshire St (Mon–Fri 7.30am–6pm, Sat 7.30am–3pm; ✆720-4754); another central branch is at 125 Mt Auburn St, in Harvard Square (same hours; ✆876-6483). The General Post Office, at 25 Dorchester Ave, by Fort Point Channel, is open 24 hours (✆654-5326).

NEWSPAPERS The *Boston Globe* (50¢) is Boston's best general daily paper; its fat Sunday edition ($2) has expanded news coverage as well as sections on art, culture, lifestyles, and a color supplement. The *Boston Herald* (50¢) is the *Globe's* tabloid competitor. To know what's on, the weekly *Boston Phoenix* ($1.50) is essential, offering extensive entertainment listings as well as good feature articles. There are also the freebies *Improper Bostonian* and *Stuff@Night*, each of which have decent, though ad-driven, features. The free *Cambridge TAB* has news articles and listings exclusively about local Cambridge events.

PARKING This can be an absolute nightmare, definitely to be avoided. Garages cost $15–20 per evening, more overnight. There are metered spots on main streets like Newbury, Boylston, and Charles, but the chances of finding one on any given evening are slim at best. Heed, too, the ubiquitous "Permit Parking Only" signs along residential streets: without the requisite parking sticker, you will be ticketed ($20) or towed ($xx).

PHARMACIES The CVS drugstore chain has locations all over the city, though not all have pharmacies. For those, try the branches at 155-157 Charles St, in Beacon Hill (open 24 hours; ℂ227-0437, pharmacy ℂ523-1028), and 35 White St, in Cambridge's Porter Square (ℂ876-4037, pharmacy ℂ876-5519).

POLICE In case of emergency, get to a phone and dial ℂ911. For non-emergency situations, contact the Boston Police, headquartered at 154 Berkeley St, in Back Bay (ℂ343-4200).

PUBLIC TOILETS There aren't too many of these around. The cleanest ones are in the visitors' center on the fourth floor of the City Hall building in Government Center, and in the National Park Service visitors' center across from the Old State House. If desperate, you can always try ducking into a restaurant or bar.

RADIO The best stations are on FM, including WGBH (89.7), which carries National Public Radio shows, plus jazz, classical and world music; WBUR (90.9), earnest leftist talk radio; WJMN (94.5), for good hip-hop beats; WFNX (101.7), mainstream alternative hits; and WODS (103.3), an oldies station.

TELEPHONES Local calls cost 20¢; just deposit your change and dial the number. To call Boston from long distance, dial 1+617 then the number. For a long distance call from Boston, dial 1+area code+number and wait for the operator to prompt you for the required payment or the option to make collect, reverse-charge, or credit card calls. Operator assistance (ℂ0), and directory information (ℂ411) are toll-free.

TELEVISION You'll find CBS on channel 4, ABC on channel 5, NBC on channel 7, and Fox on channel 25. Local channel 68 is of interest for its frequent broadcasts of regional sports action.

TIME Boston follows Eastern Standard Time (five hours behind Greenwich Mean Time). Clocks are moved forward one hour in March and back again at the end of October for daylight saving.

TRAVEL AGENTS Council Travel, 12 Eliot St, 2nd Floor, Harvard Square, Cambridge (©497-1497), specialize in student and youth travel; American Express Travel, 170 Federal St (©439-4400), provide general travel services.

CONTEXTS

A Brief History of Boston

Early exploration and founding

The first indications of explorers "discovering" the Boston area are the journal entries of **Giovanni da Verrazano** and **Estevan Gomez**, who – in 1524 and 1525, respectively – passed by Massachusetts Bay while traveling the coast of North America. The first permanent settlement in the Boston area was undertaken by a group of around thirty **Puritans**, chased out of England for their religious beliefs. They had tried to settle in Holland, but the Dutch didn't want them either, so they boarded the ship *Mayflower* to try the forbidding coast of North America, where they landed in 1620 – after a short stopover at the tip of Cape Cod – near Plymouth Bay. Within the first decade, one of them, a scholarly loner by the name of **William Blackstone**, struck out for total isolation and found it on a peninsula at the mouth of the Charles River known as Shawmut by the local Indians. He became Boston's first white settler, living at the foot of modern-day Beacon Hill with a few hundred books and a Brahma bull.

In 1630, more Puritans, led by **John Winthrop**, settled across the river from him to create **Charlestown**, named after the king of England. Blackstone eventually lured them to his side of the river with the promise of a better water supply, then sold them the entire Shawmut Peninsula, keeping only six acres for himself. The Puritans renamed the area after the town in England from which many of their company hailed: **Boston**.

The Colonial period

Early Bostonians enjoyed almost total political autonomy from England and created a remarkably democratic system of government, whose primary body was the **town meeting**, in which white male residents debated over and voted on all kind of matters. This liberal approach was counterbalanced, however, by religious intolerance: four Quakers and Baptists were hanged for their non-Puritan beliefs from 1649 to 1651. .

With the restoration of the British monarchy in 1660, the crown tried to exert more control over the increasingly prosperous Massachusetts Bay Colony, appointing a series of governors, notably the despotic **Nick Andros**, who was chased from the colony by locals in 1689, only to be reinstalled by the crown the following year. One of Andros' successors, Joseph Dudley, passed the **Molasses Act** of 1734, which placed prohibitive duties on key imports. The resultant decrease in trade was so sharp that Boston was plunged into a depression, fanning anti-British resentment.

The American Revolution

At the outset of the 1760s, governor Francis Bernard informed the colonists that their success was a result of "their subjugation to Great Britain," before green-lighting the **Writs of Assistance**, which gave British soldiers the right to enter colonists' shops and homes to search for evidence of their avoiding duties. The colonists reacted with outrage at this violation of their civil liberties, and a young Boston lawyer named **James Otis** persuaded a panel of judges headed by lieutenant governor James Hutchinson to repeal the acts. After listening to his four-hour oration, many were convinced that revolution was justified, including future US president **John Adams**, who wrote of Otis' speech that "then and there the child liberty was born."

Nevertheless, in 1765 the British introduced the **Stamp Act**, which required stamps to be placed on all published material (the revenue on the stamps would go to the Imperial coffers), and the **Quartering Act**, which stipulated that colonists had to house British soldiers on demand. These acts galvanized the opposition to the English government, a resistance based in Boston, where a group of revolutionary firebrands headed by **Samuel Adams** and known as the "Sons of Liberty," alongside more level-headed folks like **John Hancock** and John Adams, organized protest marches and petitioned the King to repeal the offending legislation. Though the King repealed the Stamp Act, he followed in 1766 with the symbolic **Declaratory Acts**, which asserted the crown's right to bind the colonists by any legislature he saw fit, and the **Townshend Acts**, which prescribed more massive tariffs on imports to the North American colonies. This was followed by a troop increase in Boston; by 1768, there was one British soldier in the city for every four colonists.

The tension erupted on March 5, 1770, when a group of British soldiers fired into a crowd of taunting townspeople. The **Boston Massacre** was hardly a massacre – only five people were killed, and the accused soldiers actually defended in court by John Adams and Josiah Quincy – but the occupying troops were forced to relocate to **Castle Island**, at the tip of South Boston. The crisis was postponed for a few years, until December 16, 1773, when Samuel Adams led a mob from the Old South Meeting House to Boston Harbor as part of a protest against a British tax on imported tea. A segment of the crowd boarded the brig *Beaver* and two other ships and dumped their entire cargo overboard, the so-called **Boston Tea Party**; Parliament responded by closing the port of Boston and passing the **Coercive Acts**, which deprived Massachusetts of any self-government. They also sent in more troops and cut off the Dorchester Neck, the

THE AMERICAN REVOLUTION

only land entrance to Boston. Soon after, the first **Continental Congress** was convened in Philadelphia, with the idea of creating an independent government for the states.

Two months after the province of Massachusetts was declared to be in a state of rebellion by the British government, the "shot heard 'round the world" was fired at Lexington on April 18, 1775, where a group of American militiamen skirmished with a company of British regulars; they lost that fight but defeated the Redcoats in a subsequent one at Concord Bridge, and the **Revolutionary War** had begun. The British troops left in Boston were held under siege, and the city itself was largely evacuated by its citizens.

The first major engagement of the war was the **Battle of Bunker Hill**, in which the British stormed what was actually Breed's Hill, in Charlestown, on three separate occasions before finally dislodging American battlements. Despite the loss, the conflict, in which the outnumbered Americans suffered fewer casualties than the British, bolstered the patriots' spirits and confidence.

George Washington took over the Continental troops in a ceremony on Cambridge Common on July 2, 1775; however, his first major coup didn't even require bloodshed. On March 16, 1776, under cover of darkness, Washington ordered much of the troops' heavy artillery to be moved to the top of Dorchester Heights, in view of the Redcoats. The British awoke to see battlements sufficient to destroy their entire fleet of warships; on March 17, they evacuated the city, never to return.

This was largely the end of Boston's involvement in the war; the focus soon turned inland and southward. After the Americans won the Battle of Saratoga in 1778, the French joined the war as their allies; on October 19, 1778,

Cornwallis surrendered to Washington at Yorktown; and the United States of America became an independent nation with 1783's **Treaty of Versailles**.

The Athens of America

Boston quickly emerged from the damage wrought by British occupation. By 1790, the economy was booming, due primarily to the maritime industry. A merchant elite developed – the "cod millionaires" – and settled on the sunny south slope of Beacon Hill. These were the Boston **Brahmins** – though that name would not be coined until seventy years later – infamous for their stuffed-shirt elitism and fiscal conservatism. Indeed, the **trust fund** was invented in Boston around then as a way for families to protect their fortunes over the course of generations.

The outset of the nineteenth century was less auspicious. Severe restrictions on international trade, notably Jefferson's Embargo Act in 1807, plunged the port of Boston into recession. When the War of 1812 broke out, old-school Federalists derided the conflict as "Mr Madison's War" and met at Hartford in 1814 to consider seceding from the union – a measure that was wisely, though narrowly, rejected. America's victory in the war shamed Bostonians back into their patriotic ways, and they reacted to further trade restrictions by developing manufacturing industries, soon becoming prominent in textiles and shoe production.

This industrial revival and subsequent economic growth shook the region from its recession. By 1820, Boston's population had grown to 43,000 – more than double its total from the 1790 census. The city remained at the forefront of American intellectual and political life, too, earning Boston the moniker "Athens of America." A controversial sect of Christianity known as **Unitarianism** – premised on the rational study of scripture, voluntary ethical behavior, and (in Boston only) a rejection of the Trinity – became the city's dominant religion (and one still practiced at King's Chapel), led by Reverend **Ellery Channing**. His teachings were the basis for **transcendentalism**, a philosophy propounded in the writings of Ralph Waldo Emerson and premised on the idea that there existed an entity known as the "over-soul," to which man and nature existed in identical relation. Emerson's theory, emphasized intuitive (*a priori*) knowledge – particularly in contemplation of nature – was put into practice by his fellow Harvard alumnus, **Henry David Thoreau**, who took to the woods just north of the city at **Walden Pond** in an attempt to "live deliberately." Boston was also a center of literary activity at this time: historical novels by **Nathaniel Hawthorne**, such as *The Scarlet Letter*, tweaked the sensibilities and mores of New England society, and poet **Henry Wadsworth Longfellow** gained international renown during his tenure at Harvard.

This intellectual flowering was complemented by a variety of social movements. Foremost among them was **abolitionism**, spearheaded by the fiery **William Lloyd Garrison**, who, besides speechmaking, published the anti-slavery newspaper *The Liberator*. Beacon Hill resident **Harriet Beecher Stowe**'s 1852 novel, *Uncle Tom's Cabin*, turned the sentiments of the nation against slavery. Other Bostonians who made key contributions to social issues were **Horace Mann**, who reformed public education; **Dorothea Dix**, an advocate of improved care for the mentally ill; **Margaret Fuller**, one of America's first feminists; and **William James**, a Harvard professor who pioneered new methods in psychology.

THE ATHENS OF AMERICA

Social transformation and decline

The success of Boston's maritime and manufacturing industries attracted a great deal of immigrants; the **Irish**, especially, poured in following the Potato Famine of 1849-50. By 1860, the city was marked by massive social divide, with overcrowded slums right by beautiful mansions. The elite that had ruled for the first half of the century tried to ensure that the lower classes were kept in place: "**No Irish Need Apply**" notices accompanied job listings throughout Boston. Denied entry into "polite" society, the lower classes conspired to grab power in another way: the popular vote.

To the chagrin of Boston's WASP elite, Irishman **Hugh O'Brien** was elected mayor in 1885. His three-term stay in office was followed by that of John "Honey Fitz" Fitzgerald, and in the 1920s, the long reign of **James Michael Curley** began. Curley was to serve several terms as mayor, and one each as governor and congressional representative. These mayors enjoyed tremendous popularity among their supporters, despite the fact that their tenures were often characterized by rampant corruption: Curley was even elected to his last term in office while serving time in a Federal prison for fraud. Still, while these mayors increased the visibility and political clout of otherwise disenfranchised ethnic groups, they did little to improve their fortunes, which were steadily worsening – along with the city's economy. The advent of railroads following the Civil War had crippled the shipping industry, and with it, Boston's prosperous waterfront. Soon after, the manufacturing industry felt the impact of competition from bigger, more efficient factories in the rest of the nation. The shoe and textile industries had largely disappeared by the 1920s, and the **Great Depression** of the 1930s made a bad state of affairs even worse. World War II turned Boston's moribund shipbuilding industry around almost overnight, but this upturn wasn't enough to prevent a massive "white flight" from the city during the 1940s and 1950s.

Recent history

A turnaround began under the mayoral leadership of **John Collins**, who undertook a massive plan to reshape the face of Boston. Many of the city's oldest neighborhoods and landmarks were razed, though it's questionable whether these changes beautified the city. Still, the project created jobs and economic growth, while making the downtown area more attractive to businesses and residents. By the end of the 1960s, a steady economic resurgence had begun. Peripheral areas of Boston, however, did not share in this prosperity. Collins' program paid little attention to the poverty that afflicted outlying areas, particularly the city's southern districts, or to the city's growing **racial tensions**. The demographic redistribution that followed the white flight of the 1940s and 1950s made Boston one of the most segregated cities in America by the mid-1970s: Charlestown's population was almost entirely white, Roxbury almost entirely black. Part of the city's remedy was **busing**, an attempt to achieve racial balance in schools by sending students from poor areas into wealthier ones and vice-versa. Opposition arose swiftly and unanimously: parents staged hostile demonstrations and boycotted the public school system. This was especially embarrassing considering Boston's history of racial tolerance. City officials scrapped the system after a few years, and the racial scars it left were healed, in part, by the policies of **Ray Flynn**, Boston's mayor during the upbeat 1980s, which proved to be one of the city's healthiest decades, both economically and socially, in recent memory.

The resurgence has spilled over into the 1990s. The ongoing **Big Dig**, a project to put I-93, the elevated highway that cuts through downtown, underground, and to date the most expensive in US history at over $1 billion per mile, doesn't look like it will be completed anytime soon. However, Boston has regained the confidence so emblematic of its storied past, and it heads toward the next century as secure as the trust funds it founded.

Architecture and urban planning

The land to which William Blackstone invited John Winthrop and his Puritans in 1630 bore almost no resemblance to the contemporary city of Boston. It was virtually an island, spanning a mere 785 acres, surrounded on all sides by murky swamps and connected to the mainland only by a narrow isthmus, "the Neck," that was almost entirely submerged at high tide. It was also very hilly: three peaks formed its geological backbone and gave it the name that Puritans used before they chose Boston – the **Trimountain** – echoed today in downtown's Tremont Street.

The first century and a half of Boston's existence saw this sleepy Puritan village slowly expand into one of the biggest shipping centers in the North American colonies. Narrow, crooked footpaths became busy commercial boulevards, though they retained their sinuous design. The pasture land of **Boston Common** became the place for public gatherings. By the end of the eighteenth century, Boston was faced with the dilemma of how to accommodate its growing population and thriving industry on its tiny geographical center. Part of the answer was to create more land. This had been accomplished in Boston's early years almost accidentally, by means of a process known as **wharving out**. Owners of shoreside property who built wharves found that rocks and debris collected around the pilings until the wharf was on dry land, necessitating the building of another wharf; Boston's shoreline moved slowly but inexorably outward.

Post-revolution development

Boston's first great building boom began in earnest following the American Revolution. Harrison Gray Otis' company, the **Mount Vernon Proprietors**, razed Boston's three peaks to create tracts for new townhouses. The land from their tops was placed where Boston Common and the Charles River met to form a swamp, extending the shoreline out even farther to create what is now known as "the flat of the hill." Left-over land was used to fill some of the city's other coves and ponds, most significantly Mill Pond, near present-day North End. The completion of the Mount Vernon Proprietors' plans made the resulting area, **Beacon Hill**, the uncontested site for Boston's wealthy and elite to build their ideal home – as such, it holds the best examples of American architecture of the late eighteenth and early nineteenth centuries, ranging in styles from Georgian to early Victorian.

This period also ushered in the first purely American architectural movement, the **Federal style**. Prime examples of its flat, dressed-down facades are prevalent in townhouses throughout downtown and in Beacon Hill. **Charles Bulfinch** was its leading practitioner; his most famous work was the 1797 gold-domed **Massachusetts State House** looming over Boston Common, a prototype for state capitols to come.

The expansion of the city

Boston continued to grow throughout the 1800s. Mayor **Josiah Quincy** oversaw the construction of a large marketplace, **Quincy Market**, behind the overcrowded Faneuil Hall building. These three oblong Greek Revival buildings pushed the Boston waterfront back several hundred yards, and the new surface area was used as the site for a symbol of Boston's maritime prosperity, the **US Custom House**. While Boston had codes prohibiting overly tall buildings, the Federal Government was not obligated to obey them, and the Custom House building, completed in 1847, rose a then-impressive sixteen stories.

Meanwhile, the city was trying to create enough land to match the demand for housing, in part by transforming its swampy backwaters into usable land. **Back Bay** was originally just that: a marsh along the banks of the Charles. In 1814, however, Boston began to dam the Charles and fill the resulting area with debris. When the project was completed in 1883, Back Bay was one of Boston's choicest addresses, drawing some prominent families from their dwellings on Beacon Hill. The layout followed a highly ordered French model of city planning: gridded streets, with those running perpendicular to the Charles arranged alphabetically. The district's main boulevard, **Commonwealth Avenue**, surrounded a strip of greenery that terminated in the **Public Garden**, a lush space completed by George Meachum in 1859, with ponds, statuary, weeping willows, and winding pathways that is the jewel of Back Bay, if not all Boston.

Back Bay's **Copley Square** was the site of numerous high-minded civic institutions built in the mid- and late-1800s, foremost among which were H. H. Richardson's Romanesque **Trinity Church** and the **Public Library**, a

High Victorian creation of Charles McKim, of the noted firm McKim, Mead and White. But the most impressive accomplishment of the century was Frederick Law Olmsted's **Emerald Necklace**, a system of parks that connected Boston Common, the Public Garden, and Commonwealth Avenue Mall to his own creations a bit further afield, such as the **Back Bay Fens**, **Arnold Arboretum** and **Franklin Park**.

While Boston's civic expansion made life easier for its upper classes, the middle and lower classes were crammed into the tiny downtown area. The city's solution was to annex the surrounding districts, beginning with **South Boston** in 1807 and ending with **Charlestown** in 1873 – with the exception of **Brookline**, which remained separate. Toward the end of the century, Boston's growing middle class moved to these surrounding areas, particularly the southern districts, which soon became known as the "streetcar suburbs." These areas, once the site of summer estates for the wealthy, were built over with one of Boston's least attractive architectural motifs: the **three-decker**. Also known as the "triple-decker," these clapboard row houses held a family on each floor, their efficiency making them commonplace in the city.

Modernization and preservation

New construction waned with the economic decline of the early 1900s, reaching its lowest point during the **Great Depression**. The streetcar suburbs were hardest hit – the white middle class migrated to Boston's nearby towns in the 1940s and 1950s, and the southern districts became run-down low-rent areas. Urban renewal began in the late 1950s, with the idea of creating a visibly modern city, and while it provided Boston with an economic shot in the arm, the drastic changes erased some of the city's most distinctive architectural features. The porn halls and dive bars of **Scollay Square** were demolished to make way for the dull gray bureaucracy complexes of Government Center. The **West End**, once one of Boston's liveliest ethnic neighborhoods, was flattened and covered over with high-rise office buildings. Worst of all, the new elevated **John F. Fitzgerald expressway** tore through downtown, cutting off the North End and Waterfront from the rest of the city.

Soon, backlash led planners to create structures that either reused or integrated extant features of the city. The **John Hancock tower**, designed by I. M. Pei and completed in 1975, originally outraged preservationists, as this Copley Square high-rise was being built right by some of the city's most treasured cultural landmarks; however, the tower managed a delicate balance. While it rises sixty stories smack in the middle of Back Bay, its narrow wedge shape renders it quite unobtrusive, and its mirrored walls literally reflect its stately surroundings, such as Trinity Church. Quincy Market was also redeveloped, and by 1978, what had been a decaying, nearly defunct series of fishmongering stalls was transformed into a thriving tourist attraction. Subsequent development has, for the most part, kept up this theme, preserving the city's 4000 acres – and most crucially its downtown – as a virtual library of American architecture.

Literary Boston: the 19th Century

America's literary center has not always been New York; indeed, for much of the nineteenth century, **Boston** held that mantle, and since then - largely due to the lingering effects of those sixty or so years of literary flowering – it has managed to retain a somewhat bookish reputation despite no longer having the influence it once did on America's reading tastes.

The origins for that period actually go back to colonial times and the establishment of puritanism. **John Winthrop** and his fellow colonists who settled here had as a vision a theocratic and utopic "City on a Hill." The Puritans were erudite and fairly well-off intellectuals, but religion always came first, even when writing: in fact, Winthrop himself penned *A Model of Christian Charity* while crossing the Atlantic. Religious **sermon**s were the real literature of the day, those and the now-forgotten explorations of Reverend Cotton Mather – such as *The Wonders of the Invisible World*, a look at the supernatural that helped foment the Salem Witch Trials – until the years leading up to the Revolutionary War, when Bostonians began to pour their energy into a different kind of sermon – that of anti-British sentiment, such as rants in radical newspapers like the *Boston Gazette*. Post-revolution, the stifling atmosphere of Puritanism remained to some extent – after all, the first theater, built in 1794, had to be billed as a "school of virtue" in order to remain open – but writers began to shake off some of its effects to explore their newfound freedom, and in certain instances, they drew upon its repressiveness as a source of inspiration.

Ironically enough, Boston's deliverance from parochialism started in the countryside, specifically Concord, scene of the first battle of the Revolutionary War. The **transcendentalist movement** of the 1830s and 1840s, spearheaded by **Ralph Waldo Emerson**, was borne of a passion for rural life, intellectual freedom and belief in intuitive knowledge and experience as a way to enhance the relationship between man, nature, and the "over-soul." The free thinking it unleashed put area writers at the vanguard of American literary expression. Articles by Emerson, **Henry David Thoreau**, **Louisa May Alcott**, **Bronson Alcott**

(Louisa's father), and other members of the Concord coterie filled the pages of *The Dial*, the transcendentalist literary review, founded by Emerson and edited by **Margaret Fuller**. *The Dial*, published in Boston starting around 1840, was merely one part of this group's output: Fuller, an early feminist, wrote essays prodigiously; Alcott produced the classic *Little Women*; Thoreau authored his famous study in solitude, *Walden*. Meanwhile, a writer by the name of **Nathaniel Hawthorne**, known mainly for short stories like "Young Goodman Brown," published *The Scarlet Letter*, in 1850, a true schism with the past that examined the effects of the repressive Puritan lifestyle and legacy.

The abolitionist movement also helped push Boston into the literary limelight. Slavery had been outlawed in Massachusetts since 1783, and Boston attracted the likes of activist **William Lloyd Garrison**, who published his firebrand newspaper, *The Liberator*, in a small office downtown during the 1820s. Years later, in 1852, **Harriet Beecher Stowe**'s slave narrative *Uncle Tom's Cabin* hit the printing press in Boston and sold more than 300,000 copies in its first year of publication. It, perhaps more than anything else, turned the nation against slavery, despite being written by a New Englander with little firsthand knowledge of the south and the slave trade.

Another involved with the cause was John Greenleaf Whittier, who also happened to be among the founding members of Emerson's famed "**Saturday Club**," the name given to a series of informal literary gatherings that took place at the Parker House Hotel beginning in 1855. Oliver Wendell Holmes and poet Henry Wadsworth Longfellow were among the moneyed regulars at these **salons**, which translated two years later into *The Atlantic Monthly*, from its inception a respected, if staid, literary and political journal. One of its more accomplished editors, **William Dean**

LITERARY BOSTON

Howells, wrote *The Rise of Silas Lapham*, in 1878, a novel on the culture of commerce that set the stage for American Realism. Around the same time, more literary salons were being held at the **Old Corner Bookstore**, down the street from the Parker House, where leading publisher **Ticknor & Fields** had their headquarters. Regulars included not only the likes of Emerson and Longfellow, but visiting British authors like William Thackeray and Charles Dickens, also published by the house and friends with its charismatic leader, Jamie T. Fields. Meanwhile, Longfellow was well on his way to becoming America's most popular poet, writing "The Midnight Ride of Paul Revere," among much other verse, while a professor at Harvard University.

In the last burst of Boston's literary high tide, sometimes resident **Henry James** recorded the sedate lives of the moneyed – and miserable – elite in his books *Watch and Ward* (1871) and *The Bostonians* (1886). His recurring theme of renunciation was well-suited to the stifling atmosphere of Brahmin Boston, where well-appointed homes were heavily curtained so as to avoid exposure to sunlight; however, his look at the emerging battle of the sexes was in fact fueled by the liberty-loving principles of Emerson and others out at Concord thirty years before.

The fact that Boston's literary society was largely a members-only club contributed to its eventual undoing. **Edgar Allen Poe** slammed his hometown as "Frogpondium," in reference to the Saturday Club-style chumminess of its literati. Provincialism reared its head in the Watch & Ward Society, which as late as 1878 instigated boycotts of books and plays it deemed out of the bounds of common decency, spawning the phrase "**Banned in Boston**." To many observers, Howells' departure from *The Atlantic Monthly* in 1885 to write for *Harper's* in New York signaled the end of Boston's literary golden age.

Ultimately the salon culture has proven more conducive to the criticism of literature than its creation. With the proliferation of universities in the Boston area, there are plenty of academics and academic presses around, though the mainstream publishing houses that were once headquartered here, like Little, Brown and Co, and Houghton Mifflin, are now based in New York and only have special divisions remaining in Boston. Mark Twain once remarked, "Tomorrow night I appear before a Boston audience – 4000 critics." Though the cadre of trendsetting authors may be gone, those critics remain.

Books

In the reviews, publishers are listed in the format UK/US, unless the title is only available in one country, in which case we've specified the country. Out of print titles are indicated by o/p.

History and biography

Cleveland Amory *The Proper Bostonians* (Parnassus Imprints US). First published in 1947, this surprisingly upbeat volume remains the definitive social history of Boston's old-moneyed aristocracy.

Jack Beatty *The Rascal King: The Life and Times of James Michael Curley, 1874–1958* (Addison Wesley UK & US). A thick and thoroughly researched biography of the charismatic Boston mayor and Bay State governor, valuable too for its depiction of big city politics in America.

David Hackett Fischer *Paul Revere's Ride* (University of Massachusetts Press/Oxford University Press). An exhaustive account of the patriot's legendary ride to Lexington, related as a historical narrative.

HISTORY AND BIOGRAPHY

J. Anthony Lukas *Common Ground: A Turbulent Decade in the Lives of Three American Families* (Vintage US). A Pulitzer Prize-winning account of three Boston families – one Irish-American, one black, one white middle class – against the backdrop of the 1974 race riots sparked by court-ordered busing to desegregate public schools.

Douglass Shand-Tucci *The Art of Scandal: The Life and Times of Isabella Stewart Gardner* (Harper Collins US). Astute new biography of this doyenne of Boston society, who served as the inspiration for Isabel Archer in Henry James' *Portrait of a Lady*. The book includes evocative photos of Fenway Court, Gardner's Venetian-style palace, now the Gardner Museum.

Dan Shaughnessy *The Curse of the Bambino* (Penguin US). Shaughnessy, a Boston sportswriter, gives an entertaining look at the Red Sox' "curse" – no championships since 1918 – that began after they sold Babe Ruth to the Yankees.

Hiller B. Zobel *The Boston Massacre* (W. W. Norton UK & US). A painstaking account of the circumstances that precipitated one of the most highly propagandized pre-revolution events – the slaying of five Bostonians outside the Old State House.

Travel and specific guides

Charles Bahne *The Complete Guide to Boston's Freedom Trail* (Newtowne Publishing US). Unlike most souvenir guides of the Freedom Trail, which have lots of pictures but little substance, this one is chock full of engaging historical tidbits on the stories behind the sights.

John Harris *Historic Walks in Old Boston* (Globe Pequot US). In most cases you'll be walking in the footsteps of long-gone luminaries, but Harris infuses his accounts with enough lively history to keep things going.

Walt Kelley *What They Never Told You About Boston (Or What They Did Were Lies)* (Down East Books UK & US). This slim book is full of fun trivia. Who would have guessed that in 1632, the Puritans passed the world's first law against smoking in public? Or that Bostonian Albert Champion invented the spark plug in 1915? You get the idea.

Architecture, urban planning and photography

Philip Bergen *Old Boston in Early Photographs 1850–1918* (Dover Publications UK & US). Fascinating stuff, including a photographic record of Back Bay's transition from swampland to swanky residential neighborhood.

Robert Campbell and Peter Vanderwarker *Cityscapes of Boston: An American City Through Time* (Houghton Mifflin US). An informative pictorial tome with some excellent photos of old and new Boston.

Lawrence W. Kennedy *Planning the City Upon a Hill: Boston Since 1630.* (University of Massachusetts Press US). This is the book to have if you want to delve deeper into how Boston's distinct neighborhoods took shape over the centuries.

Barbara Moore and Gail Weesner *Back Bay: A Living Portrait* (Centry Hill Press US). If you're dying to know what Back Bay's brownstones look – and looked – like inside, this book of hard-to-find photos is for you. They do a similar book on Beacon Hill.

Susan and Michael Southworth *AIA Guide to Boston* (Globe Pequot US). The definitive guide to Boston architecture, organized by neighborhood. City landmarks and dozens of notable buildings are given exhaustive but readable coverage.

Walter Muir Whitehill *Boston: A Topographical History* (Harvard University Press US). How Boston went from a tiny seaport on the Shawmut Peninsula to the city it is today, with detailed descriptions of the city's many land reclaiming projects.

Fiction

James Carroll *The City Below* (Houghton Mifflin US). Gripping historical novel of later-twentieth century Boston, centered on two Irish brothers from Charlestown.

Nathaniel Hawthorne *The Scarlet Letter* (Penguin UK & US). Puritan Boston comes to life, in all its mirthless repressiveness, starring the adulterous Hester Prynne.

William Dean Howells *The Rise of Silas Lapham* (Penguin UK & US). This 1878 novel was the forerunner to American Realism. Howells' tale of a well-off Vermont businessman's failed entry into Boston's old-moneyed Brahmin caste may not enthrall, but it's a good early portrayal of a hero unique to American literature: the self-made man.

Henry James *The Bostonians* (Penguin UK & US). James' soporific satire traces the relationship of Olive Chancellor and Verena Tarrant, two fictional feminists in the 1870s.

Edwin O'Connor *The Last Hurrah* (Back Bay/Little, Brown & Co). Fictionalized account of Boston mayor James Michael Curley, starring a 1950s corrupt politician, that was so popular the bar at the Omni Parker House Hotel was named after it.

John Marquand *The Late George Appley* (Buccaneer Books US o/p). Winner of the 1937 Pulitzer Prize, this novel satirizes a New England gentry on the wane.

George Santayana *The Last Puritan* (The MIT Press UK & US). The philosopher's brilliant "memoir in the form of a novel," set around Boston, chronicles the short life and education of protagonist Oliver Alden coming to grips with Puritanism.

Jean Stafford *Boston Adventure* (Harcourt Brace US). Narrated by a poverty-stricken young girl who gets taken in by a wealthy elderly woman, this long but rewarding novel portrays upper-class Boston in all its magnificence and malevolence.

Glossaries

Boston has a **language** all its own, plus a truly unmistakable regional accent. A guide to local parlance appears in this section, plus some architectural terms used in the guide; there's also a list of Boston **personalities**, from early days right up to the present.

Boston terminology and language

One of Boston's most recognizable cultural idiosyncrasies is its strain of American English, distinguished by a tendency to drop one's "r"s, as on the ubiquitous T-shirts that exhort you to "Pahk the cah in Havvid Yahd." Watch, too, for the greeting "How why ya?" or the genial assent, "shuah." The lost "r"s crop up elsewhere, usually when words that end in "a" are followed by words that begin in a vowel – as in "I've got no idear about that." When the nasal "a" (as in "cat") is not followed by an "r", it can take on a soft, almost British tenor: "after" = "ahfta." And the "aw" sound (as in "body") is inverted, like "wa": "god" = "gwad."

   If in doubt, the surest way to fit in with the locals is to use the word "wicked" as an adverb at every opportunity: "Joo guys see the Celts game lahst night? Theah gonna be wicked wasome this yeah!"

Beantown Nickname for Boston – a reference to the local specialty, Boston baked beans – that no one uses any longer.

The Big Dig The ongoing project to put the elevated highway I-93 underground.

Brahmin An old-moneyed Beacon Hill aristocrat.

Brownstone Originally a nineteenth-century terraced house with a facade of brownstone; now any row or townhouse.

Bubbler Water fountain.

The Cape Shorthand for Cape Cod

The Central Artery The stretch of I-93 that runs through downtown, separating the North End and the Waterfront from the rest of the city.

Colonial Style of Neoclassical architecture popular in the seventeenth and eighteenth centuries.

Combat Zone The once-busy strip of Washington Street just north of Chinatown designated for adult entertainment.

Comm Ave Commonwealth Avenue.

Dot Ave Dorchester Avenue. "Dot" is an occasionally used abbreviation for Dorchester.

Federal Hybrid of French and Roman architecture popular in the late eighteenth century and early nineteenth century.

Frappe Milkshake – and the "e" is silent.

Georgian Architectural style popular during the late Colonial period, highly ornamental and rigidly symmetrical.

Greek Revival Style of architecture that mimicked that of classical Greece. Popular for banks and larger houses in the early nineteenth century.

Hamburg Ground beef. A hamburg*er* is the sandwich featuring ground beef on a bun.

Hub Like Beantown, a nickname for Boston not really used.

JP Conversational shorthand for Jamaica Plain.

Mass Ave Massachusetts Avenue.

MBTA (Massachusetts Bay Transportation Authority). The agency in charge of all public transit – buses, subways, commuter trains and ferries.

MGH Massachusetts General Hospital, also "Mass General."

Packie Liquor store.

The Pike The Massachusetts Turnpike (I-90).

P-town Provincetown.

Scrod Somewhat of a distasteful generic name for cod or haddock. Almost always served breaded and sold cheap.

Southie South Boston.

Spa An independently-owned convenience store.

The T Catch-all for Boston's subway system.

Townie Originally a term for residents of Charlestown, it now refers to hardcore residents of Boston and its outlying suburbs most readily identified by their heavy accents.

Three-decker Three-story house, with each floor a separate apartment. Also called a "triple decker."

Victorian Style of architecture from the mid to late 1800s that is highly eclectic and ornamental.

Wicked The definitive word in the Bostonian patois, used to intensify adjectives, as in "wicked good."

Boston people

ADAMS Samuel (1722–1803). A standardbearer for the Revolution, Adams's patriotic pursuits included creating the Committee of Correspondence – basically a hype machine for the Revolutionary cause – in 1772, and leading the Boston Tea Party a year later. And yes, he brewed beer, too.

ALCOTT Bronson (1799–1888). Perpetually penniless father of author Louisa May, Alcott launched a series of progressive though short-lived elementary-type schools in Boston, most notably the Temple School. He also spearheaded the failed utopian community of Fruitlands, outside Boston, in 1843.

ALCOTT Louisa May (1832–1888). Writer of *Little Women* and other works that drew on her close-knit family, who lived in and around Boston. While a Civil War nurse, she was treated with mercury for a fever, beginning a painfully long demise that ended just a day after her father's funeral.

ATTUCKS Crispus (1723?–1770). Black ex-slave who was killed in the Boston Massacre of 1770, the only one of the five slain to be remembered by history, on account of his race.

BELL Alexander Graham (1847–1922). Scottish-born professor who moved to Boston in the 1870s and invented the telephone in a Boston University laboratory.

BLACKSTONE William (1595–1675). English reverend who was the first white settler on the Shawmut Peninsula, now Boston.

BOYLSTON Zabdiel (1679–1766). Boston doctor who invented a smallpox inoculation first used during the plague of 1721–1722. To allay fears about his cure, Boylston inoculated his son first.

BULFINCH Charles (1763–1844). Boston's leading architect of the Federalist style, he designed the State House and many townhouses on Beacon Hill which can still be seen today.

CHILD Julia (1912–). Cookbook author, famed for simplifying French cuisine for the middle American dinner table, who calls Cambridge her home.

COPLEY John Singleton (1738–1815). A painter best known for his portraits of prominent Colonial-era Bostonians, Copley relocated to London in 1775.

CURLEY James Michael (1874–1958). Four-time Democratic Mayor of Boston, this charismatic – and corrupt – Irish-American politician ruled for 35 years, also serving as a Massachusetts congressman and governor.

DUKAKIS Michael (1933–). Former Democratic governor of Massachusetts, born in Brookline, who used the so-called Massachusetts Miracle economic recovery of the mid-1980s as a springboard for the 1988 presidential race, in which he was roundly defeated by George Bush.

EDDY Mary Baker (1821–1910). The founder of Christian Science, a church whose world headquarters are in Boston. Healed of an injury in 1866 while reading a section of the New Testament, she was inspired to write *Science and Health*, the original Christian Science textbook.

EMERSON Ralph Waldo (1803–1882). Literary giant and renowned lecturer whose essay *Nature*, penned in Concord, signaled the birth of transcendentalism.

FANEUIL Peter (1700–1743). Wealthy merchant of French Huguenot origin who donated the eponymous town hall to the town of Boston in 1742.

FIEDLER Arthur (1894–1979). Originally a violinist, he was the conductor of the Boston Pops for about half this century.

FIELDS James T. (1817–1881). Partner in the local publishing firm Ticknor & Fields, Fields helped persuade Nathaniel Hawthorne to publish *The Scarlet Letter*.

FULLER Margaret (1810–1850). Literary critic who was the editor of *The Dial*, the transcendentalist journal of the 1840s.

FRANKLIN Benjamin (1706–1790). American statesman and inventor born and raised in Boston, he apprenticed to his brother, publisher of the independent-minded *New England Gazette* newspaper, before settling in Philadelphia.

GARDNER Isabella Stewart (1840–1919). This socialite and art collector, described once as a "millionaire Bohemienne," enjoyed shocking Boston's high society with antics such as having John Singer Sargent paint a low-neckline portrait of her and, reputedly, walking her pet lions down Tremont Street.

GARRISON William Lloyd (1805–1879). Abolitionist who at 23 made his first public address in favor of emancipation, in Boston's Park Street Church. Also the publisher of *The Liberator*, an anti-slavery newspaper.

HANCOCK John (1737–1793). Wealthy Colonial-era merchant and Declaration of Independence signer who helped finance the early Revolutionary campaign; after the war he served as the first governor of the Commonwealth of Massachusetts.

HOLMES Oliver Wendell (1809–1894). Doctor, author and pundit, Holmes coined the phrase "Boston Brahmins," describing Beacon Hill aristocrats, in a series of *Atlantic Monthly* articles entitled *Autocrat of the Breakfast Table*.

HOMER Winslow (1836–1910). Boston-born, self-taught naturalist painter best known for his watercolors of New England seascapes.

KENNEDY John F. (1917–1963) The youngest president to be elected, and the first Catholic one, Kennedy was born just outside Boston proper in Brookline. He served as Boston congressman and Massachusetts senator before gaining high office in 1960. He was assassinated on November 22, 1963.

KENNEDY Edward M. (1932–). Brother of JFK and longtime liberal Massachusetts Democratic senator.

LOWELL Robert (1917–1977). Pulitzer Prize-winning Boston-born poet whose most famous collection, *For the Union Dead*, was inspired by the Robert Gould Shaw and 54th Massachusetts Regiment statue on the Beacon Street promenade.

MATHER Cotton (1663–1728). Puritan minister who entered Harvard College at the age of 12, and proceeded to pen many esoteric books, including the 1300-page *Magnalia Christi Americana*, which traced the ecclesiastical history of America.

MATHER Increase (1639–1723). Minister (and Cotton's father) who secured a new royal charter for the Massachusetts Bay Colony in 1692; he also served some time as president of Harvard College.

MENINO Thomas (1942–). Boston's current Mayor and the first one of Italian descent.

NIMOY Leonard (1931–). Spock himself was born in Boston and attended Boston College before donning his pointy ears.

QUINCY Josiah (1772–1864). Popular Mayor of Boston in the 1820s who cleaned up Beacon Hill of prostitution and stopped development of the land that would become the Public Garden.

REVERE Paul (1735–1818). Silversmith and principal rider for Boston's Committee of Safety, he made his midnight ride to Lexington and Concord to warn the rebels that the British were coming, an event immortalized in an 1863 Longfellow poem of questionable accuracy.

RICHARDSON Henry Hobson (1838–1886). Architect noted for his oversized Romanesque Revival works such as Trinity Church.

STUART Gilbert (1755–1828). Early American painter who made his mark with a series of portraits of George Washington – one of which is replicated on the US one-dollar bill.

INDEX

Backpacking through **Europe**?
Cruising across the **US of A**?
Clubbing in **London**?
Trekking through **Costa Rica**?

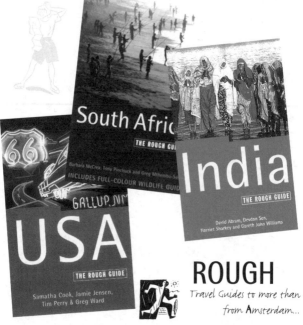

South Afric

THE ROUGH GUI

Barbara McCrea, Tony Pinchuck and Greg Mthembu-S

INCLUDES FULL-COLOUR WILDLIFE GUID

India

THE ROUGH GUIDE

David Abram, Devdan Sen,
Harriet Sharkey and Gareth John Williams

66

GALLUP, NM

USA

THE ROUGH GUIDE

Samatha Cook, Jamie Jensen,
Tim Perry & Greg Ward

ROUGH
Travel Guides to more than
from Amsterdam...

Wherever you're headed, **Rough Guides** tell you
what's happening – the history, the people,
the politics, the best beaches, nightlife and
entertainment on your budget

Malaysia
Singapore & Brunei
THE ROUGH GUIDE

Australia
THE ROUGH GUIDE
Anne Dehne, David Leffman & Chris Scott

Europe
THE ROUGH GUIDE
1999 EDITION
30 Countries • 100 Maps •
Includes Turkey, Morocco & the Baltic States

GUIDES

100 destinations worldwide
...to Zimbabwe.

Stay in touch with us!

ROUGH*NEWS* is Rough Guides' free newsletter.
In three issues a year we give you news, travel issues, music reviews, readers' letters and the latest dispatches from authors on the road.

I would like to receive ROUGH*NEWS*: please put me on your free mailing list.

NAME . . . .

ADDRESS . . . .

Please clip or photocopy and send to: Rough Guides, 1 Mercer Street, London WC2H 9QJ, England

or Rough Guides, 375 Hudson Street, New York, NY 10014, USA.

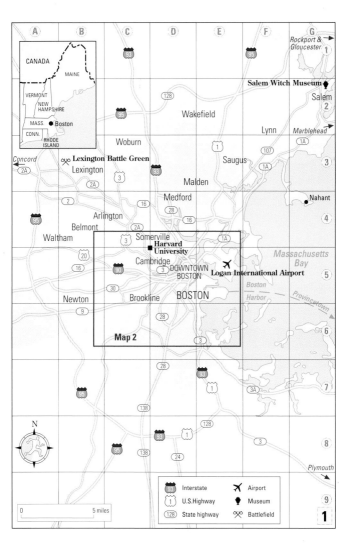

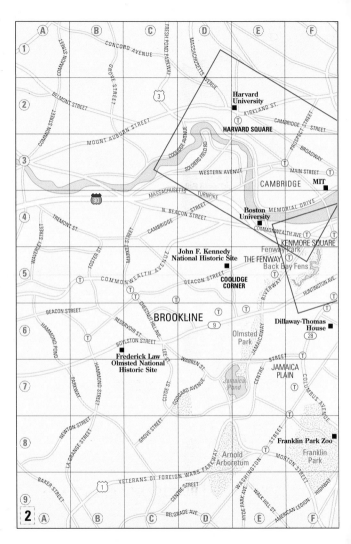

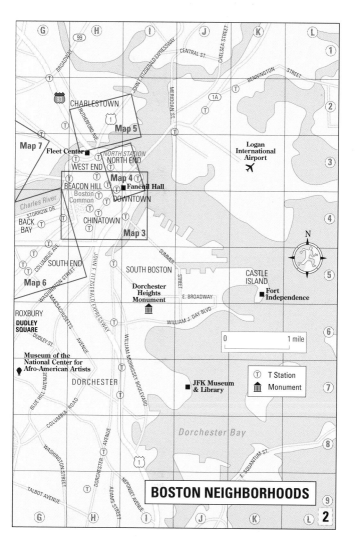

BOSTON NEIGHBORHOODS

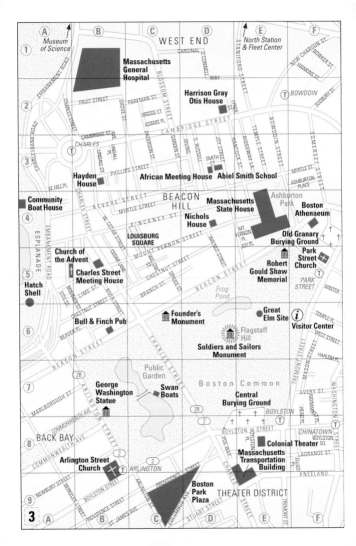

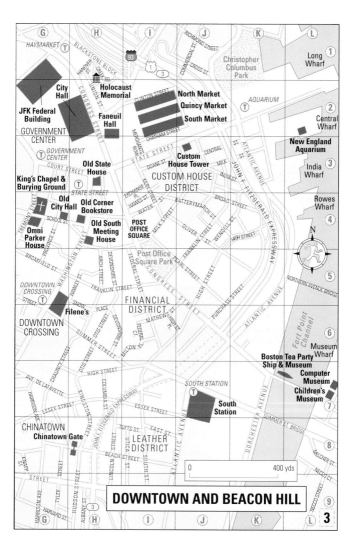

DOWNTOWN AND BEACON HILL

0   400 yds

3

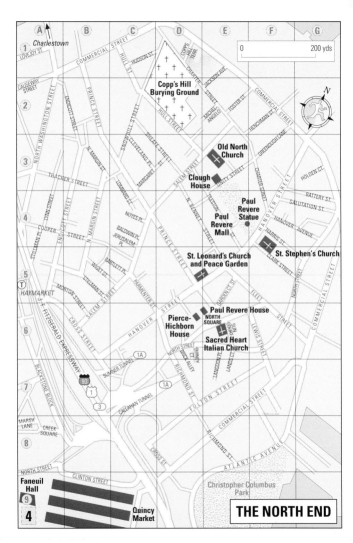

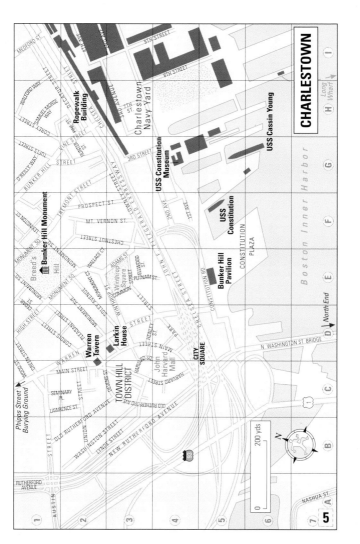

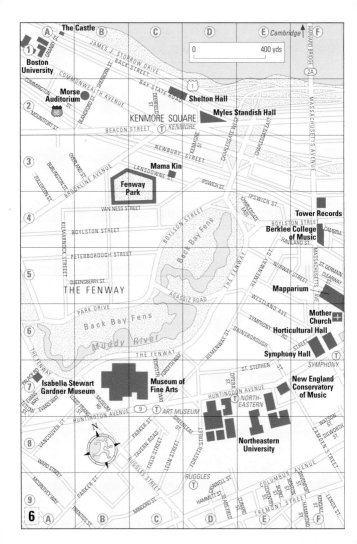

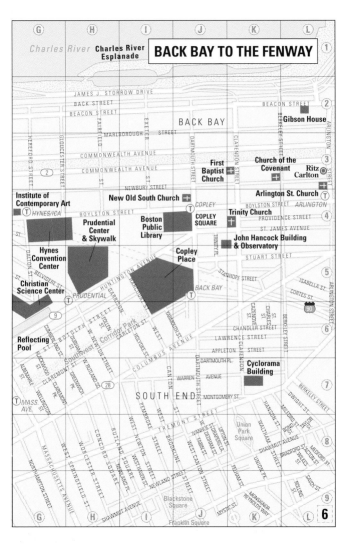

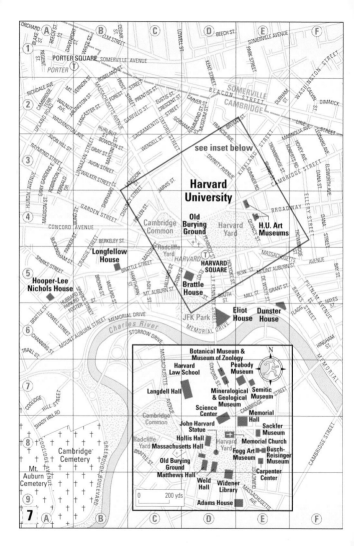

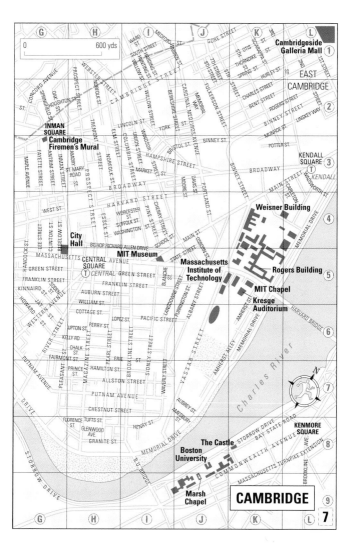

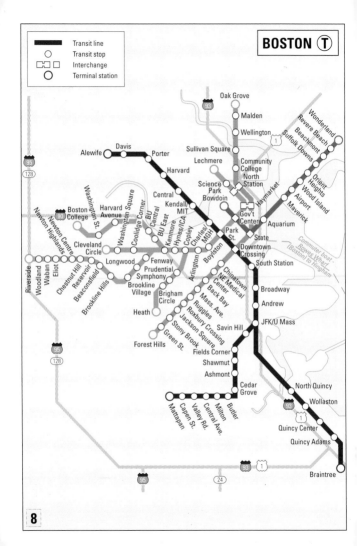

BOSTON Ⓣ

Transit line
○ Transit stop
⬚ Interchange
◎ Terminal station

8